ETHICAL DECISION MAKING IN FUND RAISING

The NSFRE/Wiley Fund Development Series

Beyond Fund Raising: New Strategies for Nonprofit Innovation and Investment by Kay Sprinkel Grace

The Complete Guide to Fund-Raising Management by Stanley Weinstein

Critical Issues in Fund Raising edited by Dwight F. Burlingame

The Fund Raiser's Guide to the Internet, by Michael Johnston

Fund Raising: Evaluating and Managing the Fund Development Process, Second Edition by James M. Greenfield

Fund-Raising Cost Effectiveness: A Self-Assessment Workbook by James M. Greenfield

International Fund Raising for Not-for-Profits: A Country by Country Profile by Thomas Harris

The Nonprofit Handbook: Fund Raising, Second Edition edited by James M. Greenfield

Nonprofit Investment Policies: A Practical Guide to Creation and Implementation by Robert P. Fry, Jr.

The NSFRE Fundraising Dictionary by National Society of Fund Raising Executives

Planned Giving Simplified: The Gift, the Giver, and the Gift Planner by Robert F. Sharpe, Sr.

The Universal Benefits of Volunteering: A Practical Workbook for Nonprofit Organizations, Volunteers, and Corporations by Walter Pidgeon

ETHICAL DECISION
MAKING IN FUND RAISING

Marilyn Fischer

John Wiley & Sons. Inc.
New York • Chichester • Weinheim • Brisbane • Singapore • Toronto

Published by John Wiley & Sons. Inc.
Published simultaneously in Canada.

No part of this publication may be reproduced, stored in a retrieval system or
transmitted in any form or by any means, electronic, mechanical, photocopying,
recording, scanning or otherwise, except as permitted under Sections 107 or 108 of
the 1976 United States Copyright Act, without either the prior written permission
of the Publisher, or authorization through payment of the appropriate per-copy fee
to the Copyright Clearance Center, 222 Rosewood Drive, Danvers, MA 01923,
(978) 750-8400, fax (978) 750-4744. Requests to the Publisher for permission
should be addressed to the Permissions Department, John Wiley & Sons, Inc.,
605 Third Avenue, New York, NY 10158-0012, (212) 850-6011, fax (212) 850-6008,
E-Mail: PERMREQ@WILEY.COM.

This publication is designed to provide accurate and authoritative information in
regard to the subject matter covered. It is sold with the understanding that the
publisher is not engaged in rendering legal, accounting, or other professional
services. If legal advice or other expert assistance is required, the services of a
competent professional person should be sought.

Library of Congress Cataloging-in-Publication Data:
Fischer, Marilyn.
    Ethical decision making in fund raising/Marilyn Fischer.
        p. cm.—(The NSFRE/Wiley fund development series)
    Includes bibliographical references and index.
    ISBN 0-471-29843-3 (cloth: alk. paper)
    1. Fund raising—Moral and ethical aspects. 2. Charities—Moral and ethical
aspects. 3.   Decision making—Moral and ethical aspects. I. Title. II. Series.
HV41.2.F57 2000
361.7'068'1—dc21   99-048186

Printed in the United States of America.
10 9 8 7 6 5 4 3 2 1

In memory of Ruth McBride Fischer
with gratitude for her gentle, giving spirit.

The NSFRE/Wiley Fund Development Series

The NSFRE/Wiley Fund Development Series is intended to provide fund development professionals and volunteers, including board members (and others interested in the nonprofit sector), with top-quality publications that help advance philanthropy as voluntary action for the public good. Our goal is to provide practical, timely guidance and information on fund raising, charitable giving, and related subjects. NSFRE and Wiley each bring to this innovative collaboration unique and important resources that result in a whole greater than the sum of its parts.

The National Society of Fund Raising Executives

The NSFRE is a professional association of fund-raising executives that advances philanthropy through its more than 17,000 members in over 148 chapters throughout the United States, Canada, and Mexico. Through its advocacy, research, education, and certification programs, the Society fosters development and growth of fund-raising professionals, works to advance philanthropy and volunteerism, and promotes high ethical standards in the fund-raising profession.

1999–2000 NSFRE Publishing Advisory Council

Suzanne Hittman, CFRE
Publishing Council Chair, Fund Raising Counsel

Nina P. Berkheiser, CFRE
Director of Development, S.P.C.A. of St. Petersburg, FL

Richard B. Chabot, PhD
Vice President, Professional Advancement, National Society of Fund Raising Executives

Linda L. Chew, CFRE
Director, Major Gifts, Alta Bates Foundation

Samuel N. Gough, CFRE
Principal, The AFRAM Group

Ann R. Hyatt, ACFRE
Director of Development/Alumni Relations,
Pace University School of Law

R. Michael Patterson
Director of Planned Giving, Trinity University

James A. Reid, PhD, CFRE
Principal Consultant, Philanthropic Resource Associates

G. Patrick Williams, MS, ACFRE
President/CEO, Lourdes College Foundation

About the Author

Marilyn Fischer, Ph.D., is an Associate Professor of Philosophy at the University of Dayton. Her areas of specialization include ethics, political philosophy, feminist theory, and philosophy of music. She is particularly interested in interdisciplinary education and team-teaches several courses with faculty from different academic disciplines. Her current research focuses on Jane Addams's philosophical writings.

Dr. Fischer has been working with NSFRE as an ethics consultant since 1990, giving workshops on ethical decision making in fund raising. She is a member of the Miami Valley NSFRE Chapter and chairs its Ethics Education Committee.

Dr. Fischer is also a professional violinist and performs regularly with the Dayton Philharmonic Orchestra. She lives in Dayton, Ohio, with her children, Cory and Kyle.

Contents

Preface

One day in 1990, I found a note in my philosophy department mailbox that said, "Call Shelley in the Development Office." I didn't know Shelley in the Development Office, and given my financial situation at the time, I could not imagine why anyone in development would have the slightest interest in me. But I returned the call. Shelley said that the local chapter of some interminable string of alphabet letters having something to do with fund raising was starting an ethics committee, and since they didn't know anything about ethics, they wondered if I, as someone trained in academic ethics, would meet with them. Since I knew nothing about fund raising, I figured there would be no harm in joining our areas of ignorance, and a mutual meeting was arranged.

The first thing I learned was that the committee members were far too modest. They knew a great deal about ethics and were highly competent ethical decision makers. With great patience, they taught me about their craft, showing me how "cultivation" was more than a gardening term, and that with practice, "NSFRE" could eventually roll off my tongue. We set about searching for an ethical decision-making model that could be adapted for fund raisers' use. We wanted a method that would build on the ethical competence fund raisers already had, would be finely tuned to the philanthropic work they did, and would be easy to remember. Because I teach ethical theory, I had many potential models tucked away in file drawers, but none of them met our criteria. So Mary Ann Fiene, the committee chair and chief visionary, suggested we make up our own. The committee and I developed the ethical decision-making model and chart, explained in Chapter 1. Shelley Outlaw, another founding member of the ethics committee and also a visionary, has for years been encouraging me to turn that chart into a book. So, Shelley, here it is.

This book is an attempt to do ethics from the inside out. This approach contrasts with much of the work done in applied ethics in which people take basic principles of abstract ethical theories and apply them directly to ethical issues in business, medicine, law, and so on. While this "start from outside and work your way in" approach can give insight, I find it unwieldy in some respects. Many philosophers developed abstract ethical theories in order to explore the meanings of basic ethical terms, for example, what it means to call an action "good" or "right." These thinkers did not intend their theories to function as guides to practical, everyday decision making. In this book, I start from inside the practice of fund raising by asking, "What conceptual tools and perspectives will best help fund raisers think through the ethical dimensions of their work?" Abstract philosophical theories and religious traditions can then function as resources rather than as starting points. I call on them frequently as we think through the ethical dimensions of fund raising.

Jane Addams (1860–1935) did philosophy from the inside out, and is in many ways a guiding spirit throughout this book. She is best known as the founder of Hull House and as an international peace activist. However, she was also a profound philosophical thinker, and her 12 books and hundreds of articles give us a method for reflecting on everyday experience. She worked in the Hull House neighborhood and with countless voluntary organizations throughout the United States and the world. From her lofty visions of a humanitarian society to neighborly advice about getting the garbage collected, Addams has much to teach us about ethics as a practical activity.

Part I of the book develops conceptual tools and perspectives that fund raisers can use to think through the ethical dimensions of their work. Chapter 1, "Thinking about Ethics and Philanthropy," starts with Addams's method of using sympathetic understanding and attention to social and temporal contexts when approaching ethical quandaries. To deepen our understanding of philanthropy as the larger framework for fund raising, I develop the idea of philanthropy as a gift economy. The chapter concludes with the ethical decision-making model our local chapter ethics committee devised, in which alternative courses of action are evaluated in light of three basic value commitments of professional fund raisers: organizational mission, professional relationships, and personal integrity.

Chapters 2, 3, and 4 take each of these three basic value commitments and explain them in terms of supporting clusters of virtues. In Chapter 2, I talk about why fulfilling the organizational mission should be at the center of philanthropic fund raising, and then set the missions of particular nonprofit organizations within the larger context of the gift economy of philanthropy. Jane Addams described her work as creating channels through which people's moral energy can flow. We can think of nonprofit organizations as such channels; in the chapter I develop the idea of clusters of virtues which energize the flow of moral energy through the philanthropic gift economy. These virtues include generosity, charity, compassion, gratitude, and mutuality.

There is a commonplace saying that fund raisers raise friends for their organizations, as well as funds. Chapter 3 focuses on networks of relationships through which philanthropic work gets done, which join nonprofit staff, donors, volunteers, and the community. Creating and preserving an atmosphere of trust is critical to healthy, long-term professional relationships. We will discuss how trust is sustained through cultivating the virtues of respect, honesty, fairness, and cooperativeness.

One's own integrity is the third basic value commitment. Sometimes, ethical dilemmas arise when we are asked or tempted to do things that gnaw at our own sense of integrity. In Chapter 4, we will look at independent judgment, responsibility, and moral courage as virtues that help to keep our integrity intact and alert.

Part II of the book focuses on specific issues that arise in fund-raising practice, which draw on all of the conceptual tools and virtue clusters from Part I. Each chapter includes general analyses of the issues involved and uses many specific case studies to show how the conceptual tools can help guide our thinking.

In Chapter 5, we start with why the principle of volunteerism belongs at the center of the philanthropic gift economy. We examine models for thinking about donors and volunteers as partners who share the organizational mission and want to contribute to furthering its work. We also look at the philosophical and religious roots of stewardship and think about how to shape ethically equitable partnerships between nonprofits and their donors and volunteers.

Nonprofit organizations and fund raisers in particular are entrusted with highly personal information about their donors and volunteers, so Chapter 6 focuses on privacy and confidentiality. We look at how privacy both protects and enables us as individuals and as members of organizations to define ourselves and to carry out our projects. I include several guidelines to use when deciding what information about donors and prospective donors to gather, what to record, and how to keep it safe.

Chapter 7 deals with conflicts of interest and other tensions on the job. The ethics of commission-based pay has been a recurring concern among philanthropic fund raisers, so I analyze it carefully in light of the three basic value commitments. We also examine tensions which arise when fund raisers move from one job to another in the same geographic location.

Corporations in partnership with nonprofits have contributed greatly to meeting basic needs and enhancing the quality of community life, yet distinctive ethical concerns arise when dealing with corporate donors. In Chapter 8, we look at matches and mismatches between corporate and nonprofit missions, and then focus on cause-related marketing and sponsorships, two prevalent forms of joint ventures between corporations and nonprofit organizations.

Chapter 9 focuses on diversity. In a sense the whole book is about diversity. Throughout the book, I draw on the intellectual resources and historical experiences of diverse peoples from around the world. Yet with demographic shifts and increasing attention to international philanthropy, it is worthwhile to reflect on just what it means to foster cultural diversity. The point of the chapter is to show how respecting diversity is not just an attitude but requires a great deal of knowledge and many participatory experiences.

I have tried to make the book adaptable for fund raisers' various purposes and needs. While the conceptual tools developed in Part I are used throughout Part II, readers should be able to find the discussions of specific topics in Part II useful by themselves. Each chapter concludes with discussion questions and additional case studies to use in chapter meetings, workshops, and discussion groups. There is an appendix with specific suggestions on what Ethics Education Committees can do and how they can contribute to local NSFRE chapters and to local communities.

Acknowledgments

Deepest gratitude goes to members of the Miami Valley Chapter of NSFRE. To the extent that this book speaks to fund raisers in the daily practice of their art, the credit belongs to members of our local Ethics Education Committee: Carla Birch, Angela Blackburn, Nestor Colon, Barry McEwen, David Nehring, Shelley Outlaw, Robin Paris, and Claudia Watson. They contributed the vast majority of the case studies in this book. Meetings with them are a joy; I always leave invigorated, with renewed appreciation for the work that fund raisers do. A special thanks goes to Mary Ann Fiene for her vision, guidance, and friendship during the early days of the committee. I am also grateful to the other members of the Miami Valley NSFRE Chapter for sharing their wisdom with me.

I thank the NSFRE Publishing Advisory Council for offering me the opportunity to contribute to the NSFRE/Wiley Fund Development Series and the NSFRE Research Council for their grant supporting this writing. I also want to thank my editor, Martha Cooley, for her patience, guidance, and encouragement through this project and Julie Sellers for her fine graphics.

Several people read the entire manuscript. Many thanks to Jane Zembaty, Helen Jackson, Charlotte Kroeker, Lilya Wagner and reviewers from the Publishing Advisory Council for their careful reading and helpful advice. I am also thankful for the support of my many colleagues at the University of Dayton who think that philosophers should spend their time in the thick of the world as well as in the ivory tower.

Finally, I am grateful to my children, Cory and Kyle, for keeping me well grounded in ongoing family life and full of hope for the gifts of the next generation.

—Marilyn Fischer

I CONCEPTUAL TOOLS FOR ETHICAL DECISION MAKING

▼ Thinking About Ethics and Philanthropy

This book is not a scholarly treatise on ethics. There are thousands of years' worth of intellectual inquiries on ethics from every part of the globe, given to us by people far wiser than I. Nor is this a how-to manual. Sometimes, when I am trying to learn a new computer skill, for example, I want boorishly explicit step-by-step instructions, but I do not believe such an approach to ethics is either possible or desirable. Instead, in this book I will suggest ways of thinking about giving and philanthropy that will help you to think through the ethical dimensions of fund raising more fully and carefully. I will offer considerations for you to take into account, but you must do the actual taking into account, using your own good judgment. The book is not to give answers, but to stimulate your thinking as you develop your own stock of imaginative resources.

This book is written for fund raisers working for philanthropic organizations and for others who appreciate philanthropy as a way of creating and enriching community life. Most people who fit this description are decent, honest, and compassionate people, who already have considerable skill in making ethical decisions and acting in ethically sensitive ways. They already strive to be trustworthy, to act with integrity, and to treat others with decency and respect. This book is intended to enable them to build on their considerable skills and to think and feel more deeply and imaginatively than they already do.

In this book I will not discuss the big, headline-grabbing scandals very much. I am skeptical whether books on ethical decision making can have much effect on people who so deeply violate the public trust. Such people will continue to come into positions of power from time to time and they will continue to violate the public trust. Preventing scoundrels from engaging in scandalous behavior does not strike me as a goal to aim at directly. This book is aimed at the vast majority of fund raisers who do want to act with integrity and would never violate the public trust on a massive scale.

I hope this book will help these fund raisers think their way carefully through ethical quandaries and shape their organizations in ethically responsive ways. We want to weave organizational fabrics so that people of ordinary decency and courage can do well. Although we are grateful to people of great moral courage who take heroic stands against massive injustice, we also would like to shape a society in which such moral heroism is not often necessary. When organizations are structured so that integrity and trust are encouraged, rewarded, and built into policies and practices, then the fabric is strong and our philanthropic institutions are scandal-resistant. Fewer people will be able to get away with the minor indecencies that are often prerequisites for major scandals. Then, if and when the scandals come, public trust in philanthropic institutions can still be preserved.

This book does not provide a utopian vision. There is wonderful utopian literature and there are stirring biographies of people who persevered through unspeakable hardship to enact their visions of justice and compassion. We need to read those books and absorb their inspiration. While we hope that philanthropy attracts visionaries, we must still find the dollars for hot meals for the elderly, for training materials for volunteer literacy tutors, and for paying the independent auditor. Fund raisers, given their flaws and fineness, working in flawed and fine institutions with flawed and fine clients, still need to carry out these everyday tasks of decency and joy here and now. There is a place for utopias and for utopian ethical theory, but we should also attend to the ethical dimensions of everyday decision making.

So in a way this is not a visionary book. It is not intended to take you to the mountaintop, give you an ecstatic vision, and then pump you up emotionally, with the hope that the high will last long enough to bring in that next grant. Instead, this book is about thinking with care and grace about everyday grit. Utopias are not brought to earth through sheer vision, but moral progress is made as relationships are carefully constructed, as planning is done with sensitivity, and as our imaginations and emotions are stretched to include the ways of those different from ourselves. My aim in this book is to help people of ordinary decency and ordinary courage to accomplish their purposes, to help them build organizations in which sainthood is not a requirement for success, but where having ordinary decency and courage is enough.

This first chapter introduces the two conceptual frameworks that give coherence to the rest of the book, and then presents an ethical decision-making model based on those frameworks. The first framework, ethics as narrative, gives a way of understanding how thinking about ethics is done. The way we tell stories gives a good pattern for the way good ethical thinking proceeds. The second gives a framework for conceptualizing philanthropy by developing the idea of a gift economy. The goal of philanthropy is to sustain and enrich a gift economy. This idea of the gift economy provides the larger setting in which fund raisers' daily activities and decisions make sense.

1.1 ETHICS AS NARRATIVE

How do we think about ethics? Ethical dilemmas arise within ongoing organizational and personal histories. A well-established agency, with policies and practices based on well-entrenched traditions, gets irritated with its new, "change-it-now" chief executive officer. Disagreement about values are at the root of decision impasses and personality clashes. As these dilemmas are resolved, the solutions and processes of arriving at them will become part of that organization's history, part of those particular individuals' patterns of working with each other. We can write stories about how ethical dilemmas arise; thinking about how to resolve them can take the form of imaginatively projecting alternate resolutions and the alternative futures they would bring.

Jane Addams's writings provide a good illustration of the way in which narrative functions as a method of thinking about ethics. Addams (1860–1935) is most well known as a founder of Chicago's Hull House and as an international peace activist. She worked with countless philanthropic organizations and did a lot of fund raising. She was also a penetratingly insightful philosopher, and her writings give us a paradigm for how to use narrative in ethical reflection. For example, in *Democracy and Social Ethics*, Addams works out her own ethical theory through telling about the people she interacted with in Chicago. She describes the lives of domestic servants, factory workers, charity visitors, and families she has known, trying to understand them from their own points of view, and placing their concerns in the ongoing contexts of their lives.[1] By approaching Addams's stories as a method for thinking about ethics, we can identify two significant dimensions of ethical reflection: sympathetic understanding and social and temporal context.

(a) Sympathetic Understanding

Addams writes, "Sympathetic knowledge is the only way of approach to any human problem ... not only by the information of the statistician, but by sympathetic understanding."[2] Living in an immigrant community, interacting with her neighbors as neighbors, and not as subjects of charity, Addams sought to understand their customs, values, determination, and failings. She listened as they articulated their own needs and desires, and then worked with them to achieve the social changes they deemed important. Addams believed that only by approaching her neighbors through sympathy, and being willing to see their world through their own eyes as much as possible, would she be able to attain the sort of understanding needed for genuine social reform.

In Addams' method, sympathy gives access to knowledge, and emotion gives the impetus for action. She tells the story of an unloved orphan, who at age 9 became a dock worker. He lived roughly, until he encountered a disabled boy, abandoned on a freighter. From that first meeting until the boy's death several years later, he was the object of the dock worker's affection. Because of their friendship, the dock worker was transformed and became a labor leader committed to social change. Addams states that only the actual experience of sympathy and affection for a particular child in need, and not abstract moral theories, could have brought about this transformation.[3]

Still, Addams knew that making changes based on sympathy alone was insufficient. She had seen how the charitable impulse could become "cruel and disastrous" if unfiltered by reason.[4] While insisting that the perspective of the objective, detached outsider was inadequate by itself, Addams and her colleagues at Hull House carefully gathered statistical information and evaluated alternative courses of action before initiating reform measures.

(b) Social and Temporal Context

Along with sympathetic understanding, Addams stresses the importance of context: People's needs and desires must be understood
within the social and temporal settings of their lives. She was highly
critical of abstract ethical theories that attempted to prescribe
actions merely by applying abstract ethical rules. Writing of a "charity visitor" who held strong ethical convictions about how people
should live, Addams writes, "Her moral concepts constantly tend to
float away from her, unless they have a basis in the concrete relation
of life."[5] Here, narrative as a method for thinking about ethics is helpful. The setting of a well-told story gives the concrete social and historical context essential for understanding the ethical dimensions
of the situation.

Part of context is a sense of temporal movement. In a well-told
story, we come to know characters as persons with unfolding lives,
who can grow and change. They enter the story with a past, and even
as the story ends, we know that their lives will continue. Much of
the poignancy of Addams's stories of prostitutes in *A New Conscience
and An Ancient Evil* emerges as she inquires into the stories of women
who appeared to be hardened and morally calloused.[6] The book is
her analysis of what was then called the "white slave trade," in which
girls and young women were lured or sometimes literally kidnapped
from Europe and brought to the United States. Through probing into
the women's pasts, she reveals the vulnerability, the tragedies, the
sheer understandable humanness of their beginnings in the trade.
Part of understanding others' view of a given situation is to place that
situation within the ongoing drama of their lives.

Telling a good story (either real or fictional) with sympathetic
understanding and plenty of contextual clues takes imagination.
Addams saw imagination as a principal ingredient in good moral
thinking, noting that "much of the insensibility and hardness of the
world is due to the lack of imagination which prevents a realization
of the experiences of other people."[7] Moving in 1889 into an immigrant neighborhood with 18 nationalities represented, Addams saw
clearly that ancient village traditions and customs could not bear the
ethical weight they had traditionally carried. Imagination was needed
to replace memory as the faculty for ethical decision making.[8]
Philosopher John Dewey, a friend and colleague of Addams and a
trustee of Hull House, writes, "Imagination is the chief instrument
of the good." He goes on to quote poet Percy Shelley, "A man to be
greatly good must imagine intensely and comprehensively."[9] Making

good ethical decisions involves many imaginings: imagining a range of future alternatives; imagining what each alternative means for the individuals, the organizations, and the communities involved; imagining the organization and the individuals not as static, but as changing and growing; and imagining the current dilemma as one phase of that growth.

At times, imagination works spontaneously, with flashes of insight; at other times, our minds need to ruminate on the possibilities until clarity emerges. We tell and retell our stories to ourselves and to others; in the process, salient features emerge, and less important details fade.

(c) Fund Raisers as Ethical Decision Makers

The ethical decision-making model presented in this book uses patterns of storytelling as a method for ethical reflection. Thinking as novelists or playwrights, we can imagine different potential outcomes and ask what each outcome would mean for the organization, the community, and the individuals affected.

A drama has a setting, a context in which some courses of action are possible while others are not. For the philanthropic fund raiser, the context centers on nonprofit organizations, existing at a given point in time, in a given community. And there are the actors: the donors, board members, fund raisers, staff, clients, volunteers, and community members. Just as playwrights imagine their way into the minds of their characters, so in ethical reflection we think our way into the minds, values, and ways of life of those affected.

The goals for resolving ethical dilemmas also fit well into the patterns of storytelling, perhaps the sort of storytelling of continuing television dramas, in which the tale never ends and a sequel is always a possibility. After resolving an ethical dilemma, we must often come back and work with the same organization and the same people. Every individual resolution becomes part of the context for the next drama, shaping the potential for further cooperation or conflict.

Fund raisers enter the drama of ethical reflection with many ethical skills already in place. Dewey writes, "Thinking is secreted in the interstices of habits."[10] This is a powerful statement, and a good expression of what most fund raisers bring to ethical reflection. Aristotle writes of virtues as habits, as skills that people acquire through cultivation and practice. In practicing courageous acts, one becomes a courageous person. Through practicing acts of generosity, the virtue itself becomes built into one's personality. Most fund raisers are compassionate, fair-minded people. These character traits are "habit-skills," already built into their personalities from a lifetime of experience. But sometimes ethical dilemmas are too complex for these moral habits to deal with spontaneously. And so the sort of ethical reflection discussed in this book functions in "the interstices of habits," building on those moral skills and character traits fund raisers already possess, and thus enhancing these skills for future use.

(d) Ethical Rules

"But wait a minute," some may say, "ethics is about following rules—the 10 commandments of the Pentateuch, the five pillars of Islam, the four noble truths of the Buddha, the one golden rule."

Ethical rules are important; they will be referred to often throughout the book. Rules about telling the truth, respecting human dignity, and working for justice should always remain uppermost in our minds. But to conceptualize ethical thinking as just a matter of applying rules to specific occasions—"sort of like a math problem with humans," as one 11-year-old put it—is too narrow.[11] Rules applied to life situations are applied within ongoing dramas, by actors with ongoing lives. When we try to apply rules mechanically, we may overlook the need for sympathetic understanding and forget that a proper application of rules must be responsive to specific features of context and peculiarities of character.

That ethical rules and storytelling are closely associated becomes more clear when we consider where ethical rules come from and how they are transmitted throughout time. Many rules come from religious and cultural traditions, the wisdom of ages distilled into short form. Those traditions often use stories to teach the rules and clarify their application. Consider the *Bhagavad-Gita*, the parables of Jesus, and the *Analects* of Confucius. Narrative judgment is inescapable. We need to decide which rules to apply in a given situation, and whether this is a case in which we should follow the rules directly, or make an exception. Aristotle describes the difficulty well, reminding us that exercising virtues entails feeling and acting "at the right times, about the right things, towards the right people, for the right end, and in the right way."[12] In thinking of ethics as storytelling, I do not want to diminish the role and significance of ethical rules, but to place them within their proper narrative setting.

1.2 PHILANTHROPY AS A GIFT ECONOMY

Like Russian dolls stacked inside each other, small stories are embedded within larger ones. Epics are fabricated out of countless individual episodes. Every nonprofit organization has its own specific mission, such as providing audiotapes for the blind, preserving rare manuscripts, or encouraging poetry readings. But these specific goals are embedded within the larger framework of the whole of philanthropy. The National Society of Fund Raising Executives (NSFRE) Statements of Ethical Principles is explicit about this. The first bullet in their list reads: "NSFRE members serve the ideal of philanthropy, are committed to the preservation and enhancement of volunteerism, and hold stewardship of these concepts as the overriding principle of professional life...."

By surveying some common definitions of philanthropy, we can sense this wider frame. The relation between micro and macro levels is clear in historian Robert Bremner's comment, "Whatever motives animate individual philanthropists, the purpose of philanthropy itself is to promote the welfare, happiness, and culture of mankind."[13] Robert Payton, founder of the Center on Philanthropy, defines philanthropy quite simply as "voluntary action for the public good," and applies anthropologist Clifford Geertz's felicitous phrase, "the social history of the moral imagination" to the history of philanthropy.[14]

History does not have a grand storymaster controlling the script, and like all historical practices, philanthropy is perhaps better described by listing what it has done, rather than trying to give a unified definition. Brian O'Connell's list reflects this history: "To discover new frontiers of knowledge; to support and encourage excellence; to enable people to exercise their potential; to relieve human misery; to preserve and enhance democratic government and institutions; to make communities a better place to live; to nourish the spirit; to create tolerance, understanding, and peace among people; to remember the dead."[15]

Above all, philanthropy is about creating and sustaining communities—communities of place, of choice, of purpose, of commitment, of interest. In *Ethics and Obedience to the Unenforceable,* John Gardner underscores the importance of community building, "We know from a lot of evidence that community not only confers identity, but a sense of belonging and allegiance, and a sense of security. But, more important, we know that communities are the ground-level generators of values."[16] Giving a gift to the jazz series, volunteering one's time in the historical museum's gift shop, and serving on the drug rehabilitation center board are all part of a long tradition of using philanthropy to build and sustain human communities.

(a) The Metaphor of the Gift Economy

Metaphors help us think. A metaphor enables us to wrap our minds around something huge and multifaceted and make our way through it. Using narrative or storytelling as a pattern for ethical reflection gives us a method of proceeding, a pattern for knowing if we have done it well. Philanthropy, too, is huge and multifaceted, and sometimes while thinking about it or acting in it we lose a sense of what it is and what it is for. Using the notion of the gift economy as a metaphor for philanthropy will help us keep track of the purpose of philanthropy and how it functions.

French anthropologist Marcel Mauss's book, *The Gift: The Form and Reason for Exchange in Archaic Societies,* published in 1925, gives us a starting point for understanding the idea of a gift economy. In it, he describes extensive and complex systems of gift exchange in Polynesia, Melanesia, and in some Native American tribes in the American Northwest. In the Trobriand Islands, a system of gift exchange (*kula*) existed alongside market exchanges (*gimwali*). Vigorous bargaining, acceptable and characteristic of *gimwali,* was thought to be ignoble and inappropriate for *kula*. The practices of *kula,* which Mauss translates as "circle," comprised vast circles of ritual giving encompassing many tribes and many islands. A chief from one island arrives on a second island and offers gifts to its chief, often bracelets and necklaces of sacred significance. The gifts are worn and enjoyed, but after some time they are given away to those on a third island, and then on to the next. The *kula* is just one part of a vast system of services and objects given and passed on.[17] Mauss describes it this way: "The process is marked by a continuous flow in all directions of presents given, accepted, and reciprocated, obligatorily and out of self-interest, by reason of greatness and for services rendered, through challenges and pledges."[18]

This one example contains features common to gift economies, although many variations exist among different cultures. The most important feature is that the exchange is not *quid pro quo,* and while reciprocity is expected, the return is not given directly to the original giver. "Serial reciprocity" describes this process well. The gift, or another item in its place, is to be passed on to a third person, and then on to another so that the gift circulates widely. To accept a gift is to accept the obligation to pass it on, to reciprocate in some way, to become a giver oneself.

The gift has vitality, a spiritual or magical significance. The Maori speak of the *hau*, the spirit of the gift, which is an active spiritual power imbuing both giver and gift.[19] In passing the gift to another, one shares a part of oneself. By circulating, the spirit of the gift is nourished and kept alive. As it moves, it fabricates and strengthens bonds of commitment and promise. The New Caledonians offer this moving description: "Our festivals are the movement of the hook that serves to bind together the various sections of the straw roofing so as to make one single roof, one single word."[20]

Unlike commodity exchanges, gift exchanges are always off-balance, never complete. The bonds created give communities historical continuity. Obligations to reciprocate from the past are carried into the present; discharging them creates future promises to continue the spiral of giving. Gift economies create the interdependencies and ties of commitment and feeling (some affectionate, others just plain sticky) that define community. Individual motives for giving may be mixed and widely varied. (Mauss describes the potlatch of Northwest American tribes as highly competitive and antagonistic. Honor and status belong to those who give the most away.[21]) Whatever the donor's motives, the giving patterns themselves are not selfish because they are not directed solely or primarily toward the giver's benefit. Neither are they selfless, because givers participate in the communities they have created.

(b) Forms of Gift Economies

Gift economies take many forms. Friendship is one form. Mauss opens his book by quoting a section of a Scandinavian epic:

> One must be a friend
> To one's friend,
> And give present for present;
> One must have
> Laughter for laughter
> And sorrow for lies.
> You know, if you have a friend
> In whom you have confidence
> And if you wish to get good results

Your soul must blend in with his
And you must exchange presents
And frequently pay him visits.[22]

Friendships grow with reciprocity, through gifts of time and concern, where no specific return is demanded, but one will inevitably be given. I invite you to dinner; later, at a time of your choosing, you offer me a cup of tea, or perhaps you share theater tickets. I take your child for an afternoon; you show my nephew your photo lab. He sends your partner prints of his hike through the canyon. And so the gifts move on, and with them, the promise that our feeling bonds will continue to be nourished. Epicurus, an ancient Greek philosopher, said, "Of the things which wisdom provides for the blessedness of one's whole life, by far the greatest is the possession of friendship."[23] This possession of friendship cannot be bought and sold in the marketplace; friendship can exist only as a gift economy.

Families are in many respects gift economies. Parents give children physical and emotional nourishment, lessons in life's joys and bumps. Children respond with spontaneous enthusiasm, giving to their parents unexpected and sometimes unrecognizable clay pots or finger paintings. But the children will grow and will pass their own acquired gifts of wisdom and care on to the next generation. In their interviews with Guatemalans living in the United States, the authors of *Philanthropy in Communities of Color* found that most of the Guatemalans they spoke with focused their giving within the family, but "family" was extensive and expansive; giving was frequent and highly responsive. Biological ties among grandparents, parents, children, aunts, uncles, and cousins are stretched by the tradition of *compadrazgo*, or ritual kinship. They share housing, food, and direct caregiving, and send money and goods to family members in Guatemala. No explicit promise of a return is needed, as family solidarity rests on traditions of reciprocal help and commitment. Many functions provided by nonprofits in the dominant American culture, such as nursing homes, hospice care, housing, and assistance to immigrants, are performed within the gift economy of the Guatemalan family.[24] (Many of those interviewed had negative impressions of the dominant culture's philanthropic organizations and giving patterns, finding them a poor substitute for family care and responsibility.)

Gift economies can reflect deeply based philosophical, religious, and cosmological belief systems. Rebecca Adamson, a member of the Cherokee tribe and president of First Nations Development Institute, thinks that giving is a far more comprehensive concept than generosity, charity, or benevolence. For Native Americans, all of creation is connected in the web of life; all are related, and so all are responsible for nourishing the relationships which themselves sustain life. Giving traditions are a way of enacting their fundamental world view.[25]

(c) Philanthropic Nonprofits as a Gift Economy

We must be careful not to think of *gift economy* as a synonym for philanthropic nonprofits, or of *market economy* as referring solely to for-profit businesses. Rather, strands of both gift and market exchanges run through both nonprofit and for-profit organizations. The products and services of many for-profit businesses respond to community needs and strengthen community vitality and growth. Many businesspeople give generously of their intelligence, creativity, and commitment to achieve these goals. Likewise, philanthropic nonprofits participate in market exchanges. Relations with suppliers and charging fees for service where the fee is not subsidized by philanthropic contributions are examples of market rather than gift exchanges. As discussed in Chapter 8, cause-related marketing and sponsorships are better understood as aspects of the market economy in which nonprofits participate, rather than as examples of philanthropic giving.

We also need to be careful not to think of nonprofits as more ethical than businesses because they seek gifts, while thinking of for-profit businesses as less moral, or even amoral, because they seek profits. The two types of organizations have different missions and different ways of generating and distributing income, but many ethical responsibilities are common to both. To treat workers with dignity, customers and clients with honesty, and the community as a treasure are ethical responsibilities belonging to all of us, which carry over into all organizational settings. In both for-profit and nonprofit organizations, people find meaning, pursue goals, and create relationships that can nourish or bruise them. Being for-profit does not exempt an organization from high ethical standards; being nonprofit does not automatically endow an organization with ethical goodness.

Nonetheless, it is fitting to describe philanthropic nonprofits as fundamentally gift economies, even as market economy threads run through them. Central features that define a nonprofit organization's structure and functions are representative of gift rather than market economies. The mission statement is a good place to start. Philanthropic nonprofits exist to advance a public purpose, to enhance the common good; private financial benefit is expressly excluded. Of course, this statement raises many ethical questions. Does an organization in fact serve the public good, or does it have a divisive, harmful effect on community well-being? Is its mission any more than a statement of lofty rhetoric, covering scurrilous activity? Admittedly, things can go wrong, well-intentioned people can misjudge their organization's impact, but the basic point still stands that the intended purpose of philanthropic nonprofits is to enhance public well-being, a giftlike quality.

Nonprofit reliance on volunteers is a clear indication of a gift economy. Many nonprofits begin as volunteer efforts; even in heavily staffed organizations, volunteers as board members hold ultimate responsibility. Volunteers give of themselves, their talents, and their time to the public good, without monetary compensation. They sustain the circle of giving, enabling nonprofits to accomplish the purposes of philanthropy.

Gift economies are precious, even though, like all human institutions, they sometimes crack, reinforce privilege and subordination, or exclude some people from the circle altogether. Yet, sustaining the giftlike quality of community building is a bottom-line responsibility of philanthropy. I worry when I see donor appeals of the sort, "Give to us, and we will give you a neon bumper sticker, three status points with your employer, and five fewer days in purgatory." Donor recognition is fine, but here the nonprofit is losing sight of the nature of the gift and turning it into a parody of a market transaction.

It will help if we identify just what is being exchanged in a gift economy, and between whom. The exchange is not a direct one from donor to nonprofit and then right back from nonprofit to donor. Now donors and volunteers may receive certain benefits in the process. They get enjoyment from participating in communal activities, performing religious duties, or receiving social status and prestige. Benefits may come, but they are not what is being exchanged. The exchanges is *not* "I will give you $100, and you give me back $100 worth of satisfactory feelings," or "I will give you four hours a week with youngsters in the hospital playroom, and you give me four hours' worth of status with my volunteer-minded friends." Remember the circle created through the *kula*, linking all those Trobriand Islanders. Gifts traveled wide and were transmuted in spirit before ever returning to the original donors, assuming they were still alive and had not lost interest.

Let us follow the donor's $100 gift to the nonprofit hospital. The hospital is a funnel, swirling the gift along with many others. Services are provided to those who need them now. The giver may at some point benefit directly from the hospital, or perhaps never. The giver may be giving this $100 in reciprocity for benefits received as a 4-H Club member years ago, in a different community. We are all beneficiaries of convoluted loops of gifts and benefits. Trying to identify which gift corresponds to which benefit in the exchange hopelessly oversimplifies the process. We may be able to identify some givings and receivings in the gift economy of a two-person friendship, but if one thinks it is time to check the accounts, that is probably a sign that something is rotten in the friendship. Reciprocity may be tilting toward exploitation. In a gift economy in which the spirit of the gift has vitality, the givings and the receivings may be widely separated in time and place, but the spirit of the gift will pervade and unify both.

At this point, some illustrations may help. One way the circle of giving expands through time is through *serial reciprocity*. When one cannot return a gift to the original benefactor, then one gives to another in need. Alumni giving is one familiar example. Alumni's college costs were paid in part by former students, anonymous to them. They discharge the debt by giving to the next generation of students.

People frequently use the phrase *giving back* to explain how gifts circulate through their community. One African American explained his sense of community responsibility this way, "I would say you need to give back to the community in which you live in order to enjoy how the community thrives. It's the same principle that a farmer has to give back a little bit of what he reaps to the soil in order for it to harvest again. You can't just take and take and take—it becomes bereft of minerals and everything else and it won't produce anymore. You have to give back in all situations, in all situations."[26]

While fund raisers in philanthropic nonprofits spend time in both market and gift economies, their primary purpose is to keep the spirit of the gift alive, to sustain and enhance the cycle of giving. Philanthropy fuels a gift economy, and fund raisers can do much to keep the spirit of giving explicitly present to public perception. Fund raisers act as both facilitators and educators. As facilitators, they can offer donors and volunteers opportunities to act on shared value commitments and work toward shared visions of community well-being; they then facilitate the movement of the gifts toward those ends. As educators, fund raisers provide information about community needs and possibilities for meeting those needs. Fund raisers also educate as the cycles of giving spiral through time. The young need to learn about philanthropy, and many of the not-so-young need some educational gaps filled in. Socrates thought of education as a form of midwifery, assisting people in giving birth to their own ideas, their own wisdom. Similarly, fund raisers often have the good fortune to help people assess and perhaps discover what they care about. They help people think about what shape they want their community to have and work out at least a part of how they want to lead their lives. By helping people make thoughtful, morally sensitive decisions about themselves and their community, fund raisers move the spirit of the gift and help to keep it vital. In Chapter 2 some of the specific virtues—generosity, charity, compassion, gratitude, and mutuality—that help the gift economy to function well will be discussed.

(d) Moral Complications in Gift Economies

Philanthropy belongs to that collection of terms, along with *family, community,* and *gifts,* which we all endorse enthusiastically until we get past the nostalgia and encounter their disquieting aspects. Robert Frost captured the weariness of family life in his poem, "The Death of the Hired Man," in which he defines home as "the place where, when you have to go there, they have to take you in."[27] Socrates never did work out a mutually harmonious accommodation with his community. The citizens condemned him to death; his friends arranged a way of escape. But Socrates refused exile, reminding his friends that his very identity was a gift from Athens. He was thoroughly enmeshed in that community, but it was a relationship better characterized by mutual irritation than by mutual love. Sometimes, community can best be defined as "made up of the people you squabble with."

Gifts come with strings attached. Communities are formed by strings; we want them, but sometimes we resent them. Ralph Waldo Emerson was keenly aware of the rub between independence and interdependence. In his essay on gifts, he says, "The law of benefits is a difficult channel, which requires careful sailing, or rude boats. It is not the office of a man to receive gifts. How dare you give them? We wish to be self-sustained. We do not quite forgive a giver. The hand that feeds us is in some danger of being bitten."[28]

The strings attached to some gifts bind too tightly—the gift functions as an extension of the donor's power. Emerson continues, "The gift, to be true, must be the flowing of the giver unto me, correspondent to my flowing unto him. When the waters are at level, then my goods pass to him, and his to me."[29] When the strings attached to the gift work to keep the waters from reaching level, to keep the waters from flowing both ways, then the gift harms community, and so must be refused.

Think about a private school in the central city that prides itself on the diversity of its student body. Many board members think it has a healthy mix of students from different racial, ethnic, and economic backgrounds. However, one influential, white board member worries that the school is becoming, as he says, "too gray." He threatens to resign from the board, taking with him his generous donations, his substantial influence in the city's financial sector, and his four, full tuition–paying children. The strings attached to his gifts of money, service, and influence threaten to distort the sort of community the school is committed to achieving.

At least once each semester, I remind my students of the truism, "You can never do only one thing." Gifts often do several things; we may applaud the obvious good they do while being oblivious to damages incurred. There are many stories of sacrificial generosity, which had the side effect of prolonging suffering. On April 12, 1861, the first shot of the U.S. Civil War was fired on Fort Sumter. On April 20, in Cleveland, the Ladies Aid and Sanitary Society was organized. Their mission was to provide blankets for all the volunteer soldiers. In carrying out this task, they discovered that many of the soldiers needed clothing. While they sewed, illness swept through the army camp, so the Society sent nurses and medical supplies. The same story could be told of cities and towns throughout both North and South. This letter, written in Virginia on August 18, 1861, could have come from any of them. "We are now very busy making clothes, knitting socks for the soldiers. Each lady proposes making one hundred garments—some are making mattresses, preparing bandages and knit nightshirts and comforts for the wounded—all are doing the most they can to add to the comforts of the soldiers."[30] Had the efforts of the Ladies Aid Societies been less prodigious, the war might well have ended sooner. By acting to relieve immediate suffering, the women's efforts indirectly prolonged the suffering of many others.

These examples of moral complications illustrate why fund raisers and others involved in philanthropy need to place individual ethical decisions within larger frameworks. In the press of the current fund drive, it is too easy to appreciate the major gift without noticing how binding the attached strings may be or how the gift masks prejudice. In the early twentieth century, the Phillis Wheatley Home in Cleveland offered shelter, safety, friendship and job training to young black women. Many white women contributed financial support to the Wheatley Home, but historian Darlene Clark Hine sees a racist underside to their generosity. It gave them a way to keep the Young Women's Christian Association exclusively white and to get more highly trained maids for themselves.[31] Nonprofit fund raisers, educators, and facilitators of the gifts that build community must sort through such strings and complications every day.

(e) The Color of Ethics

"It's such a gray area," we often hear, when difficult ethical situations come up. Gray is the color of fog, of cloudy dull skies without clarity or edges. In ethical reflection, we sometimes feel as if we are navigating in a fog with no landmarks and no sense of direction. Gray is also a color made by mixing black and white. Sometimes, in our ethical reflections, we see no clear, right answers; every alternative is tinged with negativity, evil taints the good.

"Ethics as gray" is a potent metaphor, and as with all things potent, it needs to be used with great care. Some ethical choices are clearly right or wrong and to call ethics "gray" in these cases is a way of hiding from ethical truths and ethical responsibilities. But in other cases, choices are not so clear and it is important to identify and acknowledge the ways in which ethics can be gray. In some cases, it may be true that no alternative course of action is ethically pure, and all alternatives require uncomfortable compromises. A second type of grayness arises when ethically decent people prioritize their values differently. Some members of a social service agency may want to emphasize relieving immediate needs for food and shelter; others may want to stress education and job training as long-term self-sufficiency skills. A third type of grayness arises from the way that the same acts can accomplish both ethical and unethical purposes as in the Civil War and the Phillis Wheatley Home examples.

When ethical situations look gray, it is important to sort out just which sense of grayness applies. If the real difficulty is that morally decent people prioritize their values differently, but those involved think the grayness results from good mixed with evil, organizations may become needlessly polarized. In the social service agency example, those concerned with long-term self-sufficiency can accuse the others of trying to foster dependency; those committed to meeting immediate needs can accuse the others of lacking compassion.

When an ethical quandary feels gray, thinking of ethics as storytelling can be helpful. When the full story of the ethical dilemma is told carefully, with sympathetic understanding of each person's perspective, this sort of polarization can be minimized. In the following section, a method of ethical decision making is presented that will help fund raisers construct stories in a way that clarifies the grayness and brings basic ethical commitments to the foreground. The method encourages sympathetic understanding and imagination as tools for resolving ethically troubling situations.

1.3 THE ETHICAL DECISION-MAKING MODEL[32]

Most daily decisions have an ethical dimension, and much of the time we instinctively function as competent ethical decision makers. We may not be directly conscious of it, but much of our "common-sense" decision making incorporates concern for basic ethical values such as honesty, establishing trust with others, and showing concern for their well-being. Usually, we are kind to children, fair to our colleagues, and decent to strangers.

A story will illustrate how we insert ethical concerns into our everyday lives. By examining this story, we can draw out the ethical dimensions of everyday thought, and then apply the same pattern to ethical decision making in fund raising.

After work, you pick up a four-year-old (your child, your grandchild, a neighbor, or some other youngster to whom you are attached) from day care and stop by the supermarket to find something to serve your second cousin twice removed, who just happens to be passing through town this evening. At the store you bump into a friend and stop to chat for a few minutes. You talk about the fact that if it does not rain soon your shrubs will die, about the sale on avocados in the produce department, and about getting a haircut before the fund-raising gala next week. All the while, the 4-year-old is wandering about examining boxes of granola bars.

This may look like a rare moment of idyllic calm in your over-stressed life, but what is really going on inside your head is some remarkably sophisticated ethical decision making in which you link moment-by-moment decisions to your most basic values. You let the 4-year-old wander (although always in sight) because you want him to grow up to be curious and independent. Your friend has been an important source of strength and support for years. She is the one who did your laundry for a month when your father was dying of cancer. You know her daughter has a drug problem, so as you chat through a guacamole recipe, you watch her face and listen to her tone of voice, judging if this is the day she needs for you to take an extra five minutes communing about produce sales. It has little to do with avocados, and everything to do with sustaining the friendship.

Suddenly, right when you are getting to the part about adding the lemon juice, you break off in mid-sentence and dash madly after the 4-year-old, as he gets perilously close to the pyramid of glass pickle jars. Keeping him alive and reasonably intact is also something you care about.

Here, your decisions about pickles, granola bars, and guacamole revolve around your basic values of caring for the child and sustaining your most important relationships. Much of getting through the day is a matter of negotiating life's little details in ways that support these basic values. Most of the time, at least in familiar surroundings, we successfully integrate basic values with life's minutia, without even being conscious of it. When troubling or unusually complex issues arise, however, or when we have too many responsibilities to juggle at once, it is helpful to articulate these values and deliberate about what courses of action are most consistent with our basic value commitments.

(a) Fund Raisers' Three Basic Value Commitments

In this story, caring for the child and sustaining the friendship are basic value commitments. For fund raisers in their professional capacity, three basic value commitments can be identified:

1. The **organizational mission** that directs the work
2. Our **relationships** with the people with whom we interact
3. Our own sense of **personal integrity**

The fund raiser, acting with integrity, has the task of creating and maintaining a supporting network of relationships in order to further the mission of the organization. We bring ethical sensitivity to decision making when we place particular decisions in the context of these three basic value commitments. The ethical decision-making model takes these three value commitments and uses them to construct stories about alternative ways of resolving ethically troubling situations. Here, each of the three value commitments will be described briefly, and then a sample case analysis using the model will be given. Then, I will point out how using this method incorporates the dimensions of ethics discussed in this chapter: sympathetic

ORGANIZATIONAL MISSION

FUND RAISER'S
Personal Integrity

RELATIONSHIPS
(Colleagues   Donors   Volunteers   Community)

Exhibit 1.1   Fund Raisers' Three Basic Value Commitments

understanding, social and temporal context, and sustaining the gift economy's vitality. In the chapters that follow, each of the three basic value commitments will be discussed in considerable detail.

(i) Organizational Mission

Every philanthropic organization has a mission—a social need it is trying to meet, a human good it is trying to achieve. Such purposes range from providing disaster relief to preserving rain forests; from meeting basic survival needs to enriching our spirits through artistic excellence or religious devotion. The mission justifies and directs daily tasks and decisions.

Ethical difficulties often involve misalignments between the organizational mission and daily decisions. Decisions about a university athletic program may bring glory to the school, while the athletes remain poorly educated. Professors may favor outside consulting to the point of neglecting their students. In some organizations, when glamorous fund-raising events net little income, one has to ask if their primary function is to serve the organizational mission or to provide high-class entertainment for the organization's supporters.

Many organizations have more than one fundamental purpose. A hospital, for example, may define its mission in terms of patient care, medical research, and educating future medical practitioners. While a given daily decision may not further all three goals, we can at least take care that a decision furthering one purpose does not unduly slight or injure another. Soliciting funds for long-term basic research is fine, as long as that emphasis does not diminish the quality of patient care.

Each nonprofit's specific organizational mission is embedded inside the larger framework of philanthropy. Although it is good to review and revise the mission statement periodically to make sure it advances philanthropic values, it is also helpful to assess even small-scale decisions in light of their impact on philanthropy as a gift economy. Does a particular decision revitalize the spirit of giving and move the gift along its way?

(ii) Relationships

The slogan goes that fund raisers raise friends, as much as funds. Networks of relationships with donors, colleagues, volunteers, and community members are the medium through which organizational missions are furthered. The second basic value commitment, then, is concerned with the character and quality of our relationships to each of these groups. Many ethically troubling situations are caused by or may cause fractures in workplace relationships.

Think of the qualities that characterize healthy, long-term professional relationships. Respect, honesty, and open communication are high on the list. Sensitivity, caring, and a good sense of humor also figure prominently. And trust, no doubt, is a central value—trust in the goodwill and integrity of the other, and trust that one is respected and that one's basic concerns are taken seriously. When thinking through alternative ways of resolving ethical difficulties, try to enter imaginatively into other people's way of experiencing the world. How do others, with their own idiosyncratic concerns, priorities, and values view this alternative? How would it strengthen or weaken the relationship? Not all relationships can or should be preserved; even in ethically sound decisions, some relationships may still get bruised. The point is to incorporate sympathetic understanding as much as possible, and maintain the possibility of a future healthy relationship.

(iii) Integrity

The third value commitment is to preserve and strengthen one's own sense of integrity, to express basic values in everyday actions with courage and compassion. "Ethics" comes from *ethos*, the ancient Greek word for character. Aristotle defined an ethical person as someone with a virtuous character, in whom virtues reside as deeply internalized personality characteristics. Virtues, like skills and habits, are acquired through practice. Just as a pianist acquires habits of skill-ful playing through daily practice, so we can practice being gener-ous, fair, brave, thoughtful, and honest. Through using daily decisions as opportunities for practice, we gradually nurture and develop the ethical qualities of our character.

Often, a sign of ethical trouble is that gnawing feeling that a given path of action would compromise one's integrity. You know that few of the clients in your drug rehabilitation clinic achieve the glowing success portrayed in your TV spots. Your stomach turns a bit when a donor tells you he was so moved by the spots that he wants to dou-ble his pledge. Is your fund-raising success based on dishonest por-trayals? To maintain a long-term perspective it is helpful to think of integrity as a lifetime project, always in the making. In a sense, we are continually engaged in writing our own autobiographies. Each decision, each encounter adds a few lines. The question "How should I act now?" is layered inside the larger question, "How would I like this page of my autobiography to read when I look back at it many years from now? What sort of a person will this decision incline me to become?"

(b) Using the Ethical Decision-Making Chart

Ethical reflection is an activity, carried out through conversations. Because ethically troubling situations generally involve several peo-ple, practicing ethics as a social activity enables the participants to hear the others' perceptions and ways of dealing with the difficulty. It also creates the space for collaborative decision making. Even when done alone, ethical reflection often takes the form of conver-sations with oneself, in which other voices are imagined and pro-jected. Using the ethical decision-making chart seen in Exhibit 1.2 can guide us in constructing stories and using our imaginations to think about the characters and the setting of workplace dramas.

Making a good ethical decision rests, in part, on whether the par-ticipants have asked enough good questions. Placing daily decisions in the context of these three basic value commitments is one way of ensuring that enough good questions are asked. After gathering all relevant information, you are ready to use the chart, "Ethical Deci-sion Making: Evaluating the Alternatives." Begin by writing in a few alternative ways of resolving the case. It is alright to start with alter-natives as obvious as "do it" and "don't do it." Include alternatives with which you are pretty sure you disagree. Analyzing obviously

Ethical Decision-Making Chart

Alternatives	1	2	3	4
Organizational Mission				
How does this alternative promote or detract from the organization's mission?				
basic philanthropic values?				
Relationships				
How does this alternative affect long-term relationships with colleagues, donors, volunteers, and community members?				
Personal Integrity				
In what ways does this alternative help or not help you develop into the person you want to become? How does it strengthen or weaken your own integrity?				

Exhibit 1.2   Ethical Decision-Making Chart

unethical alternatives often brings out insights that can be applied to less clear-cut solutions. Participants often find that additional and often more creative resolutions arise as they discuss the case.

Now work your way down the chart. For each alternative resolution, ask yourself:

- How does this alternative promote or detract from the organization's mission? How does it promote or detract from basic philanthropic values?
- How does this alternative affect long-term relationships with colleagues, donors, volunteers, and community members?
- In what ways does this alternative help or not help me develop into the person I want to become? How does it strengthen or weaken my own integrity?

There is no equation or formula that, if applied correctly, will yield an "ethically correct" decision. This is not a flowchart; you do not insert facts, add values, push a button, and wait for a correct solution to emerge out the other end. Ethics always involves judgment, and people of goodwill often disagree on how to interpret the facts or assess the values of a given situation. For many situations, there may be no one right answer; the ethics may be "gray" in one of the senses discussed above. But there are plenty of wrong answers, and the hope is that after reflection, the wrongness of the wrong answers will be clear. One will then be able to choose among the others with sensitivity and good judgment. If an alternative supports all three basic value commitments, you can be assured that it is ethically sound.

(c) Sample Case Analysis: The Wildlife Painting Case[33]

Consider this scenario:

> A college fund raiser has been working with an alumna, a famous wildlife painter. She agrees to do an oil painting of a nostalgic campus scene. Alumni who donate at least $100 to the college annual fund will receive reprints of the painting. After a highly successful fund-raising program, the artist presents the fund raiser with one of her original oil paintings, valued at more than $2,500. Is it ethical to accept the painting as a personal gift?
>
> The obvious alternatives are: (1) accept the painting or (2) reject the painting. We can start by analyzing just these two. (See Exhibit 1.3.)

(i) Alternative 1: Accept the Painting

Organizational Mission.   The college's fundamental purposes include educating students, contributing to the growth of scholarly knowledge through research, and serving the community. None of these are compromised in a direct or immediate way if you accept the painting. However, because you accepted the painting as a personal gift, the artist may feel you have an obligation to her. In the future, she could put you in an awkward position, which could have detrimental effects on the organizational mission. For example, she could pressure you to use your influence to get her a position on the college board of trustees. Or, she may want to establish a scholarship for students interested in studying an esoteric art form, even though the art department lacks the necessary personnel and the resources to support this study.

THE WILDLIFE PAINTING CASE

Alternatives	1	2	3	4
	Accept the painting.	Reject the painting.	Ask the artist to donate the painting to the College.	
Organizational Mission				
How does this alternative promote or detract from the organization's mission?	Mission of education, research, service. No effects unless artist feels you owe her favors that are detrimental to the college.	Little immediate effect; you avoid being compromised in ways that might hinder the college s organizational mission.	Contributes to aesthetic education; may encourage other artists to support the college.	
basic philanthropic values?	Acknowledges artist s gratitude, but removes painting from gift circulation.	Keeps the college s mission consistent with philanthropic values.	Acknowledges artist s gratitude and keeps the painting within the gift economy.	
Relationships				
How does this alternative affect long-term relationships with colleagues, donors, volunteers, and community members?	You may have compromised your relationship with the artist. Relations with colleagues may become strained.	Strengthens relations with colleagues if they see you refuse a personal favor. Artist may be offended at your refusal, but keeps open the possibility of good future relationship with the artist.	Rewards all colleagues who worked on this project. Maintains a positive and proper professional relationship with the artist.	
Personal Integrity				
In what ways does this alternative help or not help you develop into the person you want to become? How does it strengthen or weaken your own integrity?	It may be difficult to exercise independent judgment in the future.	You maintain independent judgment and exercise courage.	Increases your effectiveness as a fund raiser while maintaining your integrity.	

Exhibit 1.3   The Wildlife Painting Case

Should the artist use her influence in these ways, students and the college community could be adversely affected. She may not be qualified to be on the board, she may compromise the autonomy and good judgment of the art department, and so on.

Encouraging values such as generosity and gratitude help to sustain philanthropy as a gift economy. If you accept the painting, you acknowledge the artist's generosity and gratitude. However, you also remove the painting from circulating within the gift economy.

Relationships.   From the preceding discussion, it is clear that your relationship with the artist may be compromised. Instead of a professional relationship in which mutual concern for the well-being of the college is foremost, personal ties of obligation may have been formed. Your relationships with colleagues may also become strained. Your colleagues worked with you on the fund-raising project, yet they did not receive personal paintings. They might wonder if you have received personal gifts or favors from other donors as well. These suspicions would weaken the trust that underlies the long-term health of collegial relationships.

Personal Integrity.   You have compromised your own integrity and your ability to act with independent judgment by placing yourself in such a position with the artist. She did not merely offer you a personal gift, as between friends. By mixing personal and professional roles, the artist brings with the gift the expectation of future professional favors. By asking her to do the painting for the alumni in the first place, you gave her a lot of publicity. Alumni may like the print and want to obtain more of her work. The artist could use the personal gift as a way of pressuring you to open additional future opportunities for her. Accepting the gift this time may make it more difficult for you to act independently in future dealings.

(ii) Alternative 2: Reject the Painting

Organizational Mission.   If you reject the painting as a personal gift, you avoid putting yourself in this compromised position. You will not be in a position to detract from the college's fundamental purposes, and you further its purposes indirectly by remaining the sort of professional best able to work for the institution.

The college's mission is consistent with the purpose of philanthropy as serving the public good. Although the artist's own sense of generosity may be dented if you refuse the painting, you keep the college on firm ground to encourage philanthropic giving from others.

Relationships.   If colleagues knew you had been offered and had rejected the painting, this would strengthen the trust and respect they have in you, and thus strengthen your working relationships. Your relationship with the artist may become strained, but she has placed you in a position in which a healthy relationship is impossible. The strain may be temporary; rejecting the painting may be the only way to make a future good relationship with her possible.

Personal Integrity.   You have used this experience as practice for strengthening your own integrity, even though it may have been difficult.

By the time you work through these two alternatives, it is likely that someone will suggest, "How about asking the artist to donate the painting to the college? It would look great hanging in the college theater lobby." So, let us add this alternative to the chart.

(iii) Alternative 3: Ask the Artist to Donate the Painting to the College

Organizational Mission.   One aspect of educating students and serving the community is to enhance people's aesthetic sensibility. Displaying the painting in the college theater serves this purpose and also acknowledges the artist's generosity and gratitude. The painting remains within the philanthropic gift economy so that visitors and members of the college community can enjoy it.

Relationships.   Accepting the painting for the college rewards all your colleagues who worked on this project, rather than giving special recognition just to you. This would strengthen the spirit of camaraderie among you and your colleagues, which would have a positive effect on future endeavors. Other artists and potential donors may also feel encouraged to support the college in analogous ways.

The artist may not have had ulterior motives in offering you the painting. She may simply have appreciated the opportunity to work with you and help the college. She may not have realized that in offering the painting as a personal gift, she is placing you in a compromised position. By suggesting she donate the painting to the college, you offer her a way to show her appreciation, without the sense of embarrassment she may feel if you simply refuse the painting as a personal gift.

Personal Integrity.   Part of your own sense of personal integrity is to be an effective, diligent professional. Encouraging the artist to donate the painting is well in keeping with your role as fund raiser. Rather than placing a block in the cycle of giving, you have facilitated its movement.

In this case study, the strongest alternative is to encourage the artist to donate the painting to the college. If she refuses, then you should refuse to accept the painting as a personal gift.

While working through this case, someone may ask, "Suppose it's a lousy painting?" That is a good question, and it gives you a new case to analyze. So, take out a fresh copy of the chart and begin anew.

1.4 THE MODEL, ETHICS AS NARRATIVE, AND PHILANTHROPY AS A GIFT ECONOMY

One rarely hears inefficiency praised as a virtue, but in thinking through ethically troubling situations, thinking slowly has its advantages. One virtue of the chart is that by following it through systematically, one is forced to think slowly and attend to reasons and details that might otherwise be overlooked. Also, by going through the chart one alternative at a time, the polarizing effects of a debate format can be avoided. Sometimes, debates about ethics are fruitful, but too often, the effect is to further entrench disagreement. For good ethical reflection, it is important not to be defensive about one's own position and to be willing to enter into others' ways of thinking and feeling. Even people who initially advocate, and may continue to advocate, different alternatives will be able to uncover areas of agreement as they work their way through the chart, instead of simply arguing back and forth about their own preferred solution. Articulating areas of agreement may encourage creative compromise, enabling people to come up with new resolutions that all can endorse.

Thus, focusing first on the organizational mission is a good strategy, as people probably agree on its content and importance. Starting from clearly expressed, shared commitments, rather than polarized differences, bodes well for a healthy decision-making process.

There are several ways in which using the chart encourages sympathetic understanding. Articulating the organization's mission and its relation to the goals of philanthropy, and affirming shared commitment to those goals, gives an initial basis for sympathy and goodwill. Also, because the goal of evaluating the effect of each alternative on the fund raiser's relationship with various groups is to strengthen long-term relationships, sympathetic understanding emerges as one enters imaginatively into the perspective of office colleagues, board members, volunteers, donors, and community members.

Social contexts will be articulated as the stories are told. Good ethical reflection involves careful attention to both factual details and basic values (remember the supermarket). As you work through the chart slowly, it is likely that different interpretations of the facts will emerge, along with value differences. In some discussions, ethical differences evaporate as people realize that apparent value clashes are really just different interpretations of facts, or different collections of facts relevant to the case.

The temporal dimension is present throughout. Placing the organizational mission in the context of broader philanthropic values is a good way of checking whether the mission stays true through time or whether it has drifted. By focusing on long-term relationships, the bumps caused by immediate disagreements are more easily recognized and kept in perspective. Finally, thinking about integrity in terms of our continuing autobiographies better equips us to accept temporary discomfort with serenity. "If I don't say just what I think the donor wants to hear, we won't get this gift this time" will not seem so compelling as a reason to cheapen one's sense of integrity.

Finally, this method helps us to remember that what is important about philanthropy is that it serves public purposes by keeping the philanthropic gift economy functioning. Reviewing the mission clarifies the public purposes being served. Keeping philanthropic values firmly in mind helps us resist those short-term gains that compromise long-term consistency with philanthropic purposes.

DISCUSSION QUESTIONS

1. Trying to define philanthropy is both intriguing and frustrating, especially if we try to find a definition that fits giving traditions outside the dominant U.S. culture of the past two centuries. Take Robert Payton's frequently quoted definition, "Voluntary giving is for the public good." (Payton is fully aware of the complications in his definition.) *Voluntary* is generally defined in contrast to nonvoluntary taxation. *Public* is generally defined as "outside the family."

  a. In ancient Greece, many governmental tasks were carried out "voluntarily" as part of aristocratic privilege and obligation. When philanthropy and government are so deeply intertwined, is it still philanthropy?
  b. If a nonprofit social service agency receives all its funding from government grants, is it a philanthropic agency? Is it part of the gift economy?
  c. In many societies, the line between family and public is not clearly drawn. How, for example, do we understand giving traditions within Guatemalan families? Should they be considered philanthropic?

2. In this chapter, fund raisers were described as educators and facilitators of gifts. Michael O'Neill, director of the Institute for Nonprofit Organization Management, goes further by describing fund raisers as "moral trainers," who inculcate the virtues of generosity and responsibility in those with whom they work.[34] Some might object, saying that moral training is better left to parents, friends, and religious communities. Is moral training part of a fund raiser's job?

NOTES

1. Jane Addams, *Democracy and Social Ethics* (New York: Macmillan, 1907; reprint ed., Cambridge, MA: Harvard University Press, 1964.

2. Jane Addams, *A New Conscience and an Ancient Evil* (New York: Macmillan, 1912), p. 11.

3. Jane Addams, *The Spirit of Youth and the City Streets* (New York: Macmillan, 1909; reprint ed., Urbana: University of Illinois Press, 1972), pp. 155–6.

4. Jane Addams, *Newer Ideals of Peace* (New York: Macmillan, 1906), p. 160.

5. *See* note 1, p. 68.

6. *See* note 2, *A New Conscience and an Ancient Evil.*

7. Jane Addams, *Democracy and Social Ethics*, p. 9.

8. Jane Addams, *The Second Twenty Years at Hull House* (New York: Macmillan, 1930), p. 367.

9. John Dewey, *Art as Experience* (1934); reprinted in Jo Ann Boydston (ed.): *John Dewey: The Later Works, 1925–1953*, vol. 10 (Carbondale and Edwardsville: Southern Illinois University Press, 1987), pp. 350, 351.

10. John Dewey, *The Public and Its Problems* (1927); reprinted in Jo Ann Boydston (ed.): *John Dewey: The Later Works, 1925–1953*, vol. 2 (Carbondale and Edwardsville: Southern Illinois University Press, 1988), p. 335.

11. Carol Gilligan, *In a Different Voice* (Cambridge, MA: Harvard University Press, 1982), p. 26.

12. Aristotle, *Nicomachean Ethics,* trans. by Terence Irwin (Indianapolis: Hackett, 1985), p. 44.

13. Robert H. Bremner, *American Philanthropy,* 2nd ed. (Chicago: University of Chicago Press, 1988), p. 3.

14. Robert Payton, *Philanthropy: Voluntary Action for the Public Good* (New York: Macmillan, 1988), p. 40.

15. Brian O'Connell, *Philanthropy in Action* (New York: Foundation Center, 1987), p. 8.

16. John Gardner, "Summary of Statement to IS Committee on Values and Ethics," in The Nation's Voluntary and Philanthropic Community: *Ethics and Obedience to the Unenforceable* (Washington DC: Independent Sector, 1991), p. 145.

17. Marcel Mauss, *The Gift: The Form and Reason for Exchange in Archaic Societies* (1925), trans. by W. D. Halls (New York: Norton, 1990), pp. 21–31.

18. *Id.*, p. 29.
19. *Id.*, p. 11.
20. *Id.*, p. 21.
21. *Id.*, p. 37.
22. *Id.*, p. 2
23. Epicurus, *The Epicurus Reader,* trans. by Brad Inwood and L. P. Gerson (eds.) (Indianapolis: Hackett, 1994), p. 34.
24. Bradford Smith, Sylvia Shue, Jennifer Lisa Vest, and Joseph Villarreal, *Philanthropy in Communities of Color* (Bloomington: Indiana University Press, 1999), pp. 49–68.
25. Ronald Austin Wells, *The Honor of Giving: Philanthropy in Native America* (Indianapolis: Indiana University Center on Philanthropy, 1998), pp. 30, 36.
26. Bradford Smith et al., *Philanthropy in Communities of Color,* p. 18–19.
27. Robert Frost, "The Death of a Hired Man," in *Robert Frost's Poems* (New York: Washington Square Press, 1970), p. 165.
28. Ralph Waldo Emerson, "Gifts," *The Essays of Ralph Waldo Emerson* (1841) (Cambridge, MA: Harvard University Press, 1987), p. 312.
29. *Id.*, p. 313.
30. Anne Firor Scott, *Natural Allies: Women's Associations in American History* (Urbana: University of Illinois Press, 1992), pp. 69–70.
31. Darlene Clark Hine, "'We Specialize in the Wholly Impossible,' The Philanthropic Work of Black Women," in Kathleen D. McCarthy (ed.): *Lady Bountiful Revisited* (New Brunswick, NJ: Rutgers University Press, 1990), p. 80.
32. Some of the material in this section is taken from my article, "Ethical Fund Raising: Deciding What's Right." *Advancing Philanthropy* (Spring 1994), pp. 29–33. I thank *Advancing Philanthropy* for permission to use this material here.
33. This case analysis is intended to apply to western organizational settings. There are many societies in which personal gifts have different cultural meanings than portrayed here. The analysis would be different in those societies.
34. Michael O'Neill, "Fundraising as an Ethical Act," in Marianne G. Briscoe (ed.): *Ethics in Fundraising: Putting Values into Practice, New Directions for Philanthropic Fundraising,* no. 6 (San Francisco: Jossey-Bass, Winter 1994), pp. 3–14.

Organizational Mission and the Wider Frame of Philanthropy

"How does this alternative promote
or detract from the organization's mission?

How does it promote or detract
from basic philanthropic values?"

2.1 ORGANIZATIONAL MISSION

In Chapter 1, ethics was described as a form of storytelling. Non-profit organizations have many stories to tell, full of characters, stretched out over time. The organizational mission is the theme of the story, the sustaining thread that gathers and gives unity to all of the details. The mission statement defines, directs, and justifies the organization. It defines by stating just what the organization is trying to accomplish; it directs by being the touchstone in light of which programs are developed. It justifies by showing that the purpose to be achieved is for the public good, and that donors, by contributing, can share in a common philanthropic endeavor. This chapter will look at dimensions of the first basic value commitment on the ethical decision-making chart: the commitment to organizational mission and philanthropic values. In assessing whether an alternative is consistent with the organization's mission, three dimensions are particularly important: clarity, consistency and efficiency.

(a) Clarity of the Mission

Clarity is an important criterion for a good mission statement. If the mission is not clear, misunderstandings are likely to arise. Donors may think they are contributing to a given purpose, while the funds may be used for something else. If an organization's mission is not clear, it is sometimes difficult to tell if, or when, ethical problems arise. Consider this case:

> **Mission Drift?:** A small private school's mission is to provide education in Spanish and French. The marketing committee recently redesigned its literature, emphasizing the economic benefit of the school to the community, in addition to the inherent value of bilingualism. Donations from businesses increased as businesses found that potential employees from other countries were more willing to relocate once they knew about the school. At a recent meeting on the upcoming capital campaign, a board member suggested, "What about using slots in the school as part of our fund raising? For every $10,000 a corporation donates, we could guarantee an employee's child a slot in the school."

Is there an ethical issue here? That depends on whether the mission goes beyond providing education in Spanish and French to those who can pay. Does the school's mission include maintaining a certain mix of students in terms of economic or ethnic diversity? Is the school for academically gifted students only? If the answer is "yes" to these or similar questions, then the mission could be compromised by the proposal. Unless the mission is clearly stated, it is difficult to determine whether an ethical problem exists.

(b) Consistency with the Mission

Along with clarity, consistency with mission is important; ethical problems arise when fund-raising practices are inconsistent with the mission. Consider this example:

> **Mission Match?:** One of your responsibilities, as coordinator for special events for Organization X, is to plan a golf tournament. In your small, Midwestern town, a condom manufacturer, Safe Choices, Inc., is one of the primary employers. A representative from Safe Choices, Inc. offers to underwrite the entire golf event.

Is there an ethical issue here? It depends on the mission of Organization X. If X is a family planning clinic, then it is a great match. If X is an experimental theater company or a blood bank, there is no problem. But if X is religiously affiliated, with official and long-term commitments opposing artificial birth control methods, then there is a serious ethical issue. Accepting a gift from such a donor is inconsistent with the organization's mission and could lead to questions about the organization's integrity.

This case, as written, sounds simple. But many times, it is hard to determine whether a funding source is consistent with an organization's mission. Consider Boys and Girls Clubs' $60 million sponsorship and marketing arrangement with Coca-Cola.[1] The Boys and Girls Clubs' mission reads, "To inspire and enable all young people, especially those from disadvantaged circumstances, to realize their full potential as productive, responsible and caring citizens."[2] Critics charge that because Coke has no nutritional value, and because caffeine has been linked to hyperactivity, this marketing arrangement encourages poor nutritional habits. This is contrary to the mission of helping children realize their full potential.[3] Alternatively, some argue that the match between mission and marketing arrangement is acceptable. Soft drinks are unobjectionable as long as children learn to enjoy them in moderation and cultivate good nutritional habits. (The ethical dimensions of corporate sponsorships will be examined more fully in Chapter 8.)

This case illustrates how clarity of mission is not just a matter of crafting the language of the mission statement, so as to pass muster with a writing teacher. The mission is not just words on a piece of paper. An organization's mission is dynamic, a part of its continuing, living story. Just as the mission shapes and guides the organization, so the mission itself is shaped and guided by the ongoing actions and decisions of its members. If people want to know if jay-walking is permitted on a certain street, they do not just check the law books; they also watch the daily activity on the street. Children learn quickly that "I want it done now," means different things, when uttered by different people. The meaning of an organization's mission gets clarified and amplified day by day.

Mission statements must of necessity be general. Even if Boys and Girls Club had thought about nutritional balance when they wrote their mission statement, they decided wisely to leave it out. If they covered every contingency ahead of time, their mission statement would be as thick as the New York City phone book. What the mission means in practice is something that participants must decide over and over again.

Sometimes, unconscious assumptions are so deeply embedded in a mission that we do not realize they are there. Consider this case; the agency is fabricated, but the issue is real.

Fired Volunteer: While she was recovering from a mastectomy, Lynn Jefferson was very grateful to her neighbor, who offered support by sharing her own experiences of surgery and recovery with her. Lynn wanted to support other women in the same way, so she signed on as a volunteer with the Breast Cancer Recovery Association, whose mission is "to give hope while healing." At the first volunteer training session, Lynn felt like she was "fired." The trainer told her, "We want volunteers who look normal. A breast cancer patient's first concern is whether she will look normal again, so we do everything to assure her that she can. Since you don't wear a prosthesis, how are you ever going to give women hope?"[4]

The association's mission to give hope during recovery was circumscribed by a conventional view of normal female appearance. Many women share this view. But there are women, like Lynn Jefferson, who do not agree, and would like to be living examples that breasts are not essential to a woman's psychological well-being. The organization's definition of normalcy, though unstated, was made a part of the mission through the actions of its members.

There are ethical issues here: Is the organization's adherence to this particular definition of "normal" appropriate? Should it be placed explicitly in the mission statement? The point is that we should pay attention to what we do every day, because our actions determine what the mission means.

(c) The Mission Defines Efficiency

We want to "get things done." We want to use our time and money, and our volunteers' and donors' time and money, wisely. To squander these resources is inefficient and contrary to good stewardship.

What does efficiency mean? We need to remember that efficiency is a dependent variable. What counts as efficient is determined by the goal to be achieved. Parents learn that while it is almost always more efficient at any given time to do a given household task themselves, this is not an efficient way to teach children to be responsible, skilled, and independent. Parents must learn to tolerate inefficiency in terms of getting the specific task done (often by sitting on their hands and holding their tempers), in order to achieve the goal of raising their children to be competent adults. Efficiency is defined by the goal.

Martin Luther's famous "95 Theses" were part of a fund-raising dispute over efficiency. In the early sixteenth century, John Tetzel established his fame as a phenomenally successful fund raiser for the Catholic Church by selling indulgences. Donor recognition took the form of remission of sins for oneself or one's relatives. Tetzel's highly effective fund-raising slogan was, "As soon as coin in coffer rings, the soul from purgatory springs." On October 31, 1517, Luther nailed his 95 Theses to the church door at Wittenberg Castle. Indulgences, he claimed, were not an efficient method for attaining the goal of eternal salvation. Scripture gives no basis for buying one's way into heaven, Luther wrote, and added, "Why does not the Pope, whose riches are at this day more ample than those of the wealthiest of the wealthy, build the one Basilica of St. Peter's with his own money, rather than with that of poor believers?"[5] Indulgences raised funds in a way contrary to the Church's organizational mission and goals.

Goals include processes. Changing the process often alters the goal. Susan Ostrander gives a contemporary example in *Money for Change*, her study of the Haymarket People's Fund. She writes "Haymarket's mission in the larger society is to create, through its grants and its own internal structure, a democratic system based on collective ownership and control of resources; an equitable distribution of wealth and power; an end of all exploitation of some people by others; and freedom from oppressions of class, race, ethnicity, gender, and sexual orientation."[6] Founded in 1974 by George Pillsbury and funded by people of inherited wealth, Haymarket is committed to breaking the pattern typical of many philanthropic organizations, in which those with the money also have the power. At Haymarket, grantmaking decisions are made by local funding boards made up of grassroots community leaders. These people live in the same communities as the groups being funded, so they have inside knowledge of the issues and challenges being addressed. As the organization grew, members realized that they had to move from an informal, consensus-based collective structure to a more formal one. Throughout their discussions, they tried to ensure that concern for efficiency not distort their mission. At one point, a staff member suggested that changing the number of local funding boards from nine to six would cut down on the amount of administrative work required. One funding board member strongly objected, saying, "I think this idea of consolidation could destroy what Haymarket is."[7] This more "efficient" funding board arrangement would sacrifice the close relationship between grantmakers and grantees, which was at the heart of Haymarket's mission. The proposal was rejected.

Haymarket's concern with donor education gives us a second example of why it is important to keep sight of the mission. When efficiency in fund raising is assessed solely in terms of dollars obtained, then the mission is in danger of being distorted. Ostrander explains Haymarket's "political education" component of donor relations this way: "It requires dealing openly with issues of class and race as part of raising and giving money. It requires a way of thinking about social movement philanthropy that systematically incorporates knowledge about class, race, and gender—not simply as interpersonal behaviors that marginalize certain groups, but also as institutionalized structures of privilege and domination that affect the daily lives of all people."[8] Here, political education is an essential part of presenting Haymarket's mission to prospective donors. Without this knowledge, donors who lack Haymarket's commitment to redistribution of social power could create tension, by trying to exercise the kind of power that often accompanies wealth. Thus, fund raising efficiency is calibrated by Haymarket's goal of establishing relationships with donors who share Haymarket's vision of social change.

2.2 THE WIDER FRAME OF PHILANTHROPY

Jane Addams often spoke of the work of Hull House as creating channels through which people's moral energy can flow.[9] This is a wonderfully expressive metaphor for philanthropic organizations. Whatever the specific mission, the larger purpose is to create channels through which people's creativity, skill, and understandings of "the good life" can find expression. This ties in well with the notion of a gift economy: By creating and sustaining the channels for moral energy, gift economies are themselves sustained.

In this section, we will first look at some of the ways in which voluntary associations have functioned as channels for moral energy, and then discuss just a few of the virtues that are particularly serviceable in sustaining gift economies. This will give us a good sense of the ways in which philanthropy provides the frame in which the missions of specific nonprofits reside.

(a) The Expressive Dimension

Voluntary associations have been a significant channel for what has been called the *expressive dimension*. True, we are biological beings, tethered to a physical environment, but as we find our way within it, we use the arts, culture, and religious symbols and ceremonies to make sense of who we are. Artists have often spoken of artistic inspiration as a gift. Plato's metaphor is particularly vivid: "[Poets] gather their strains from honied fountains out of the gardens and dells of the Muses; Thither, like the bees, they wing their way. And this is true. For the poet is a light and winged and holy thing, and there is no invention in him until he has been inspired and is out of his senses, and the mind is no longer in him ..."[10] We smile at Plato's last phrase, but the arts themselves, as well as religious understandings, have long been regarded as gift economies themselves. So it is particularly appropriate that many philanthropic associations use gifts to encourage the gifts of artistic and religious expression.

(b) Social Reform Movements

Consider this list of social reform movements: abolition of slavery, prison reform, humane treatment of the mentally ill, women's suffrage, civil rights, environmental concerns. The list goes on, and nonprofit associations, through voluntary service and funding, fueled them all. The residents of Hull House, with their neighbors as partners, investigated and experimented with child care, child labor reform, health clinics, sanitation, factory conditions, educational methods, and recreational opportunities. Addams believed that the settlement's role was that of social innovator. Hull House would run the experiments and then turn successful projects over to the community.[11]

In retrospect, it is easy to applaud the vision of the suffragists and the courage of the abolitionists. However, in the middle of the fray, there is little consensus on whether a given cause counts as moral reform or moral decline. The public needs time and space to work these things out in nonviolent ways. Abortion, gun control, religion in the schools, and other ethically complex issues are debated by caring people with deep commitments to clashing views. The path to (if not the maze of) social reform is full of bumps, detours, and dead ends. Gift economies of voluntary associations have been crucial to social reform. They are the pathways through which people work toward causes they care about, even while the wisdom of their causes is debated.

(c) Tolerance and Pluralism

People disagree; some celebrate what others despise. In twelfth century Germany, the nuns at Hildegard's Benedictine abbey danced and wore bright jewels. Neighboring bishops frowned; how could such exuberance be worshipful? The history of religious tolerance in England contains an instructive paradox. The seventeenth century Puritans who championed religious tolerance *among* groups were not the least bit tolerant of diverse beliefs and practices *within* their own group. They just did not want other groups to have legally coercive powers over their own tight, intragroup authoritarian reins. Through the efforts of these intolerant people, religious tolerance gradually made its way.[12]

Once we get past the bumper sticker version of "celebrate diversity," we realize that part of the celebration is figuring out how to tolerate ways of living we find distasteful. Although the ideal of social harmony is alluring, I appreciate philosopher Michael Walzer's sober assessment, "Tolerance brings an end to persecution and fearfulness, but it is not a formula for social harmony."[13] He goes on to discuss how the best protection against intolerance is participation and engagement. The gift economy of philanthropy is a place where people who are deeply divided by beliefs and practices can act on their commitments and come to tolerate those who disagree.

2.3 ARISTOTLE'S PATTERN FOR VIRTUE

Because our concern is how fund raisers, working through nonprofit organizations, can contribute to sustaining gift economies, the next sections will focus on those virtues that are particularly germane to facilitating the movement of gifts. Through these virtues, we come to care for the continuing good of the community; through these virtues, we are able to resist attempts to treat gifts as market commodities. In the next two chapters, virtues particularly germane to sustaining strong, healthy professional relationships and one's own integrity will be discussed. Virtues often grow alongside each other, their branches intertwining, so this way of dividing up lists of virtues is to an extent artificial. Many virtues that contribute to strong relationships also support personal integrity and help sustain gift economies.

This section will describe Aristotle's general analysis of what virtues are. The next two sections will present two clusters of virtues, organized by how they sustain the gift economy. The first cluster is called *virtues of gifts as outgoing;* this cluster includes generosity, charity, and compassion. The second cluster is called *virtues of gifts of return*, and includes gratitude and mutuality. In Chapter 1, ethics was described as a form of storytelling. So, in describing these virtues, I will tell stories of traditions in which these virtues have flourished.[14]

What are virtues? In Chapter 1, Aristotle's conception of virtue was mentioned, but this theory is worth a closer look. Aristotle explains moral virtues with an analogy to a craftsperson's skills. In ancient Greece, crafts were at the heart of economic production. Skilled potters provided the means for transporting water from well to home. The craft of hand weaving was essential for fabric and clothing. A skilled craftsperson needs a cognitive understanding of the craft, as well as physical skills developed through much repetition. These two features interact. Exercising a skill is not the blind application of rules, but as one's hands practice at the wheel or loom, one's perception and understanding become more nuanced. One becomes skilled by practice, and as one becomes more practiced, exercising the skill becomes more pleasurable.

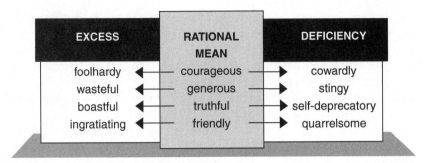

EXCESS	RATIONAL MEAN	DEFICIENCY
foolhardy ←	courageous →	cowardly
wasteful ←	generous →	stingy
boastful ←	truthful →	self-deprecatory
ingratiating ←	friendly →	quarrelsome

Exhibit 2.1 Aristotle's Conception of Virtue

Virtues for Aristotle are well-established character traits or dispositions to act, which have both intellectual and affective components. If placed on a continuum, the virtues fall at a mean between the extremes of deficiency and excess, with reason determining where the mean is. (See Exhibit 2.1 for Aristotle's pattern of virtues and vices.) Take courage, for example. A young child is flailing out in the lake. On the beach, Lee watches, shaking in fear, even though he is a good swimmer. He is not courageous, but has the deficiency of cowardice. Karen dives right in, even though she cannot swim. Aristotle would say she suffers from excess and is foolhardy, rather than courageous. Edwin calmly assesses the situation, and then either dives in, if he can swim sufficiently well, or quickly goes for help. His courage is exhibited by rationally assessing the situation, and then acting on his assessment, in order to save the child. He has shown virtue by feeling and thinking and acting "at the right times, about the right things, towards the right people, for the right end, and in the right way."[15]

Establishing virtues as part of one's character takes practice. One becomes courageous, just, or honest by performing courageous, just, or honest acts. Although this may be difficult at first, as the virtue-skills develop, exercising them becomes pleasurable. To a skilled potter, shaping the clay on the wheel gives pleasure to hands and mind. Likewise, acting courageously, justly, or honestly is pleasurable for the person who possesses those virtues as well-established parts of his or her character.

One point needs to be clarified. It is true that virtues have motivational force. For example, we commonly say, "Alisha gave to the Red Cross because she is a generous person," or "Juan volunteers because he is so compassionate." We must be clear, though, that virtues are deeper than motives. Virtues, in the sense that Aristotle meant, are enduring, stable features of one's personality. They form the palette of colors through which we see the world, and they shape how we think and how we feel connected to the whole. Donors and volunteers often act from a variety of motives; acting from virtues of character is certainly compatible with mixed motives. A genuinely generous person may also appreciate the thank you note, the recognition plaque, the sense of continuing the family tradition, or of belonging to the workplace team. Still, we must be careful in our minds not to reduce the virtues to a subset of motives.

This point is not trivial. The question, remember, is "What sustains a gift economy, what nourishes the spirit of the gift?". If the spirit of the gift dies, philanthropy become a version of a market economy. We can turn the question around and ask it this way: "What motives, if removed, would kill the spirit of the gift? Take out desires for status and recognition, and the spirit of the gift lives. Eliminate generosity, compassion, and mutuality, and the gift dies.

I doubt that we need to encourage people to desire more status and recognition. A few people, generally labeled as having "low self-esteem," may benefit from learning to enjoy recognition more than they do already do, but in general, people's desire for recognition is not in short supply. I am not at all arguing against giving donor recognition. Showing appreciation for gifts is a fine and decent thing to do. What is objectionable is to think about donor relations primarily from the perspective of "What self-interested motivations can we latch onto and milk, in order to get them to give?" It is not the mission of philanthropic organizations to increase people's desire for recognition. But as fund raisers for organizations committed to sustaining the gift economy of philanthropy, especially organizations located in a competitive, materialistic society, we do need to take extra care about virtues that nourish the spirit of the gift.

2.4 THE CLUSTER OF VIRTUES OF GIFTS AS OUTGOING

Because the missions of specific nonprofits are continuing threads in the larger story of philanthropy, the first question on the ethical decision-making chart asks us to assess how well each alternative serves both the organizational mission and philanthropic values. We need to assess how each alternative nourishes or damages those virtues that sustain the spirit of the gift. The first cluster of virtues

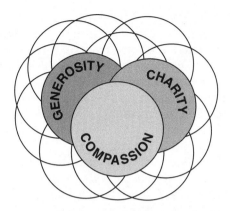

Exhibit 2.2   Cluster of Virtues of Gifts As OutGoing

includes generosity, charity, and compassion as illustrated in Exhibit 2.2. These virtues encourage people to initiate gift giving, to give birth to the spirit of the gift and to set it in motion.

(a) Generosity

Aristotle's account of generosity is a good place to begin. In ancient Greece, the class structure was hierarchical and included slaves, wage laborers, and citizens. Female citizens, who were always under male guardianship, spent most of their time secluded in the household and did not participate in public, political affairs.[16] Among male citizens, men of wealth often gave generously to public projects. Holding public office was both a responsibility and an honor for the aristocracy. These men were not paid for serving the public in this way. In fact, financing the functions of the office was an expected part of the job, so in effect, most state functions were financed "voluntarily." This may sound familiar to board members who volunteer their time, knowing full well that giving financially is part of their responsibility. In ancient Greece, lists were published to honor the givers. Sometimes, the lists were arranged by amounts given, not unlike today's tiers of donor clubs.

These wealthy citizens funded temples, gymnasiums, public baths, religious festivals, and construction projects. They contributed to subscription funds to stabilize prices of essential commodities such as corn and oil. While the poor were not singled out as recipients of "charity," they often benefitted from this method of public funding. For example, when his city was in financial difficulty, Empedon of Akraephia, in 42 c.e., gave supplies of corn and oil, and interest-free loans, as part of a festival to Apollo. All residents of the city, free and slave alike, received a measure of corn and half a measure of wine. A statue was set up in his honor with the inscription, "The city of Akraephia to Empedon ... for their (sic) generosity and benefactions to her."[17]

Health care and education were funded the same way. Epicurus (341–271 b.c.e.) gives us an early example of alumni giving. He founded a school and wrote in his will, "And I entrust the school in the garden in perpetuity to those who are its members ... and their successors, so that they too may maintain the garden in the way which is most secure, just as it is maintained by those to whom the members of my philosophic school bequeath it."[18] In Rome at the end of the first century, c.e., Pliny the Younger offered a challenge grant. While he could have paid the complete bill for some children's elementary education, he said he would add a third to what parents contributed, reasoning that if their own money was involved, they would treat the matter more responsibly.[19]

This gives the social context for Aristotle's discussion of generosity. The spirit of a gift economy is clear in a letter ascribed to Aristotle, where he wrote, "Giving and returning is that which binds men together in their living, as some give, others receive, while others again make a return gift for what they have received."[20] In his discussion of generosity, Aristotle was thinking of male Athenian citizens, and how they gave of their wealth. Generosity follows Aristotle's pattern for virtues as a mean between the excess of wastefulness and the deficiency of being ungenerous or stingy. The mean between these extremes is determined through reason, aiming "to give to the right people, the right amounts, at the right time."

Aristotle says that generous people aim for moral excellence in giving, and because generosity as a virtue is inculcated into their character, they take pleasure in giving and do not value being wealthy for its own sake. Generosity is assessed relative to a person's ability to give, and not the absolute amount of the gift. To enjoy receiving honor for giving, even to display one's wealth does not diminish having the virtue of generosity, as long as moral excellence in giving is one's main motivation. But to display wealth for the sake of display, or in order to bring honor to oneself, is not generosity, but arrogance.[21]

There are a number of features of Aristotle's account of generosity that are particularly germane to fund raisers. First, Aristotle emphasizes that as a virtue, generosity is built into a person's character, and so provides a sturdy basis from which specific motives arise. His analysis is subtle but not cynical. Generosity is compatible with enjoying honor and recognition, but the presence of these self-interested motives does not negate the genuineness and the central importance of generosity. The second feature is the way Aristotle connects generosity to a reasoned perception of the situation. To give the wrong amounts, at the wrong times, and to the wrong causes is wasteful and not generous. This underscores the importance of fund raisers as educators. Donors need to read the case statement, know the full story, and even check with the Better Business Bureau before making a gift. All of this information gathering belongs to the virtue of generosity. Finally, a generous person gives with pleasure. For Aristotle, exercising generosity is enjoyable because it flows out from a virtuous character. Fund raisers as facilitators can enable donors to give rightly, and provide the opportunity for them to take pleasure in exercising generosity. Aristotle would appreciate the definition of fund raising that Hank Rosso, founder of The Fund Raising School, used, "Fund raising is the gentle art of teaching the joy of giving."

Aristotle writes about generosity in terms of giving money, but we can expand this to include giving of one's time and talent as a volunteer. Here, generous people give with pleasure, with the principle aim of benefitting others. Generous volunteers carefully assess the needs of the organization and the clients, so that they serve the right persons, at the right times, and so forth.

Here, it is easy to see how generosity nourishes the spirit of the gift and sustains the gift economy. Because generosity springs from a person's character and makes giving pleasurable, acts of generosity will be performed repeatedly. When giving is done at the rational mean between extremes, the right causes will receive the right amounts, at the right times. Organizational missions will be well served; the gift economy of philanthropy will be well nourished.

(b) Charity

In many religious traditions, including Islam, Buddhism, Hinduism, and Judaism, almsgiving has been and remains an integral part. The historical origins of the Christian conception of charity date back to ancient religions of the Middle East. For example, Baal, the Syrian god, equated justice with charity. In ancient Egypt and in the Bible's Old Testament, charity, understood in terms of pity or mercy for the poor, was considered a religious duty. In ancient Egypt, there were altars to which the poor could flee to obtain sanctuary. For both Egyptians and Hebrews, human charity paralleled their gods' mercy toward the poor.[22]

In Medieval Europe, this notion of charity was adapted into a Christian world view that framed the people's understandings of their lives and duties. Life was a journey toward the goal of eternal salvation and everlasting blessedness with God. Charity played a role in the task of working out one's salvation. Until the twelfth century, charity was largely administered through the bishops and monasteries; after that, municipal involvement in charity increased. The *Rule of Benedict*, which provided a pattern for monastic life from the sixth century on, links love of God explicitly with charity to the poor. Chapter 4 begins with the commandments, "Love the Lord God with your whole heart, your whole soul and all your strength, and love your neighbor as yourself," and quickly continues, "You must relieve the lot of the poor, clothe the naked, visit the sick and bury the dead. Go to help the troubled and console the sorrowing."[23] Chapter 53 instructs the monks, "All guests who present themselves are to be welcomed as Christi.... All humility should be shown in addressing a guest on arrival or departure. By a bow of the head or by a complete prostration of the body, Christ is to be adored because he is indeed welcomed in them."[24] For the next 600 years, giving alms and supporting hospitals and hospices was a liturgical matter, a part of religious ritual expressing love for God. The poor, including those who became voluntarily poor by entering monasteries, were regarded as symbols of Christ; their prayers on behalf of donors and their relatives were of special potency.[25]

Many wills included charitable bequests. These were often composed on the deathbed, with a priest in attendance. It was understood that these bequests contributed to the salvation of the donor's soul, and could shorten the stay in purgatory of the donor's parents, who had gone on before.[26]

Medieval thinkers worked out elaborate mappings of Christian virtues. By the twelfth century, parallel lists of sevens had evolved spelling out the dimensions of charity. There were the seven corporeal works of mercy: "feeding the hungry, giving drink to the thirsty, clothing the naked, sheltering the homeless, visiting the sick, ransoming captives, and burying the dead"; and seven spiritual works of mercy: "instructing the ignorant, counseling the doubtful, admonishing sinners, bearing wrongs patiently, forgiving offenses, comforting the afflicted, and praying for the living and the dead."[27]

This sets the context for St. Thomas Aquinas's monumental writings on theology and Christian ethics. For the corporeal virtues, Aquinas follows Aristotle's pattern of the virtues as habits, acquired through practice, and following the dictates of reason, while avoiding extremes of excess and deficiency. Aquinas places Aristotle's schema within a Christian context. Earthly virtues needed to be supplemented by theological virtues, which could not be attained through human effort, but were infused into the soul as a gift of God's grace. People needed these infused virtues of faith, hope, and charity, in order to attain their supernatural and ultimate goal of eternal salvation in the life to come.[28]

What can fund raisers learn from this medieval Christian view of charity? In this account, what moves the gift and infuses the spirit of the gift is service to ideals and to people's conception of their ultimate good. Charity was a virtue in service to God, but as service to God, it encircled the community. Acts of charity served the self, in the sense of contributing to personal salvation, but these acts were not self-serving in the sense of bringing short-term, immediate gain. Instead, they were part of the whole trajectory of a good life, and so repeated as part of that pattern.

Thus, medieval fund raisers, often priests, nuns, and monks, were educators and facilitators. They taught the people that charity was a virtue that served life's ultimate meaning, and they facilitated the cycling of gifts to serve the community. The gifts returned to the donors, through a wide circle, in the form of eternal salvation.

In ancient Greece and medieval Christendom, attitudes toward the poor were different, and the social structures supported through giving were different. Yet there are similarities in Aristotle's understanding of generosity and Aquinas's conception of charity. In both cases, the cycle of giving is wide and is sustained through virtues which are well-established in a person's character. In both cases, gifts ultimately return to the donor, but on their way they nourish the larger community.

(c) Compassion

In 563 B.C.E., at the time of Siddhartha Gautama's birth, a sage told the king that his son would either be a great king or a great spiritual leader. The king wanted his son to follow in his steps, so he hid all signs of suffering from him. But as a young man, Gautama saw a diseased, deformed man, then a corpse, and wondered about the cause of suffering. He renounced his life of luxury and became an ascetic, practicing meditation and yogic discipline. Enlightenment came to him at age 36, and from then on he was called the Buddha, or "the awakened one." For the rest of his life, he taught the four noble truths and the eightfold path. Binding all of his teaching was compassion. The Buddha taught, "Just as a mother would protect her only child even at the risk of her own life, even so let one cultivate a boundless heart towards all beings. Let one's thoughts of boundless love pervade the whole world—above, below and across—without any obstruction, without any hatred, without any enmity."[29]

For Buddhists, self-grasping, or the self-centered aversion to suffering, is at the root of all harm. Through compassion, we come to realize that all beings suffer in the same ways; through compassion, we can sympathetically imagine ourselves in their place. Sogyal Rinpoche, a contemporary Tibetan Buddhist, describes the Buddhist practice of Tonglen as a kind of exchange. "The Tonglen practice of giving and receiving is to take on the suffering and pain of others, and give them your happiness, well-being, and peace of mind."[30]

Along with recognizing people's suffering and feeling sympathy for them, a compassionate person also works actively to alleviate others' suffering. In Tibetan iconography, the Buddha of Compassion has 1,000 eyes with which to see others' pain and 1,000 arms reaching out to help them.[31]

A pure compassion for all living things, arising from selfless detachment, is the Buddhist path toward enlightenment. Compassion (*karuṇā*) and wisdom (*prajñā*) are like two wings of a bird, the saying goes. The root of *karuṇā* means "the anguished cry of deep sorrow that elicits compassion."[32] When a person already knows other people and has affection for them, compassion is a natural response to their suffering. *Prajñā*, or wisdom, is realizing that the idea of the individual self is a fiction. At the deepest level of reality, all distinctions between oneself and other selves are as illusory as attempting to cut the sky in half with a knife.[33] Through meditation, we can attain *prajñā*, and thereby extend compassion to all living things, friends and strangers alike.[34] When we know that boundaries between selves are illusory, self-centered concerns vanish. Compassion gives us a kind of equality with all others, based on our shared humanity.

Although Western conceptions of compassion do not depend on denying boundaries between individual selves, they are rooted in similar conceptions of equality and shared humanity. Addams's notion of sympathetic understanding and Dewey's comments about imagination discussed in Chapter 1 are helpful here. Through imagination, we can enter sympathetically into what others think, feel, fear, and suffer. We realize that we share common human capacities and troubles, and through compassion we wish to relieve others' pain.

With both Buddhist and Western understandings of compassion, we can see how compassion moves the spirit of the gift. Compassion dissolves the bonds of egoism, whether we enter imaginatively into another's way of experiencing the world or, with the Buddhists, deny that boundaries between selves have ultimate significance. As the needs, cares, pains, and joys of others take precedence over our own, we give and thus keep the spirit of the gift in motion.

The Buddhist understanding of compassion sounds close to altruism. One might think of altruism as the exemplar of virtues of gifts as outgoing. Altruistic acts are selfless; they are done purely for the good of another, with no expectation of a return. We commonly think that in acting altruistically a person chooses to go far beyond what is normally expected, (the technical philosophical term is "*supererogatory*"), making these acts particularly praiseworthy.

But altruism is problematic. Not everyone is so sanguine about altruism. If the self is illusory, as Buddhists believe, then we have a metaphysical basis for saying that compassion is altruistic. But there are doubters who claim that altruism is a psychological impossibility. People are self-interested all the way down, they say. People who appear to be acting altruistically are really enjoying the psychic rewards of their actions, the warm glow inside, the praise and recognition.

Others worry about the contexts in which altruism is praised, particularly when the context includes a hierarchical society. Writer bell hooks gives us this telling description of a purely altruistic person: the black mammy. "The mammy image was portrayed with affection by whites because it epitomized the ultimate sexist-racist vision of ideal black womanhood—complete submission to the will of whites.... They saw her as the embodiment of woman as passive nurturer, a mother figure who gave all without expectation of return, who not only acknowledged her inferiority to whites but who loved them."[35] It is no accident that women who desire to nurture their own talents and strive for achievement are so often criticized as selfish, and as lacking the feminine virtue of altruism.

Is altruism the highest virtue, a supererogatory version of generosity, charity, and compassion all rolled into one? Consider how the medieval Jewish philosopher, Moses Maimonides, ranked eight ways of giving. The lowest level is to give grudgingly; the next level, to give meagerly, then in response to a request; and so on, up to the seventh level in which the donor does not know who the recipient is, and the recipient does not know the source of the gift. It sounds as though we are getting progressively more altruistic as we go up the levels. But listen to how Maimonides explains the highest level of giving. It is "to take hold of a Jew who has been crushed and to give him a gift or a loan, or to enter into partnership with him, or to find work for him, and thus put him on his feet that he will not be dependent on his fellow-men."[36] Now, a more contemporary version of this is the adage about teaching people to fish, rather than giving them fish. What is striking about Maimonides' highest level of giving is the phrase about entering into partnership. Selfless altruism has given way to community participation. The best gift is one that welcomes others to share in one's life and work.

These examples lead to two questions: (1) Does altruism exist? Is it a psychological possibility at all? and (2) If altruism exists, is it part of a gift economy, or does it fall outside, as purely detached, selfless giving?

In thinking about these questions, let us consider Kristen Renwick Monroe's study, *The Heart of Altruism: Perceptions of a Common Humanity.* Monroe interviewed several people who had rescued European Jews during the Nazi occupation, often at great risk to themselves and their families. She analyzed taped narratives and data from survey questionnaires, looking for common socioeconomic or psychological traits. None of the factors one might predict turned out to be common among the rescuers. Some of the rescuers had strong religious backgrounds and commitments; others did not. In the interviews, the rescuers denied that religion was relevant to their altruistic acts. Other factors that turned out not to be relevant were family background, wealth, occupation, family position, birth order and family size, and the closeness of the community.[37]

Psychic income was not an explanation. The rescuers did not want public praise or recognition. They insisted that they had not done anything extraordinary, and in fact, most said they felt nothing—no warm glow. Did they engage in a cost–benefit analysis in deciding whether to rescue? The answer was an unequivocal "no." They considered risks tactically as they decided how to hide the Jews, but they did not consider risks at all when deciding whether to rescue the Jews.[38]

In fact, what is most interesting about the rescuers is that they claimed there was nothing to decide, there were no alternatives to choose between. They did not deliberate at all. It was very simple:

The Jews needed help, so of course, they helped. The one thing all the rescuers shared was that they saw themselves deeply linked with all of humanity. Tony, a Dutch rescuer, expressed this eloquently, "I was to learn to understand that you're part of a whole, and that just like cells in your own body altogether make up your body, that in our society and in our community, that we all are like cells of a community that is very important.... And you should always be aware that every other person is basically you. You should always treat people as though it is you, and that goes for evil Nazis as well as for Jewish friends who are in trouble."[39]

This shared humanity was the rescuers' core perspective, the lens through which all else was seen. We are all one, and thus helping those in need is normal, expected, spontaneous, and uncalculated. None of the rescuers interviewed said they were Buddhist, but their shared perspective of our common humanity resonates with the Buddhist understanding of compassion.

If Monroe's analysis is correct, then the two questions posed above are answered. Yes, altruism exists, and yes, it is part of a very special sort of gift economy, based on our shared humanity. But the altruism of the rescuers does not fit Aristotle's pattern of the virtues. There was no practice phase; altruists did not find rescuing hard at first, and then gradually become more skillful, as it worked its way into their characters. I do not know why some people are altruistic or how they got to be that way, but I am grateful for their gifts to us all.

2.5 THE CLUSTER OF VIRTUES OF GIFTS OF RETURN

In the gift economy, the gifts come back. Often, they take a circuitous journey, during which time some folks leave the circle of giving through death or disinterest, and other folks enter through birth or new community affiliation. As gifts return, people often benefit before they have a chance to make an initial donation. This second cluster contains the virtues of gratitude and mutuality, as seen in Exhibit 2.3. These virtues express our understanding that as beneficiaries we need to make gifts of return.

(a) Gratitude

Samantha gives a birthday bouquet of wildflowers to her Uncle Sigmund. Sigmund is grateful for the gift itself, he is grateful to Samantha

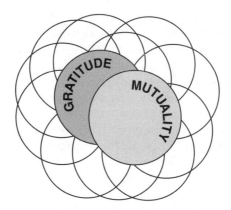

Exhibit 2.3   Cluster of Virtues of Gifts of Return

for remembering, for taking the time to pick the flowers and arrange them, and especially for feeling the emotional bond with him that the gift represents. It is fitting for him to say thank you, to write a note, or perhaps to send the flowers on to Aunt Cecilia in the nursing home. It is not fitting for Sigmund to say to Samantha, "Tell me exactly what these are worth, and I will repay you." That would turn the gift into a commodity, destroying its spirit and vitality as a gift.

So gratitude is a virtue of philanthropy as a gift economy. It expresses emotional links of appreciation for those who have given and is an impetus to continue the cycle of giving by seeking appropriate forms of return. So many times we cannot make a return to the original giver. Samantha as a child enjoys Girl Scouts, school trips to the symphony's young people's concerts, and a home renovated through volunteer labor. As she grows, she comes to realize the complexity of the web of benefits, and she is grateful to the friends and strangers who designed and strengthened that web. Perhaps her appreciation is for these specific benefits; perhaps it will grow into a general gratitude for the world as a tangle of gifts, past and present. Perhaps she will read in Emerson's essay, "A man is a bundle of relations, a knot of roots whose flower and fruitage is the world."[40] She will see herself as a bee, drinking nectar from those flowers, and creating honey for others to enjoy.

We are familiar with the phrase "debt of gratitude." The sense of the phrase is clear enough—grateful for what we have been given, we owe a return. Philosopher Claudia Card, however, worries that the metaphor of indebtedness is not quite right. It evokes images of moral bookkeeping: of accounts kept, interest calculated, and legal and economic exactness. She suggests instead the metaphor of trusteeship.[41] We can think of Sigmund as a trustee of Samantha's beneficence, rather than as a debtor. This suggestion fits well into the roles we assume in the gift economy of philanthropy. While both trusteeship and indebtedness entail obligations, trusteeship is a responsibility of privilege and honor, rather than an undesirable condition one would just as soon get rid of. Trustees often have discretion on how to carry out their responsibilities; good judgment rather than matching amounts is the appropriate response. A trust of gratitude better represents the openness of the beneficiary-turned-donor response.

Aristotle's paradigm of the virtues is appropriate here. It is easy to think of people (perhaps ourselves, at times) who are deficient in gratitude. It may sound odd to think of people having too much gratitude. Addams gives us a good example in her discussion of protective labor legislation for children. She writes that those who regard such protections as fulfilling charitable rather than democratic obligations exhibit "kindly contempt" toward the recipients.[42] When just treatment based on dignity and respect is called for, expecting gratitude is a form of kindly contempt; and returning gratitude is a sign of internalized oppression.

Gratitude fits in well with fund raisers' roles as educators and facilitators. When fund raisers talk about philanthropy, telling stories of how their organizations have grown and whom they have benefitted, they encourage the virtue of gratitude. Nonprofits as "channels through which moral energy can flow" give people the opportunity to fulfill their responsibilities as trustees of gratitude.

(b) Mutuality

The virtue of mutuality expresses the realization that an individual's well-being and the community's well-being are deeply intertwined. Mutuality is expressed through cooperation and interdependence. It is similar to reciprocity and fairness in that it includes balancing benefits and treating people fairly, but it goes deeper. Mutuality is based on a profound appreciation for how our fates and our very identities are bound with those of others. Mutuality is thus a virtue of gifts of return in the way it combines a sense of responsibility for the continuing health of the whole, with an appreciation of how one's own well-being is a gift from the community.

Mutuality fits well into Aristotle's schema for the virtues. It is a rational mean between narcissism and self-effacement. Reason and feeling both have a role; by seeing your place in the whole and feeling linked with others, you develop an internalized sense of responsibility toward the community's well-being.

Imagine a crocodile with two heads and a single stomach. For the Akan, the largest ethnic group in Ghana, this siamese crocodile is a symbol of the relationship between individuals and society. Two heads, one stomach—in a community, there is individual distinctiveness, and there are times of conflict and disagreement. Yet we share a common stomach; we are fed through the same channels, and if we do not share, we die. Individuals can flourish only if the community as a whole is kept healthy, only if each individual mouth takes responsibility to feed the common stomach with foods nourishing to all.[43]

This metaphor expresses the Akan's communal ethics, which we will use as a context for understanding the virtue of mutuality. The Akan have many proverbs that explain the need for mutual cooperation: "One finger cannot lift up a thing." "If one man scrapes the bark of a tree for medicine, the pieces fall down."[44] The Akan's conception of moral goodness is built on this realization of interdependence. Something is good if it contributes to the well-being of the community as a whole. Kindness, faithfulness, compassion, and hospitality are all valued as character traits leading to social harmony. The Akan's two categories of evil reveal tellingly how communal well-being is the primary good. *Bōne* or ordinary evil, brings harm to particular individuals. But *musuo* is extraordinary evil because, as one Akan describes it, "*musuo* is an evil which is great and which brings suffering ... to the whole community, not just to the doer alone."[45]

Moral education is a matter of character development. For the Akan, as for Aristotle, moral character develops through practice and habituation. Through proverbs, folktales, and living example, children are taught to be responsible for their own moral behavior and undertake responsibility for the well-being of the community as a whole.[46]

From the seventeenth century until today, giving traditions among African Americans have exemplified this tradition of mutuality. Many Africans were brought from the regions of the Akan and from other tribes that shared their communal metaphysics. Slave traders could not strip Africans of their oral traditions: the music, rhythms, poetry, stories, and ritual practices that expressed their communal ethics. This spirit of community was evident in the way slaves organized themselves in plantation slave quarters and in the scores of mutual aid societies African Americans formed well before the end of slavery. The African Masonic Lodge in Boston and the Free American Society in Philadelphia were founded in 1787. By the early 1800s, there were several hundred such societies. Few of these societies applied for state charters and many met clandestinely, as such organizations were illegal in many states. The aim of the societies was to give aid and relief to any community members in need; mutuality was the governing spirit behind their efforts.[47]

Phrases such as "racial uplift" express this sense of mutuality. In the 1890s, African American women formed clubs for education, service to the elderly, literacy, cultural endeavors, and political activism. By 1917, the National Association of Colored Women represented 50,000 women and over 1,000 clubs. The association's motto was "lifting as we climb."[48] Although club members were primarily middle-class black women, they did not view their work with poor blacks as charity or altruism. Instead, in the spirit of mutuality, they felt a deep kinship, believing their own fate was deeply tied to the fate of their poorer brothers and sisters. Mary Church Terrell, well educated, wealthy, and one of the organization's founders, wrote, "Self-preservation demands that [black women] go among the lowly, illiterate and even the vicious, to whom they are bound by ties of race and sex ... to reclaim them."[49] Health care, education, child care, job training, and cultural advance were among their missions, lifting the race as they themselves climbed.

Mary McLeod Bethune (1875–1955) was also one of the founders of the National Association of Colored Women, and served as special advisor on minority affairs to President Franklin Roosevelt. She begins her story of how she founded Bethune-Cookman College in Florida, by recounting, "Mother was of royal African blood, of a tribe ruled by matriarchs.... Throughout all her bitter years of slavery she had managed to preserve a queenlike dignity." Bethune goes on to tell of the early days of the school: "We burned logs and used the charred splinters as pencils, and mashed elderberries for ink. I begged strangers for a broom, a lamp, a bit of cretonne to put around the packing case which served as my desk." Her ingenuity and persistence in fund raising offer a strong antidote to any contemporary fund raiser experiencing burnout. Bethune ends the account by returning to her African heritage of mutuality, "For I am my mother's daughter, and the drums of Africa still beat in my heart. They will not let me rest while there is a single Negro boy or girl without a chance to prove his worth."[50]

Mutuality links us in the circle of giving as both beneficiaries and donors. Holding this double role propels the gift through the gift economy of philanthropy. Fund raisers as educators and facilitators have daily opportunities to exhibit mutuality and to encourage others to practice this virtue, thus instilling vitality in the spirit of the gift.

2.6 FUND RAISERS AND THE VIRTUES OF PHILANTHROPY

What can we learn about the practice of fund raising from this excursion through the virtues of gifts as outgoing and the virtues of gifts of return? When fund raisers exercise these virtues themselves and design fund-raising practices that encourage these virtues in others, philanthropy can flourish as a gift economy. Generosity encourages informed, thoughtful giving, where giving is pleasurable. Charity reminds us that philanthropic giving serves moral and religious ideals, and that both our inward commitments and outward activities should exemplify these ideals. With compassion, as with Addams's sympathetic understanding, we enter into the perspectives of others, so our giving is a way of identifying with their joy and suffering. With gratitude, we demonstrate through our giving that we appreciate the gifts from which we ourselves have benefitted. Finally, with mutuality, our giving reflects our place in the larger community and our responsibility for the well-being of the whole.

All of these virtues point to the realization that "Who am I?" and "Who are we?" are parts of the same question. As these virtues foster sensitivity and responsiveness to others, the boundaries of ourselves become permeable. Lao-tzu gives us a poignant portrayal of such receptivity in his description of a Tao master:

The ancient Masters were profound and subtle.
Their wisdom was unfathomable.
There is no way to describe it;
all we can describe is their appearance.
They were careful
as someone crossing an iced-over stream.
Alert as a warrior in enemy territory.
Courteous as a guest.
Fluid as melting ice.
Shapable as a block of wood.

Receptive as a valley.
Clear as a glass of water.[51]

Through exercising these virtues of the gift as outgoing and of the gift of return, we can shape ourselves and our philanthropic practices so that we and they can be "channels through which people's moral energy can flow." These virtues will sustain the gift's vitality and keep it moving through the gift economy of philanthropy.

DISCUSSION QUESTIONS

1. Come up with as many examples as you can of how fund raising and nonprofits have adopted the language of business and the market economy. Examples might include referring to donors as investors, gifts as investments, volunteers as "unpaid staff," organizational accomplishments as "returns on investment," and so on. What are the advantages of this linguistic shift? What ethical concerns should we have about this? Do you think using this vocabulary subtly shifts the attention of donors and staff away from the spirit of philanthropy and toward a market economy mentality?

2. Do you think altruism exists, or do you side with those who say altruism is psychologically impossible? Do you think altruism is a virtue that we can develop if we work at it, or are altruistic people, like Monroe's rescuers, somehow unique?

3. Think of several examples of fund-raising practices in your organization. In what ways and to what extent do they encourage philanthropic virtues? Do they in any way hinder or obstruct these virtues? In what ways do they provide opportunities for fund raisers to educate and facilitate philanthropy as a gift economy?

CASE STUDIES

Fams Go High Tech. Vera Leanwell plans tours for the Great Plains Historical Society, whose mission is "to preserve love for and knowledge of the past, as we make our way into the future." She is ecstatic about her "fam," or familiarization trip invitation from Futures Now, a tour operator who specializes in tours to high-tech locations. Travel planners are invited to go, all expenses paid, with no obligation. Of course, the trip is not supposed to be just a free vacation. Futures Now uses fam trips as a way to familiarize travel planners with their services, hoping that the planners will book a tour with them for their organization. Vera and her family are technology enthusiasts, so this fam trip really piques her interest. Although she enjoys her job at the Historical Society, she gets irritated by the stodgy board members, who refuse to see that history did not end with the nineteenth century. Would accepting the invitation be inconsistent with the mission of the Historical Society?

Board Perks. As fund raiser for the ballet, you are in charge of the donor appreciation program. After each performance, you host an expensive catered reception for all major donors. The few donors who attend enjoy the reception; however, you are concerned that the majority of those who attend are board members. They, along with the ballet chief executive officer, seem to think that schmoozing with the powerful is a perk of board membership, even though they themselves are not major donors. You would like to discontinue the receptions, but are quite sure that you will face serious board opposition. What should you do? Do these receptions serve the organizational mission of the ballet?

Sliding Scale. Your social service agency offers counseling to clients on a sliding scale, with a $10 per session minimum fee. Some families have run up bills as high as $200. Understanding that they simply cannot pay, your agency simply writes off the bills. An influential board member is appalled by this practice, and complains to you, "We wouldn't have to work so hard to raise money if the staff would just make those clients pay their bills." Does the board member misunderstand the mission of the organization?

Library Services. The public library has just hired you as their first development officer. Tax money is insufficient for purchasing new books, maintaining the old facility, and updating technology resources. You are enthusiastic about the library's mission of taking its services to the public. Your latest project is working out an arrangement with a shopping mall to open a library branch in a vacant mall shop. The project is going well, except for two sticky points. The library has helped many unemployed people with resume building and job searches, but the mall management does not want you to offer this service at the branch. They tell you, "We don't want any bums hanging out at our mall." Also, you provide meeting space for discussions of most anything people want. The mall wants to get the list of topics ahead of time to make sure they fit in with the mall's image. You foresee potential problems here. *Image* is defined in terms of what paying customers find acceptable, and in your community, this could exclude many topics of recent discussions, such as gay and lesbian rights, survivalist groups, and drug needle sharing programs. Would agreeing to these concessions be contrary to the library's mission?

Clients' Best Interest. Your organization, which serves the homeless, runs a counseling program that is minimally operable. You know that the clients of the program could receive better service elsewhere. Listing job training and home maintenance skills as higher priorities, the executive director and the board are not willing to make the comprehensive changes required to improve the counseling program. A donor calls and tells you that his nephew just had his life turned around, thanks to a counseling service at his workplace. He wants to show his gratitude by donating a substantial sum to your counseling program. You are concerned that if your organization accepts the money and uses it as designated, clients (and hence, the mission) will not be well served. How should you respond to the offer?

NOTES

1. Susan Gray and Holly Hall, "Cashing In on Charity's Good Name," *Chronicle of Philanthropy* (July 30, 1998).
2. Boys and Girls Clubs Web site, http://www.bgca.org.
3. Irving Warner, "Marketing Deals Shouldn't Be Child's Play," *Chronicle of Philanthropy* (September 24, 1998).
4. This case is based on Sharon Batt, "'Perfect People': Cancer Charities," in Rose Weitz (ed.): *The Politics of Women's Bodies* (New York: Oxford University Press, 1998), pp. 137–146.
5. Quoted in John McKay, Bennett D. Hill, and John Buckler, *A History of Western Society*, 4th edition, vol. 1 (Boston: Houghton Mifflin Co., 1991), pp. 425–427.
6. Susan A. Ostrander, *Money for Change* (Philadelphia: Temple University Press, 1995), p. 4.
7. *Id.*, p. 116.
8. *Id.*, p. 166.
9. Jane Addams, *A Modern Lear, Survey 29*, 1912, pp. 131–137; reprinted by Jane Addams's Hull House Museum, 1994, p. 23.

10. Plato, "Ion" *The Dialogues of Plato,* vol. 4, trans. by Benjamin Jowett, (London: Begelow, Smith & Co., n.d.), p. 287.
11. Jane Addams, *Democracy and Social Ethics* (New York: Macmillan, 1907; reprint ed., Cambridge, MA: Harvard University Press, 1964), pp. 163–164.
12. In seventeenth century England our modern idea of religious toleration among individuals virtually did not exist. For a study of the early historical development of religious freedom and toleration in the United States see Thomas J. Curry, *The First Freedoms: Church and State in America to the Passage of the First Amendment* (New York: Oxford, 1986).
13. Michael Walzer, *On Toleration* (New Haven, CT: Yale University Press, 1997), p. 98.
14. There are many excellent philosophical analyses of moral virtues. Aristotle's account in the *Nichomachean Ethics* continues to instruct after 2,500 years. Two contemporary favorites include Edmund L. Pincoffs' discussion in *Quandaries and Virtues* (Lawrence, KS: Kansas University Press, 1986), and Mike W. Martin's focus on virtues and philanthropy in *Virtuous Giving* (Bloomington, IN: Indiana University Press, 1994).
15. Aristotle, *Nicomachean Ethics,* trans. by Terence Irwin (Indianapolis: Hackett, 1985), p. 44.
16. Sarah B. Pomeroy, *Goddesses, Whores, Wives, and Slaves: Women in Classical Antiquity* (New York: Schocken Books, 1975), pp. 57–92.
17. A. R. Hands, *Charities and Social Aid in Greece and Rome* (Ithaca, NY: Cornell University Press, 1968), p. 182.
18. *Id.,* p. 201.
19. *Id.,* p. 128.
20. *Id.,* p. 32.
21. Aristotle, *Nicomachean Ethics,* pp. 85–93.
22. A. R. Hands, *Charities and Social Aid in Greece and Rome,* pp. 11, 13, 77, 80–81.
23. Benedict, *The Rule of Saint Benedict in English,* Timothy Fry (ed.) (Collegeville, MN: The Liturgical Press, 1982), pp. 26–27.
24. *Id.,* p. 73.
25. Suzanne Roberts, "Contexts of Charity in the Middle Ages: Religious, Social, and Civic," in J. B. Schneewind (ed.): *Giving: Western Ideas of Philanthropy* (Bloomington: Indiana University Press, 1996), p. 34.
26. *Id.,* pp. 37–38.
27. *Id.,* p. 28.

28. Aquinas, Thomas, *Summa Theologica* (New York: Benzinger Brothers, 1947). J. B. Schneewind's book (*see* note 24), especially the chapters by Roberts, Schneewind, and Ryan, is particularly helpful in tracing the history of charity in western thought from the medieval period to the early twentieth century.

29. The Buddha did not write down any of his teachings. They were transmitted orally until the first century B.C.E., when they were first written down. Walpola Sri Rahula, *What the Buddha Taught*, revised ed. (New York: Grove Press, 1974), p. 97.

30. Sogyal Rinpoche, *The Tibetan Book of Living and Dying* (New York: HarperCollins, 1992), p. 202.

31. *Id.*, p. 187.

32. Taitetsu Unno, "Karuṇā" in Mircia Eliade (ed.): *Encyclopedia of Religion*, vol. 8 (New York: Macmillan, 1987), pp. 269–270.

33. Shantideva, *The Way of the Bodhisattva*, trans. by the Padmakara Translation Group (Boston: Shambhala, 1997), p. 181.

34. Geshe Kelsang Gyatso, *Ocean of Nectar: Wisdom and Compassion in Mahayana Buddhism* (London: Tharpa, 1995), pp. 20–21.

35. bell hooks, *Ain't I a Woman* (Boston: South End Press, 1981), pp. 84–85.

36. Quoted in Mike W. Martin, *Virtuous Giving* (Bloomington: Indiana University Press, 1994), p. 97.

37. Kristen Renwick Monroe, *The Heart of Altruism: Perceptions of a Common Humanity* (Princeton, NJ: Princeton University Press, 1996), pp. 130–136.

38. *Id.*, p. 156.

39. *Id.*, p. 92.

40. Ralph Waldo Emerson, "History," *The Essays of Ralph Waldo Emerson*, 1841 (Cambridge, MA: Harvard University Press, 1987), p. 20.

41. Claudia Card, "Gratitude and Obligation," *American Philosophical Quarterly*, vol. 25, no. 2 (April 1988), pp. 115–127.

42. Jane Addams, *Newer Ideals of Peace* (New York: Macmillan, 1906), p. 153.

43. Kwame Gyekye, *African Philosophical Thought: The Akan Conceptual Scheme*, revised ed. (Philadelphia: Temple University Press, 1995), pp. 159–160.

44. *Id.*, p. 156.

45. *Id.*, p. 133.

46. *Id.*, pp. 151–152.

47. James A. Joseph, *Remaking America* (San Francisco: Jossey-Bass, 1995), chapter 5. *Also see* Adrienne Lash Jones, "Philanthropy in

the African American Experience," in J. B. Schneewind (ed.): *Giving: Western Ideas of Philanthropy* (Bloomington: Indiana University Press, 1996), pp. 153–178.

48. Paula Giddings, *When and Where I Enter* (New York: Bantam, 1984), pp. 95–102.
49. *Id.,* p. 97.
50. Mary McLeod Bethune, "A College on a Garbage Dump," in Gerda Lerner (ed.): *Black Women in White America: A Documentary History* (New York: Vintage Books, 1972), pp. 134–143.
51. Lao-tzu, *Tao te Ching,* trans. by Stephen Mitchell (New York: Harper & Row, 1988), p. 15. The *Tao*'s influence on Chinese philosophy is incalculable. Although there is no doubt that Lao-tzu existed, there is considerable debate over when he lived. The estimated dates range from the sixth to the third century, B.C.E. See Wing-Tsit Chan, trans. and compiler, *A Source Book in Chinese Philosophy* (Princeton, NJ: Princeton University Press, 1963), pp. 136ff.

▼ 3 Professional Relationships

"How does this alternative affect long-term relationships with colleagues, donors, volunteers, and community members?"

Professional relationships provide the channels through which we sustain the gift economy of philanthropy. We further our organizations' missions through establishing networks of relationships, linking colleagues in the office with donors, volunteers, and community members. Through these relationships, we exercise compassion, charity, generosity, mutuality, and gratitude, the virtues of philanthropy as a gift economy. So the health of our professional relationships strongly affects our ability to fulfill our organizations' missions and maintain the giftlike nature of philanthropy.

Sustaining healthy, long-term, professional relationships also helps to shape who we are. Our thought patterns, our emotional responses, and our warts and wisdom all develop through our associations with others. Even a poet in seclusion exercises creativity by reworking the language and metaphors of past literary artists. Scientists working alone in the laboratory discover and invent by using their predecessors' gifts of equipment, scientific concepts, and formulas. Aristotle says that "good people's life together allows the cultivation of virtue."[1] Becoming virtuous is not a solitary quest, but a shared endeavor.

This chapter describes how trust provides the atmosphere for healthy relationships—the oxygen they must breathe to survive. Trust is not a virtue, but its purity is maintained by a cluster of what can be called *virtues of relationships*. Many virtues belong in this cluster; here, the focus will be on four particularly important ones: respect, honesty, fairness, and cooperation. In Chapter 5, the concepts of trust and virtues of relationships will be used to examine ethical dilemmas that arise among fund raisers, donors, and volunteers.

3.1 WHAT IS TRUST?

"Trust makes philanthropy possible."[2]

Think of how gifts move in the gift economy of philanthropy. Givers have no guarantee that the gift will return to them. If they give with the virtues of gifts as outgoing or the virtues of gifts of return, their giving is centered on the well-being of others and on the public good.

Now compare this with a market exchange. I go to Van's Fan Shop and exchange $20.00 for an electric box fan. With the fan, I get express warranties and implied warranties, along with an extensive body of law in place to interpret and enforce them. If the fan is the wrong size, if the motor short-circuits, or if I simply decide I do not want it, I can return it, according to the terms of the sale. All of this contractual machinery is the framework within which market exchanges take place. All of this gives me a sense of security so that I buy the box fan, all boxed up, without first checking every screw and circuit before purchasing it.

The gift economy does not work this way. I give $80.00 to the modern dance troupe, the temple, or the teen center. The thank you note arrives with no warranties. If I later decide I do not like the dance concerts, or the rabbi at the temple, or the policies at the teen center, I do not ask for my donation back (although I may not give another one). There are no refunds, except perhaps in cases of egregious fraud. It is true that there are many legal regulations that frame nonprofit work, but to a large extent the warranty in philanthropy is trust. We trust that the gift will be used wisely, in keeping with the donor's intent, to fulfill the organizational mission and for the public good. The relationships that make up the gift economy of philanthropy must be full of trust, and staff and volunteers must be trustworthy if, as the epigram at the beginning of this section states so succinctly, philanthropy is to be possible at all.

Trust is not a virtue in Aristotle's sense. It is not a disposition or character trait. Except when "trust" is used as a synonym for self-confidence, you do not "have" trust in and of yourself the way you can have generosity or courage, for example. If you "have" trust, it is someone else's trust that is entrusted to you. Trust needs the word "in" after it. Having trust is different from having the virtue of trustworthiness. A person could be trustworthy, without anyone actually trusting in him or her. (This could happen, for example, under an oppressive regime, such as Nazi Germany.) So trust is inherently relational. Trust is held *between* people, *between* a person and an organization, or even between people and something as amorphous as "the public trust."

Reliance is part of trust, but trust is not the same as reliable predictability. I can predictably rely on totally self-absorbed neighbors to keep their property tidy because they care about their home's resale value, but I do not trust them. To trust them, I would need to know that they felt goodwill toward me, that they took my interests seriously and would not manipulate me or treat me trivially to gain their own advantage.[3]

Trust is open-ended; it involves granting others discretion. Audra trusts Jasper to care for her children in her absence. She leaves a list of instructions (make sure Josey eats her spinach before having a cookie; put Tyler to bed by 8:00) but she cannot possibly write down all that might go wrong or instruct Jasper on how to deal with every contingency. What if the pet iguana eats the spinach before Josey gets to it? What if the clock battery runs down at 7:15? What Audra does, in trusting Jasper, is to trust his discretion. She trusts he will take the children's well-being seriously and make wise judgments on their behalf, no matter what goes unpredictably or wrong.

In trusting Jasper, Audra makes herself vulnerable to him. He is in a position to harm what she cares about most. Trust is about making oneself vulnerable to another, while believing that the other will not take advantage of one's vulnerability. People who are physically and emotionally self-sufficient do not need trust, because they are impervious to harm from others. But most of us are not so self-sufficient, and we do not want to be. Most of us agree with Epicurus that friendship is most blessed, and we treasure those relationships in which trust is strong. Philosopher Annette Baier sees the handshake as symbolizing trust. "The Romans, I am told, had an armshake rather than a handshake—they grasped each other by the elbow, thereby immobilizing each other's strong right arm." An oath was included in the Roman armshake. "Should I prove faithless, then may my right hand lose its cunning, as it has at this moment in your hand's grip!"[4] Our handshake is the armshake's descendant and still demonstrates how vulnerability is part of trust.

We can now see why the dimensions of trust cannot be specified in a contract. Trust is based on goodwill; it applies to unspecifiable areas of discretion, and it entails vulnerability. Philosopher Sissela Bok suggests a helpful metaphor for trust: *"Whatever* matters to human beings; trust is the atmosphere in which it thrives."[5] Trust is atmospheric. It is the oxygen supply that relationships need to breathe, and without breath there is no life.

How is the atmosphere of trust kept healthy? How do we prevent pollutants from poisoning it? Trust is not the sort of thing that we can work on directly. An adolescent shows poor judgment and asks his parents, "What do I need to do to regain your trust?" They respond by listing a lot of other things. "Be honest, be cooperative, check with us first, and take your responsibilities seriously" is just the beginning of the list.

We can make the same point using the NSFRE Code of Ethical Principles and Standards of Professional Practice. The code uses the word *trust* only once, and that is at the end of the preamble: "Such individuals practice their profession with integrity, honesty, truthfulness and adherence to the absolute obligation to safeguard the public trust." Trust is not mentioned in any of the particular provisions of the Statements of Ethical Principles or the Standards of Professional Practice. The specific provisions direct members to "put charitable mission above personal gain," to "treat all people with dignity and respect," to "value privacy and freedom of choice," to "disclose ... all conflicts of interest," to "ensure ... proper stewardship of charitable contributions," and so on. All of these specific provisions taken together sustain an atmosphere of trust. Through basing daily decisions and actions on these provisions, fund raisers can safeguard the public trust.

3.2 THE CLUSTER OF VIRTUES OF RELATIONSHIPS

Most fund raisers already have many ethical decision-making skills. Recall Socrates' remark that philosophy is a form of midwifery; his calling was to help people uncover what they already knew. So as we think about trust, try to work with examples from your own experience. Think of people you trust completely, of people you mostly trust, and of people with whom trust is problematic. Keep in mind the questions we are asking: What virtues strengthen our ability to further the organizational mission? What characteristics of professional relationships encourage the movement of gifts through the gift

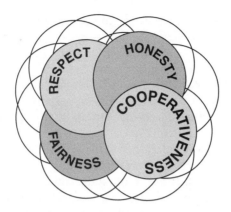

Exhibit 3.1   Cluster of Virtues of Relationships

economy? Or, simply stated, what characteristics of relationships strengthen trust?

Trust can be thought of as the oxygen supply of relationships, as sustained by a cluster of virtues, called *virtues of relationships*. If all the virtues in this cluster could be listed the list would be very long and would include the virtues of philanthropy as a gift economy, discussed in Chapter 2, as well as virtues of integrity, discussed in Chapter 4. In this section, the focus will be on four specific virtues that support trusting relationships: respect, honesty, fairness, and cooperativeness. (See Exhibit 3.1.)

(a) Respect

Healthy, sustained relationships are based on mutual respect among the participants. We can think of respectful relationships as having these three characteristics: They are grounded in a deep belief in every person's fundamental moral worth, they pay attention to particularities, and they show generosity in judgment.

(i) Fundamental Moral Worth
There are many ways of expressing a deep belief in fundamental moral worth. Some religions speak of people being made in the image of God. Eighteenth century philosopher Immanuel Kant describes moral worth by saying people are "exalted above all price," and that their "existence has in itself an absolute value."[6] The United

Nations Universal Declaration of Human Rights is based on a commitment to moral worth. Article One explains it this way: "All human beings are born free and equal in dignity and rights. They are endowed with reason and conscience and should act towards one another in a spirit of brotherhood." This is the basis for declaring that all people are entitled to life, liberty, personal security, freedom from slavery and torture, freedom of thought and conscience, an adequate standard of living, and so on.[7]

Death is the great leveler. It comes to us all, regardless of wealth or poverty, virtue or vice. In the early planning stages of Horizon Hospice in Chicago, Frank Duda wrote a draft of the hospice's goals on the back of an envelope. These goals indicate a clear dedication to fundamental moral worth: "Patients come first. Patients will be pain-free and alert. Health care should be patient controlled and patient oriented. And patients will never die alone."[8]

(ii) Attention to Particularity

Fundamental moral worth is ascribed to everyone, regardless of individual characteristics. Yet I also want people to show respect by recognizing that I am "me," a particular, peculiar individual. We want others to respect our basic humanity, but we also want them to respect our individual uniqueness.

Here, sympathetic understanding and attention to context, the main ingredients of ethics as narrative, are particularly important. To respect someone's individual uniqueness is to know what they value, what gives them joy and pain, who is important to them, and what customs or conventions have particular significance. These things change over time, so we need to understand people within the context of their life stories.

How do we come to know what we need to know in order to respect individuals' uniqueness? We listen and we try to imagine, not just what *we* would feel in others' shoes, but what *they* feel, given their personal history and their social context.

This is particularly important for respecting people who are from different social, economic, and cultural backgrounds from oneself. In discussions of diversity today, we often hear that all groups deserve to "have a voice." But having a voice requires more than just having places and spaces to talk. For one person or group to have a voice, others must hear what is being said.[9] To *hear* people means to take into account what they say, and to alter one's own thoughts, feelings, and reactions accordingly.

Karen Fiser explains how part of living with multiple sclerosis is not being able to predict what her pain and energy levels will be like. If people do not understand this, when she is late for an appointment, they assume she is irresponsible and cannot plan her time well. Here, respecting her means paying attention to her particular bodily condition so that one does not make false or disparaging assumptions about her character.[10]

Donors have many different reasons for requesting anonymity in their giving and it is helpful to understand their concerns from within their own personal and cultural perspectives. Jews have a long and rich history of commitment to philanthropic giving, to give back to their community (*tzedakah*) and to "heal the world" (*tikkum olam*). In their article on diversity among women donors, Susan Weidman Schneider and Gretchen von Schlegell write, "Jewish women may be particularly uneasy about being visible as donors. Historically, anti-Semitism has linked Jews and money. Jewish women have been victims of this bigotry in the form of "Jewish-American Princess" jokes, with their pernicious amalgam of anti-Semitism and misogyny."[11] Here, understanding these Jewish women donors in the context of the history of anti-Semitism is part of showing them respect.

Respecting someone's particularity also means acknowledging the limits of one's ability to imagine another's place. How many of us feel insulted when, at a time of loss, someone without the same experience says, "I know just how you feel." They do not know how you feel, and pretending they do cheapens your pain. Addams lived with her immigrant neighbors; she worked with them, celebrated with them, and sometimes even delivered their babies. She tried to enter their lives through sympathetic understanding as much as she possibly could. Yet she freely admitted she could never enter that space completely. Because of her economic position, she did not have to worry about illness or old age the way her neighbors did. She understood how her privilege altered her perceptions, noting, "The lack of these two securities are the specters which most persistently haunt the poor."[12] Respecting what we cannot imagine is also part of respecting particularity.

(iii) Generosity in Judgment
Philosopher John Dewey gives us this felicitous phrase.[13] We respect people by showing them generosity in judgment, by thinking of people's capacities not as static and fixed, but as having the potential to

grow and change. This means viewing people within the past and future narratives of their lives, imagining them as young, as old, as joyous, and as sorrowful. This does not mean that irresponsible behavior or incompetence should be overlooked. But, before arguing with someone with whom we disagree, we should ask ourselves, "What do I need to know about this person's values, worries, and personal history, so I can find the place from which their views make sense?" This will not eliminate disagreements, but it may create a space for working through the issues together.

Here is a sample case to think through.

> **Estate Changes:** Mr. Harrigan, an elderly gentleman whom you have been cultivating as a planned giving prospect, notifies you that he has changed his will so that your organization will receive approximately 75 percent of his estate when he dies. Several days later, the council president of the church he has attended all his life walks into your office and asks you to persuade Mr. Harrigan to change his mind. Apparently, during the recent church building program, Mr. Harrigan has verbally promised to pledge the majority of his estate to that effort. Before the pledge was received in writing, he had a petty argument with the coordinator of the building program. What should you do?

It sounds as though Mr. Harrigan's decision was made more in anger than by calmly assessing his own values and commitments. We need more details about Mr. Harrigan, his family, and the history of his involvement in the two nonprofits before proposing specific ways of resolving the tensions. If nothing is done, trust will be seriously undermined and relations between the two nonprofits and between the nonprofits and Mr. Harrigan will remain strained. The starting point, however, should be mutual respect for all parties involved. When respect is based on appreciating deep moral worth, attending to particularity, and having generosity in judgment, there is a basis for trust. The three taken together demonstrate that the participants have goodwill, that they will not take advantage of each other, and that when vulnerabilities arise, they will not cause harm.

(b) Honesty

Honesty is the next virtue that sustains trust and keeps the atmosphere of trust breathable. When honesty characterizes a relationship, the participants demonstrate their respect for each other and provide a sound basis for continuing their trust.

But what does honesty require? "Tell the truth, the whole truth, and nothing but the truth" is one possible response. It sounds so simple, and sometimes it is easy to know what the truth is that needs to be told. Having the courage to tell that truth is the hard part.

But knowing "what the truth is that needs to be told" is not always simple, and anyone who has lived a few years is well acquainted with the difficulties. First, what is "the whole truth?" Limited by time, geography, bias, and forgetfulness, we can never know what "the whole truth" is. Second, how much of the truth should we tell? Specific kinds of relationships call for different degrees of revelation. Casual acquaintances are not entitled to know the truths of intimacy; even intimates may not need to know some truths that we must tell strangers, for example, if the strangers are nurses and doctors seeking a diagnosis to save our lives. In keeping with many professional codes of ethics, information openly shared among certain colleagues is kept from others, protected by promises of privacy and confidentiality.

Thus, there may sometimes be good reasons for withholding the truth. Honesty is a profound virtue, but it is not the only virtue. The altruistic rescuers, spontaneously and without regret, lied to the Nazis who asked if they might happen to be hiding Jews that day. Their lies were justified by the lives they saved.

We know and experience these difficulties with truth telling, yet we still uphold honesty as a prime virtue. It is true that honesty is a virtue of personal integrity. Deception creeps into the liar's soul and splits it; liars are appropriately called "two-faced." But honesty is also a virtue of relationships and of communication. Eleventh century Islamic mystic Al-Ghazálí gives us a method for discovering how important honesty is. "If you want to know the foulness of lying for yourself, consider the lying of someone else and how you shun it and despise the man who lies and regard his communication as foul." He writes about controlling various body parts, and says about the tongue: "It is the part of your body with most power over you and over the rest of creation. It is, above all, the slanders of the tongue which throw men into Hell on their noses." We also need to guard our hands, "for the pen is one of man's two tongues." The hands must observe honesty as scrupulously as the tongue.[14]

"Deceit and violence—these are the two forms of deliberate assault on human beings."[15] This is strong language, but true. Sissela Bok wrote this statement in the 1970s, at a time when informed

consent was debated intensely in medical circles, and when physicians rarely questioned their prerogative to tell paternalistic lies to
their patients. While physicians treated their obligation to tell the
truth cavalierly, Bok found that to the patients, honesty mattered
more than anything else. If physicians were not honest with them
about their condition, they could not make thoughtful, autonomous
decisions about their lives, and sometimes, about their own deaths.

Consider what honesty requires in this case:

Showcase Clients: You are the new director of development for
an agency serving at-risk youth. The agency's past success in raising funds rests in part on 15-second TV spots that showcase former clients who go on to graduate from college. The executive
director is enthusiastic about this type of publicity. However, you
know that most of the youths who participate in your programs
are not "showcase clients." In fact, most of them have deeply
rooted emotional, physical, and family problems. You worry that
potential donors are being misled. What should you do?

The executive director could try to justify the ads by saying that
they do not contain bald-faced lies. The young people in the ads were
helped by your agency and did graduate from college. Besides, the ads
are effective; they tug on donors' heartstrings and wallets and bring
in the needed funds so that the agency can serve the community.

Nonetheless, the ads are misleading in that they misrepresent
your agency to the public, to potential donors, and to the youths in
your program. Use Al-Ghazálí's technique and compare what you
know to be true with what the listeners and viewers hear and see.
Do these two perspectives match? In this case, the ads manipulate
donors and undermine their ability to make fully informed decisions
about their charitable donations. Sustained public trust in the agency
rests on the agency's willingness to present itself honestly to potential donors even if misleading representations are more profitable in
the short term.

(c) Fairness

Treating people fairly is a fundamental part of maintaining the
atmosphere of trust that sustains long-term, professional relationships. We often associate fairness with treating people equally. Aristotle built on this idea by defining justice in terms of equality and

proportionality: Equals should be treated equally, and unequals in proportion to their inequality. Intuitively, this idea is clear. Quincy and Justine both work in the library shelving books, but Justine works twice as many hours as Quincy, and so should be paid twice as much.[16]

Ethics is not mathematics; there is no blanket rule of equality that applies to every case. The first task is to decide which variables to use in assessing equality and proportionality. In some situations, treating people equally means treating each person or unit the same. In board decisions, each board member gets one vote, rather than a variable number of votes proportional to longevity on the board, fund-raising ability, or degree of commitment. In some cultural traditions, equality based on this sense of sameness is important. In the late 1980s when the presidents of the member colleges of the American Indian College Fund discussed how to distribute funds among the 26 tribal colleges, they had to decide what understanding of fairness would guide the distribution. Should distribution be proportionate to size of the student body? Proportionate to need as demonstrated by grant proposals? They decided that each school would receive an equal sum, regardless of school size. As board chairperson Hansen observed, "Only that [option] is consistent with 'Indian way'—sharing resources equally regardless of how limited they may be."[17]

In other situations and cultural traditions, other features are important in deciding equality and proportionality. In a family of six children, ranging in age from 6 to 16, household chores are distributed fairly when they are based on each child's developmental abilities, and not in terms of the actual amount and type of work accomplished. When the music club is deciding how to award scholarships to summer music camp, the club members must wrestle with complex formulas reflecting ability, need, and potential to benefit from the experience.

Philosophers have long pondered these complications; we cannot possibly review or resolve them all here. So, let us focus on two dimensions of fairness that are particularly germane to sustaining trust within professional relationships: a sense of sharing responsibility and equal concern for growth.

(i) Sense of Sharing Responsibility

Special event week craziness has arrived. Does it seem that every year, the same people stay late, give up lunch breaks, and attend to last-minute details? One sign of fairness is that everyone has a sense of sharing responsibilities. While job descriptions enumerating each person's responsibilities set the stage for fairness, judgment beyond that is required. Fund raisers work amidst swarms of details, which often rise up unpredictably. Knowing that coworkers will assume their share of responsibilities is important to maintaining trust among colleagues.

It is easy to say that, other things being equal, unanticipated work burdens should be shared in the office, especially during high-pressure times. But consider this version of the story:

> "I'm getting really tired of this," Sadie mutters to Shaw. "The fund-raising gala is in one week. I've worked evenings and week-ends since I can't remember when. Willis always leaves right at 6:00 to pick up his kids at day care, and yesterday he ran out at 10:00 in the morning so he could take his youngest to the doctor for an ear infection. On the way out, he handed me a list of eight phone calls that just had to be made right then."
>
> "I can sure relate to that," Shaw agrees. "Last week Inez all at once took two days off, trying to find a nursing home for her mother, who has Alzheimer's. She said the elder day care pro-gram she had her in just can't handle her anymore. I'm sorry for her, of course, but why should we have to handle all the extra work, just because we are single, and all our relatives are healthy?"

There is a trust issue here. With this kind of resentment in the air, workplace relationships are apt to deteriorate. In thinking through this case, it is helpful to use the two main features of ethics as narrative: sympathetic understanding and attention to social and temporal context. Here are some contextual points to consider in try-ing to sort through what fairness means in this case.

First, we need to take a long-term view. Sadie and Shaw are thinking only of the present when they describe themselves as the people without caretaking responsibilities, and Willis and Inez as the people with caretaking responsibilities. Sadie and Shaw should think instead in terms of life spans. They may not have caretaking respon-sibilities now, but they may well have them in the future, at a time when Willis and Inez are relatively free of them. (This is not to say that caretaking responsibilities even themselves out in the long run. Some people simply have larger family commitments than others. Also, historical gender-role patterns are still playing themselves out. Even though many men do take their caretaking responsibilities very seriously, in general, women still perform more than their share of this work.)

The second contextual point is to remember the historical roots of contemporary work and family life patterns. Many of these patterns were established at a time when employers assumed that workers had few, if any, direct caretaking responsibilities themselves. It was assumed that workers had wives at home to care for the domestic needs of the workers and their children. This assumption has always been false, and particularly inapplicable to poor, immigrant, and nonwhite American families.[18] Many contemporary solutions are basically patch-up attempts on this flawed background. Other patterns also work against combining employment with caretaking responsibilities. Today's school hours were originally set to accommodate the needs of farm families. Geographical patterns separating workplace locations far from residential areas increase the difficulty of coordinating work and family responsibilities.

When Sadie and Shaw keep these points in mind, they will realize that the situation itself is difficult, and that they should not direct their resentment against Willis and Inez personally. Nonetheless, Sadie and Shaw do have justified complaints. When unanticipated, extra work is a fully anticipated part of the job description, Willis and Inez need to do what they can, when they can, to make sure that the burden does not fall on those with more flexible time schedules.

Fair resolutions to these sorts of tensions are an important element in maintaining trust among colleagues. Section 3.3 will discuss how having fair agency-wide policies is essential for maintaining interpersonal trust. In addition to Sadie, Shaw, Willis, and Inez's good-faith efforts to distribute the extra work among themselves, this problem also needs to be addressed by workplace policies that respond to issues of both shared workplace responsibilities and the demands of responsibilities outside the office.

(ii) Equal Concern for Growth

Earlier we discussed Aristotle's point that justice is defined in terms of equality and proportion, and that equality can be determined using a number of different variables. Dewey is critical of assessing people's equality in ways that ignore what is unique and distinctive about each individual. Instead of thinking about treating people equally with analogies like dividing up a pie, he directs us to think of sharing in a game, a play, or family life in which each person has a distinctive role. A jazz ensemble gives us a particularly appropriate image of equality as participation and continuous individual growth.

All the musicians are committed to the shared goal of making great jazz. When the trumpet solos, the pianist lays back and vamps, although plenty of subtle interplay is going on between them. Then the bass player takes the tune and bends it inventively. The drummer picks up on the bass player's inventions and adds a unique voice. The voices are equal in participation and equal in that each member's individual creativity is encouraged and enhanced.[19] It is precisely people's different talents and perspectives that enrich the communal effort. Dewey writes, "One person is morally equal to others ... when his values with respect to his own possibilities of growth, whatever they are, are reckoned with in the social organization as scrupulously as those of every other."[20]

Notice how directly Dewey's concept of equality leads back to trust. We treat people fairly when we consider their own good and their own potential for future growth as important variables in the relationship. In fund raising, this suggests that part of treating colleagues and volunteers fairly is to encourage continuous learning and skill development. This demonstrates respect for each person's capacities and appreciation for what they can contribute, and so supports an atmosphere of trust.

(d) Cooperativeness

Jane Addams was suspicious of heroes. During the early years at Hull House, Chicago was full of labor union activity. Addams was often called upon to negotiate strikes. In *A Modern Lear*, her analysis of the Pullman strike, Addams describes George Pullman's double role as capitalist and philanthropist. Not only did he provide jobs for his workers, he also built them a model town where they enjoyed dwellings and amenities far finer than other workers. Pullman was baffled when the workers went on strike; he could not imagine how they could align their sympathies with the union movement, when he had been so generous to them. The root of Pullman's problem, Addams writes, was that his model town was not a cooperative venture. Pullman tried to be good *to* the workers, but he did not consult them, and did not attempt to discover how they defined their own needs or values. Addams compares a heroic reformer to a solitary mountain climber, who soon leaves the rest of the folks far behind. By contrast, when efforts at reform are characterized by widespread cooperation, "progress (is) slower perpendicularly, but incomparably greater because lateral."[21] If the common good is truly to be common, it must be reached through active cooperation and widespread participation.

The final virtue we will discuss in the virtues of relationship cluster is cooperativeness. Cooperation fits in well with the other virtues in the cluster. Cooperating with others shows them respect. For cooperation to be effective, participants must attend to each other's particularity and show generosity in judgment. We enact fairness through cooperation, by sharing responsibilities and caring about each others' growth.

Addams's term for cooperation was *associated effort.* At Hull House, this was the basis for reform efforts of all sorts, even reforms about garbage. In the summer of 1894, the residents at Hull House were alarmed when they saw death rate statistics for their neighborhood. Garbage was the major culprit. The Hull House Women's Club, made up of neighborhood women, began investigating conditions in the alleys. After two months, they filed reports of 1,037 violations to the health department. Addams applauded her neighbors' commitment and persistence over that long, hot Chicago summer. "For the club woman who had finished a long day's work of washing or ironing followed by the cooking of a hot supper, it would have been much easier to sit on her doorstep during a summer evening than to go up and down ill-kept alleys and get into trouble with her neighbors over the condition of their garbage boxes."[22] Addams and the other Hull House residents were participants in the investigation, but it was not *their* investigation; it was planned and carried out by residents and neighbors as a mutual, cooperative venture.

Aristotle identifies two virtues that we can put in the category of cooperation. He admits he has trouble coming up with appropriate names for these virtues, but his descriptions are clear enough. The first he calls *mildness,* and places it between the excess of irascibility and the deficiency of "inirascibility." What he means by mildness is keeping an even temper, except in cases in which it is right to get angry, that is, where rational judgment indicates that anger is the appropriate response. People who get angry without thinking, get angry over trifles, or stay angry longer than warranted are irascible. People who overlook insults and do not get angry when warranted are "inirascible."[23]

The second virtue relevant to cooperation Aristotle calls *friendliness,* although here again he admits that the language is awkward. Friendliness lies between the excess of being ingratiating and the deficiency of being quarrelsome.[24] Disagreements and discomforts occur routinely in cooperative work. To get angry at the wrong time over the wrong issue subverts the effort; not to get angry at all might result in letting sloppy work or poor planning slip by.

"Amicable cooperation ... is itself a priceless addition to life."[25] Dewey's high esteem for cooperation follows directly from his understanding of equality as equal concern for growth. Fairness, he said, is to take seriously everyone's capacities for growth in whatever areas they can grow. He thinks that disagreement is an inevitable and healthy part of the process. The opposite of cooperation is not disagreement, but force or coercion. "To cooperate by giving differences a chance to show themselves because of the belief that the expression of difference is not only a right of the other persons, but is a means of enriching one's own life-experience, is inherent in the democratic personal way of life."[26]

This case presents a good opportunity for cooperation:

Wealth and Perception: "Purple Sage Estates" has been in the family for five generations. From cattle ranch to oil magnate mansion, to summer estate of a computer guru, "Purple Sage" has always been a home of gracious elegance and wealth. Now Patricia Pinion, the last surviving family member, wants to give it all to Mesquite Community College. She requests that the mansion, private golf course, and swimming pool be maintained for visiting dignitaries. You are thrilled at the offer of choice real estate, but worry that your economically strapped students will resent their lack of access to the college's showpiece, and the public will be less willing to vote for levies to support the college. What do you do?

As it stands, Pinion's offer is rife with possibilities for mistrust. The college needs the continuing goodwill and trust of the community, its alumni, and current and future students. If Pinion insists that only visiting dignitaries use the property, then the college may need to turn down the gift. But if Pinion and the college community are open to cooperation, many creative possibilities open up. Many departments and programs in the college could work together to create educational opportunities for the students. Programs in restaurant and hotel management, sports and recreation facilities management, and parks and wildlife management could all benefit from using the property. Through cooperation, trust among various members of the college community can be preserved and strengthened.

Just four of the virtues that support the atmosphere of trust—the oxygen supply of healthy workplace relationships—have been discussed. There are many more. When fund raisers are asked to list traits of healthy working relationships, in addition to those discussed here, people often add competence and a sense of humor. These belong in the cluster of workplace virtues, as well. It is reasonable to trust someone's discretion when they have competence; otherwise, it is unreasonable. Aristotle includes wit on his list of virtues, and we all know how a good sense of humor can recalibrate emotional thermometers. The cluster of virtues of relationships is large; fostering them makes philanthropy possible.

3.3 WHERE IS TRUST?

"To live in a complex society without going mad, we must have trust in systems, too."[27]

Our discussion of trust and the virtues of relationships has focused on interpersonal trust. But we can add other locations of trust, which are particularly important in modern, bureaucratic societies. Sociologist Ann-Mari Sellerberg studied trust in rural and urban settings in Sweden and contrasted the forms of trust she found there. Rural life revolved around interpersonal trust. Farmers enjoyed doing business with people they knew and had little confidence in people they did not know. In urban settings, people trusted bureaucratic institutions, such as banks and large retail stores, even though they knew very few of the people who worked there. In a complex society, it is impossible to rely on interpersonal trust alone; trust in institutions is absolutely necessary.[28] In this section, two levels of institutional trust important for fund raising and philanthropy will be discussed: agency trust and system trust.

(a) Agency Trust

Agency trust is the trust people have in a nonprofit organization, beyond their trust in particular individuals in that agency. Imagine this sad scenario: A 45-year-old graduate of Littleworth College goes to a job interview. The prospective employer sees the college's name, and exclaims, "What a joke that place that has become! They haven't offered a decent education in twenty years!" As a college's administrators and faculty change over time, one reason (among many) for maintaining quality is to sustain its trust with alumni so that their degrees do not become worthless.

Much of agency trust involves constructing and maintaining bureaucratic structures of accountability. This is not a book on non-profit management, but a few examples can be provided to illustrate the ethical dimension of management and the importance of designing policies that foster trust within an organization.

(i) Consistency between Policies and Mission

All nonprofits should have policies based on respect, fairness, and so on. In addition, agencies must be particularly careful that their policies are consistent with their own particular mission. For example, an agency working to improve a low-income, racially diverse community needs to be particularly sensitive about the composition of its work force and board. An agency dedicated to family issues must be careful that it does not ask its staff to sacrifice their own families for the sake of their clients.[29]

(ii) Policies Suitable to an Agency's Stage of Maturity

Joan Flanaghan points out the stages of a nonprofit's growth: "Leaders of nonprofit organizations improve our society, first, as outside reformers, then as creators of better models of care and as advocates for mainstream funding, and finally, as managers of the best programs."[30] Cooperation takes different forms in different stages of agency maturity. Imaginative flights of fancy can spread and grow informally throughout a small, new organization, but they must be carefully guided through all the deliberately designed channels of a mature agency. If the communication channels are not clear, people who should be consulted may be overlooked, with a resulting loss of trust.

(iii) Oversight Checks

There is a story of an organization's president who shuffled donations around, creating the illusion that several building projects were in good financial shape. Surely, as an individual, he was untrustworthy. But there was a deeper problem. Financial checks and controls were not in place, so the president was able to continue these practices for a long time before they were detected. Even then, the board refused to call him on it. The grounds for both interpersonal trust and agency trust were shaky. Adequate agency monitoring is an important support structure for sustaining agency trust, as well as stopping untrustworthy individuals.

It is not easy to decide how much oversight is appropriate. Even healthy relationships of trust can bear only so much monitoring.

Employees are rightly suspicious when a supervisor says, "I trust your judgment, but you must check every little detail with me before acting, and by the way, I'm monitoring every word you type on your computer." In trying to eliminate the vulnerability to harm that comes along with granting others discretionary powers, the supervisor has also eliminated the basis for trust. Too little oversight invites untrustworthy opportunists; too much oversight invites cynicism and resentment.

(iv) National Offices and Affiliates

When an "agency" is a large national or international organization with many affiliates, maintaining agency trust is a complicated affair. Trustworthy local branches feel the impact when the national office violates trust. Think of the damage done to local United Way affiliates when news of then President William Aramony's misuse of funds reached the public.

Tensions affecting trust can arise in other ways as well. The national office may want to standardize fund-raising efforts to consolidate costs and present a uniform image. Affiliates may feel that the national office's approach is not well suited to their particular community. Individual donors, corporations, and foundations may not appreciate being solicited by both the national office and a local affiliate at the same time.[31]

Interpersonal trust and agency trust are mutually supportive; the loss of one diminishes the other. The virtues that support trust—respect, honesty, fairness, and cooperation—need to be built into agency policies so that practices reflecting these virtues are encouraged and rewarded as part of everyday, routine operations. Agency trust provides a platform for interpersonal trust, but it can never replace it. There can never be enough policies to address every contingency, so trustworthy individuals in relationships of trust will always be needed to exercise discretion for the good of the whole.

(b) System Trust

Pollsters are fond of asking, "How much do you trust the media? big business? the government?" These systems are more than simply lists of individual journalists, businesses, or government agencies and personnel. Although none of them functions as a tightly knit system, it is still sensible to use singular nouns to refer to them. Those of us who remember the days of Presidents Eisenhower and

Kennedy remember when entering public service was assumed to be an honorable thing to do. Lyndon Johnson's lies about United States' involvement in Vietnam, the Watergate cover-up, and questionable campaign financing have all damaged the public trust in government per se, and not just in those politicians who made egregious moral errors. When my students show spontaneous, almost automatic cynicism about government, I hardly know what to say. I want students to believe that public service is honorable, yet I know that their cynicism is well founded. When the NSFRE Code of Ethical Principles refers to the "obligation to safeguard the public trust," it is referring to system trust, to the public's warranted ground for trusting philanthropic nonprofits collectively. The "system" here is the gift economy of philanthropy itself. When the Foundation for New Era Philanthropy collapsed and when United Way President Aramony's financial dealings became public, morally decent nonprofits worried that these scandals would diminish public trust in nonprofits in general, in addition to the harm done to local affiliates. Donors and volunteers need to be able to trust that the system as a whole will function well. They need to know that if a particular agency is untrustworthy, they can take their philanthropic giving elsewhere. Without this assurance, the gift economy of philanthropy collapses.

Professional and agency codes of ethics play a role in sustaining system trust. A code gives the public a clear indication of what the profession or agency stands for, and what behaviors will not be tolerated. Codes cannot create trust when it is unwarranted, but they can give guidance and they can contribute to sustaining trust in an already trustworthy system.

3.4 INTERTWINED LEVELS OF TRUST

Interpersonal trust, agency trust, system trust—the three of them together are the oxygen supply of trust in philanthropic nonprofits. (See Exhibit 3.2) The three levels of trust are intertwined; system trust and agency trust are built by the actions of countless individuals, in countless interpersonal interactions, day by day. Interpersonal trust is easier to maintain if agency trust is already in place.[32] System-wide distrust diminishes public trust even in completely trustworthy agencies or individuals.

This makes thinking about trust complex. In working through the question about relationships on the decision-making chart, we

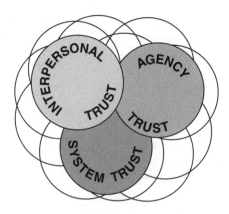

Exhibit 3.2 Three Levels of Trust

need to take into account not only maintaining trust between individuals, but also maintaining trust in individual agencies, and in the system of philanthropy as a whole.

We want our organizations to be structured and operated so that people of ordinary decency and courage can do well. Agency trust, based on responsible and responsive policies, and system trust, linking trustworthy agencies, provide an atmosphere in which trusting interpersonal relationships can breathe easy. When all three levels of trust function well, we are well equipped to sustain the gift economy of philanthropy.

DISCUSSION QUESTIONS

1. Philosopher Annette Baier writes, "Trust is much easier to maintain than it is to get started and it is never hard to destroy."[33] Think of an example of a professional relationship in which trust was damaged and then repaired. What specific measures contributed to restoring trust between the parties involved?

2. Too little monitoring and too much monitoring are both damaging to trusting relationships. Think of a particular example of a monitoring or oversight policy in your workplace. How does it support or diminish agency trust? What would the effect on trust be if the amount of oversight were increased? diminished?

3. The kind of system trust discussed in this chapter is *intrasystem* trust, or trust in the gift economy of philanthropy. Think about the notion of *intersystem* trust. Do you see cynicism about business or government carrying over into and damaging the trust people have in philanthropic nonprofits? Do nonprofits act in ways to contribute to that? Here are a few possibilities: Many of my students in business ethics are very cynical about advertising. To them, it is completely obvious that the point of advertising is to manipulate people into buying products. If philanthropic nonprofits use marketing techniques that too closely mimic advertising, will that be a conduit for cynicism? If nonprofit marketing techniques too closely mimic the "soundbite" techniques that pass for political speeches today, is that another channel for cynicism? What can nonprofit organizations and associations like NSFRE do to defend the philanthropic gift economy from cynicism migrating in from other systems?

CASE STUDIES

Early Perks. Your alumni association tours have generally been well received, but often have to run with a person or two fewer than budgeted for. Now you have a trip you know will be a winner. "Rare Religious Manuscripts of Eastern Europe" should be a big draw with graduates of your prestigious professional schools in library science and theology. The brochures are at the printers. A member of the university's board of trustees, a very major donor to the university who commands a lot of attention, calls you and wants to give you a deposit right away. She wants to use the trip as a present to her theologian husband and six members of their extended family, all university librarians. You hesitate, thinking it wouldn't be fair to other alumni to fill slots before the brochures go out. What do you do?

Bait and Switch? Historically, Jane Addams University has had many vocationally oriented programs, such as social work, medical technology, financial planning, and so on. However, the current administration is seriously considering changing the orientation of the university into a more prestigious, academic institution. Enrollments in the medical technology program have been declining, while a similar program at a nearby medical arts college is gaining a national reputation. A proposal for dropping the program is included in the five-year plan, which the board will consider at their next meeting. The vice-president for advancement, who favors the university's vocational orientation, asks you to solicit Sylvia Service, a wonderfully wealthy, terminally ill medical technology graduate who is in a position to give a large donation to the program. (The university's stated policy is that should programs cease to exist, designated funds will be used for other purposes.) You know Ms. Service is strongly committed to medical technology education. What do you do?

Unfulfilled Pledge. Several months ago Mr. Generous Donor ("GD"), a highly successful local business owner, and his wife, Penelope, pledged the lead gift in your college's capital campaign. Many of your college graduates work in GD's business, and he has always appreciated the fine preparation they receive at the college. It is now halfway through the campaign. You learn that GD has just died, and that Penelope has no intention of honoring the pledge. "GD was married more to his work than to me. Now it's my chance to support the charities I care about," she tells you. Some of the college trustees want to sue Mrs. Donor. How would you advise them? How will your decision affect interpersonal trust and agency trust?

Peaches and Cream. You are the fund raiser for an outdoor, summer drama company. Your marketing director solicits advertising support for your season program booklet from Peaches N' Cream, a local gourmet ice cream business. The ice cream shop receives much of its business from customers who drop in after performances. The owner of Peaches N' Cream is ready to purchase a large advertisement for $1,000 without knowing of the state's proposed road construction plans, which will reroute theater patrons to an alternate road, totally bypassing the ice cream business. Should you mention this before completing the deal?

Future Mayor? Five years ago you were contacted by an IRS agent, regarding Dotty Dodge. The IRS wanted to prosecute attorney Dodge for tax evasion. The evidence was convincing, but the agent was frustrated because a crucial witness could not be located. As CEO of your small nonprofit you had worked closely with Dodge, who had served as treasurer of your board. You told the agent that you did not have any information to help him locate the key witness. You were relieved that Dodge's term on the board was just about to expire. Now, five years later, Ms. Dodge is running for mayor, and is heavily favored to win. No mention of this part of her past has surfaced during the campaign. Do you have a responsibility to the community to "do" anything regarding this information?

NOTES

1. Aristotle, *Nicomachean Ethics*, trans. by Terence Irwin (Indianapolis: Hackett, 1985), p. 259.
2. Mike W. Martin, *Virtuous Giving* (Bloomington: Indiana University Press, 1994), p. 48.
3. Annette C. Baier's account of trust is most helpful. See *Moral Prejudices: Essays on Ethics* (Cambridge, MA: Harvard University Press, 1995). Chapter 6, "Trust and Antitrust," is particularly insightful.
4. *Id.*, p. 177.
5. Sissela Bok, *Lying: Moral Choice in Public and Private Life* (New York: Vintage Books, 1978), p. 31n.
6. Immanuel Kant, *Groundwork of the Metaphysic of Morals*, trans. by H.J. Paton (New York: Harper & Row, 1964), pp. 95, 102.
7. The "United Nations Universal Declaration of Human Rights" can be found at http://www.un.org/Overview/rights.html.
8. Joan Flanagan, "Horizon Hospice: From Zero to $2.7 Million a Year." in Michael Seltzer (ed.): *Fundraising Matters: True Stories of How Raising Funds Fulfills Dreams. New Directions for Philanthropic Fundraising*, no. 1 (San Francisco: Jossey-Bass, Fall 1993), p. 117.
9. Margaret Urban Walker, *Moral Understandings: A Feminist Study in Ethics* (New York: Routledge, 1998), p. 167.
10. Karen Fiser, "Philosophy, Disability, and Essentialism." in Lawrence Foster and Patricia Herzog (eds.): *Contemporary Philosophical Perspectives on Pluralism and Multiculturalism* (Amherst: University of Massachusetts Press, 1994), pp. 88–89.
11. Susan Weidman Schneider and Gretchen von Schlegell, "Richness in Diversity." in Abbie J. von Schlegell and Joan M. Fisher (eds.): *Women as Donors, Women as Philanthropists. New Directions for Philanthropic Fundraising*, no. 2 (San Francisco: Jossey-Bass, Winter 1993), p. 139.
12. Jane Addams, *Twenty Years At Hull House* (New York: Macmillan, 1912; reprint ed., Urbana: University of Illinois Press, 1990), p. 80.
13. John Dewey, *The Moral Writings of John Dewey*, revised ed., James Gouinlock (ed.): (Amherst, New York: Prometheus Books, 1994), p. 192.
14. Al-Ghazáli, *The Faith and Practice of Al-Ghazáli*, trans. by W. Montgomery Watt (Oxford, Oneworld Publications, 1994), pp. 48, 147, 155.

15. Sissela Bok, *Lying: Moral Choice in Public and Private Life* (New York: Vintage, 1978), p. 18.

16. Aristotle, *Nicomachean Ethics*, trans. by Terence Irwin (Indianapolis: Hackett, 1985), pp. 123–125.

17. Ronald Austin Wells, "'The Future Is in Our Minds': The American Indian College Fund." in Michael Seltzer, ed., *Fundraising Matters: True Stories of How Raising Funds Fulfills Dreams. New Directions for Philanthropic Fundraising*, no. 1 (San Francisco: Jossey-Bass, Fall 1993), p. 84.

18. For a fascinating discussion see Stephanie Coontz, *The Way We Never Were: American Families and the Nostalgia Trap* (New York: Basic Books, 1992).

19. I am grateful to Kathleen Higgins for this metaphor. After Higgins presents the idea of the jazz ensemble as an image for social interactions, she suggests the progressive jazz solo as a pattern for race relations. See Kathleen Marie Higgins, *The Music of Our Lives* (Philadelphia: Temple University Press, 1991), pp. 174–182.

20. John Dewey, *The Moral Writings of John Dewey*, revised ed., James Gouinlock (ed.): (Amherst, New York: Prometheus Books, 1994), p. 191.

21. Jane Addams, "A Modern Lear." *Survey*, vol. 29 (1912); reprinted by the Hull House Museum, 1994, p. 23.

22. Jane Addams, *Twenty Years At Hull House* (New York: Macmillan, 1912; reprint ed., Urbana: University of Illinois Press, 1990), pp. 164–166.

23. Aristotle, *Nicomachean Ethics*, trans. by Terence Irwin (Indianapolis: Hackett, 1985), pp. 105–106.

24. *Id.*, pp. 107–109.

25. John Dewey, *The Moral Writings of John Dewey*, revised ed., James Gouinlock (ed.): (Amherst, New York: Prometheus Books, 1994), p. 270.

26. *Id.*, p. 270.

27. Trudy Govier, *Social Trust and Human Communities* (Montreal and Kingston: McGill-Queen's University Press, 1997), p. 29.

28. *Id.*, pp. 24–25.

29. Dennis R. Young, "Nonprofit Organizations and Business: The Conflict and Confluence of Managerial Culture." in Royster C. Hedgepeth (ed.): *Nonprofit Organizational Culture: What Fundraisers Need to Know. New Directions for Philanthropic Fundraising*, no. 5 (San Francisco: Jossey-Bass, Fall 1994), p. 84.

30. Joan Flanagan, "Horizon Hospice: From Zero to $2.7 Million a Year." in Michael Seltzer (ed.): *Fundraising Matters: True Stories of How Raising Funds Fulfills Dreams. New Directions for Philanthropic Fundraising,* no. 1 (San Francisco: Jossey-Bass, Fall 1993), p. 111.
31. Marilyn Dickey, "Fund-Raising Friction." *Chronicle of Philanthropy,* vol. 10, no. 24, (October 8, 1998), pp. 33, 38.
32. Annette C. Baier, *Moral Prejudices* (Cambridge, MA: Harvard University Press, 1995), p. 111.
33. *Id.,* p. 107.

4 ▼ Images and Virtues of Integrity

"In what ways does this alternative help or not
help you develop into the person you want to become?
How does it strengthen or weaken
your own integrity?"

Why do we care about integrity? Ralph Waldo Emerson points out an answer: "Nothing is at last sacred but the integrity of your own mind."[1] Integrity is as close as it gets to identifying the moral quality of your own self, your one absolutely constant companion. You can change jobs, move to a new location, find new friends, and sometimes even acquire a new family. You can take a vacation; get away from colleagues, donors, and volunteers; and shelve the mission statement for awhile. But you can never request a leave of absence from yourself. You are the one to whom you are ultimately accountable. What makes the "could you face yourself in the mirror tomorrow morning" test compelling is the fact that *your own* face is the one that is going to appear in the mirror. Much as we might wish it, no one else's face will show up there. So we care about our own integrity; we must face it every day.

There is a consolation prize. I am ultimately responsible to and for myself; that is my face I will see in tomorrow's mirror, but I also have special access to sculpting tools. New parents are quickly cured of the illusion that their young children are infinitely malleable. Others stubbornly resist our makeover plans for them. But we have the power to shape ourselves. We can fashion our own integrity so that the face in tomorrow's mirror is a welcoming sight.

4.1 IMAGES OF INTEGRITY

Integrity, integer, integrate. The *Oxford English Dictionary* defines integrity as "wholeness, entireness, completeness." Integrity shares the same root with integers, or whole numbers, and with integration, a harmonious blending of parts. People often think of integrity in terms of coherence, where all of one's parts fit together into a coherent, unified whole. This image has much to recommend it, so two ways of understanding integrity's wholeness as a kind of coherence will be discussed at length: coherence as a harmony of the parts of the soul, and coherence as acting in fidelity to ideals. This image of integrity as wholeness also has limitations, so we will seek other images to supplement it.

(a) Integrity as Harmony of the Soul

The ancient Greeks defined harmony in terms of bringing dischordant parts into an orderly whole. Their goddess, Harmonia, was the daughter of Ares, the god of war, and Aphrodite, the goddess of love. Harmony is an achievement, a matter of overcoming strife between disparate parts. Plato uses this perspective as he constructs his image of a virtuous soul. (For Plato, *soul* includes a person's entire psychological makeup, and is not a theological soul.) He started with the obvious fact that we do experience internal conflict. The surgeon says, "Do not eat or drink anything for eight hours prior to surgery." If surgery is scheduled for 4 P.M., one generally experiences a great deal of internal conflict, trying to keep the doctor's directive. The "appetitive" part of your soul fills you with the desire to drink. (The appetites include bodily desires and desires for wealth.) The rational part of your soul understands the reason for abstinence. Which part wins out depends on what Plato calls the spirited or passionate part of the soul, the part that gives us the energy and resolve to act. If the spirited part allies itself with the rational part, we have the courage to act on wise choices; if it allies itself with bodily desires, reason's cautions are ignored. Using Plato's image of the soul, a person of integrity is one whose soul is in harmony. In a harmonious soul, reason rules with the spirited part as its ally, and the appetitive part follows and obeys. For

Plato, a harmonious soul is a virtuous soul. The four Greek virtues—wisdom, courage, temperance, and justice—are found in this configuration. Wisdom is achieved when reason rules, for wisdom is knowledge of each part's role in a harmonious soul, and knowledge of how the parts benefit from working well together. Courage is "holding on" and following reason's wisdom even when tempted by pain or pleasure to let the appetites take over. Temperance (sometimes translated as *moderation* or *harmony*) is the friendly agreement among the three parts of the soul that reason should rule. Justice is achieved when each part of the soul keeps to its proper task, and does not try to usurp the role of another.[2]

Plato's image is profound and expresses much of what we mean by integrity. Internal conflicts make up the drama of everyday life. Having the wisdom to know what to do and the courage to follow wisdom's dictates is the mark of a person of integrity. Plato describes such a person this way: "He is master of himself, puts things in order, is his own friend, harmonizes the three parts like the limiting notes of a musical scale.... He binds them all together, and himself from a plurality becomes a unity."[3] Integrity is thus a kind of wholeness achieved through harmonizing the parts of one's soul, all following the rule of reason.

That integrity is an achievement is clear in Plato's Myth of the Charioteer, his metaphor for the soul's journey. The charioteer (reason) has a difficult task. One horse, which is usually identified as the spirited part of the soul, loves honor and is willing to obey the charioteer's commands. Trouble comes from the second horse, generally identified as the appetitive part of the soul. We easily recognize our desires in Plato's apt description: "The other is crooked of frame, a massive jumble of a creature, consorting with wantonness and vainglory ... hard to control with whip and goad."[4]

Another image of the soul as a charioteer is found in the *Katha Upanishad*, a Hindu Holy Scripture, although the roles are assigned a bit differently. The chariot is the body, the charioteer is the soul, and the horses are the senses.

> Who knows not how to discriminate
> With mind undisciplined the while,
> Like vicious steeds untamed, his senses
> He cannot master,—he their charioteer.
>
> But he who does know how to discriminate
> With mind controlled and disciplined,

Like well-trained steeds, his senses
He masters fully,—he their charioteer.[5]

In both of these writings, the charioteer achieves a smooth ride through careful training and vigilant control. By analogy, integrity and moral virtue are achieved when the parts of the soul fit together harmoniously under reason's rule.[6] For fund raisers, a person of integrity knows what is wise and just; desires for personal gain or reward remain firmly in the background. Reason keeps the organization's mission and the giftlike nature of philanthropy clearly in view. Courage is being spirited enough to face conflict and risk rejection, holding firm to what reason indicates. The glory of getting the big gift does not overshadow one's wisdom and persistence in making sure that how one gets the gift is in keeping with the mission and the larger purposes of philanthropy.

(b) Integrity as Fidelity to Ideals

A second way of thinking about integrity as coherence is in terms of fidelity to ideals. Coherence is achieved when one's outward actions flow from one's inward commitments. The discussion in Chapter 2 of charity as a virtue of gifts as outgoing gives us a good example. In the medieval monasteries, love for God defined the ideal of charity; the monks demonstrated fidelity to that ideal through charitable actions toward others. St. Francis of Assisi is a clear example of living in fidelity to one's ideals. This thirteenth century monk devoted his life to imitating the life of Jesus in its poverty and simplicity and in bringing the message of the gospel to the poor. In a person of integrity, outward actions flow from commitment to moral ideals. This, too, is applicable to philanthropic fund raising. The ideal is sustaining philanthropy as a gift economy; by working to further one's organizational mission, we demonstrate fidelity to that ideal.

(c) Integrity as Reliable Accountability and Flexible Resiliency

In many circumstances, the image of integrity as wholeness, both as harmony and as fidelity to ideals, is adequate. However, the image of integrity as wholeness does not apply in every case. The problem with integrity as wholeness is that it does not fit into the life stories of many of us. Using the features of ethics as narrative—sympathetic understanding and knowledge of social and temporal context—will help us see this point. The two problems with integrity as wholeness are its isolated focus on the individual, and its static quality.

All that we do takes place in a social environment, and many of our deepest commitments are commitments to care for and be responsible for others. This is at the essence of philanthropy as well. Wholeness in terms of harmony within oneself or guiding one's actions in fidelity to inner ideals does not take this environmental context sufficiently into account.

One clue to the problem is to look more closely at where Plato's harmonious soul and the medieval charitable monks lived. Plato explains his theory of the soul in the context of devising his utopian vision of a just state, the *Republic*. The pattern of the just state matches perfectly the pattern of the harmonious soul. Reason rules via philosopher kings, whose wisdom entitles them to absolute political authority. (Plato feared that in a democracy, incompetent people would be elected. He had a point.) The *Rule of Benedict*, which so clearly spells out the connection between charity as love for God and charity as service to humankind, was written for monastic communities, that is, places where integrity as fidelity to ideals was the pattern for one's community, as well as for one's own soul. Because we are social beings, it is easier to achieve coherence in one's own soul if everyone else is living by the same pattern. Neither of these patterns addresses the difficulties of living coherently in a society that does not mirror the harmony or fidelity of one's own soul.

The definition of integrity as internal harmony is not finely tuned to the fact that many of us have multiple identities. Our own personal identity draws heavily on the groups with whom we share heritage and commitment. We typically identify with several groups. For example, Hassan is Catholic, Egyptian, currently American working class, and a jazz afficionado. He appreciates Walt Whitman's line, "I am large; I contain multitudes."[7] Integrating these multitudes gets tricky, because some of the groups with which one identifies may not fit companionably together. Philosopher Maria Lugones gives a particularly poignant account of why it is difficult for her to achieve inner wholeness. She is a Latina lesbian, at home in and committed to her own Hispanic culture, even though she finds that her community is often hostile to her identity as a lesbian. The lesbian communities she appreciates do not share her Latina heritage. She works this out by thinking of herself as "multiplicitous," as dwelling in the borderlands. Her personal identity contains both parts, and she is committed to both communities, but the two parts are in tension.[8]

Should Lugones stop worrying about negotiating through the troubles of her disparate communities and shift her focus to achieving inner harmony between her own disparate parts? Inner harmony work is fine to an extent, but there are dangers in focusing too much on oneself, even on one's moral self. Jane Addams worries about this: "When the entire moral energy of an individual goes into the cultivation of personal integrity, we all know how unlovely the result may become." She suggests we turn our focus away from our own individual wholeness, and onto our activities in connection with others.[9] Philosopher John Dewey gives a withering critique of what he terms *spiritual egotism*, in which people become so self-absorbed with their own character that they ignore the conditions around them. Working on their own integrity becomes a way of escaping the troubles of the world.[10]

We need a way to understand integrity that makes sense to us in the context of our lives as social beings with multiple identities, living in multiple communities, and with multiple commitments to other people. Rather than focusing on inner wholeness, Philosopher Margaret Urban Walker suggests that we think about integrity by starting with the question, "How do I relate to, care for, and act responsibly to others?" Walker suggests phrases like *reliable accountability, sturdiness,* and *flexible resiliency* as core concepts for integrity. Others can count on us; we respond to their needs and concerns in dependable ways. We have the flexibility to adapt to whatever challenges come our way and the resilience not to be thrown by them.[11] With these changes in emphasis, integrity is still about the shape of one's character, but it is one's character in relation to others and to one's commitments to the community. Lugones is committed to and hence accountable to both Latina and lesbian communities. As she moves between them, she is resilient and sturdy; members of both communities can count on her love and participation. She can be a person of integrity without needing to achieve inner harmony.

In the context of our commitments as professional fund raisers, we can think of integrity less as a state to be achieved and more as a term for living a life that exhibits many of the virtues we have discussed so far: generosity, charity, and compassion, the virtues of gifts as outgoing; gratitude and mutuality as virtues of gifts of return; and respect, honesty, fairness, and cooperativeness as virtues of relationships. We can think of integrity as a "master virtue" that pulls into service a long list of other specific virtues. These virtues working together make a person sturdily and reliably accountable.[12]

(d) Our Garden Is the World

A second limitation of the image of integrity as wholeness is that it aims for an essentially unchanging state. Once the charioteer gets those horses under control, the ride is smooth and unvaried. All along we have been talking about the temporal context of our lives and how growth takes place as we meet new challenges from the social environment. So we want to think about integrity in ways that make the potential for growth a central part of the definition.

Dewey gives us some wonderful suggestions on how to do this. Connecting integrity with one's place in the ever-changing environment, he writes, "In short, the thing actually at stake in any serious deliberation is ... what kind of person one is to become, what sort of self is in the making, what kind of a world is making."[13] This perspective fits in well with the final question on the ethical decision-making chart: "In what ways does this alternative help or not help you develop into the person you want to become?" The emphasis here is on continual growth. We can think of each decision and each day as additional entries in our autobiographies. But note the context. In making ourselves, we also make the world. Self and environment are intertwined and mutually constructed. The notion of integrity as incorporating growth and change is implicit in Dewey's wonderful twist on cultivating one's garden. At the end of Voltaire's eighteenth century satire, Candide finds happiness in cultivating his garden away from the world. At the end of *Individualism Old and New*, Dewey also has a garden, but note the difference: "To gain an integrated individuality, each of us needs to cultivate his own garden. But there is no fence about this garden: it is no sharply marked-off enclosure. Our garden is the world, in the angle at which it touches our own manner of being."[14]

We can welcome the challenges a changing environment brings us and view them as opportunities for both self and world transformation. To clarify this, let us use the human body as a source of analogy. We can think of a person's skin as a barrier, something that clearly delineates that person from the rest of the world. By contrast, we can switch our focus and see the body as a point of continuous exchange. Oxygen, water, plants, and animal products are constantly taken in, transformed as the body is transformed, and then the waste products eliminated. Without this constant interchange, we have no life, as the *Maitri Upanishad* expresses so bluntly: "Food is indeed the highest form of the Self; for the breath of life is made up of food. Now, if one does not eat, one cannot think, hear, feel, see, speak, smell or taste, and so one loses one's vital breaths."[15]

Likewise, our psychological selves are in constant interchange with the social and temporal environment in a process of mutual shaping and being shaped. We need to understand integrity in a way that resonates with this openness to growth. Integrity as "reliable accountability," "sturdiness" and "flexible resiliency" is a good beginning. The next section will describe three virtues of integrity that aid us in being open to change, yet still provide filters to keep out moral pollutants. First, let us go back to that book of ancient Chinese wisdom, the *Tao te Ching.* Lao-tzu gives us an image of the self that has both sturdiness and dynamism.

> The mark of a moderate man
> is freedom from his own ideas.
> Tolerant like the sky,
> all-pervading like sunlight,
> firm like a mountain,
> supple like a tree in the wind,
> he has no destination in view
> makes use of anything
> life happens to bring his way.[16]

I find this description compelling, except for the part about not having a destination in view. But the other images speak to me. Yes, we should hold to our ideals and commitments firmly like a mountain. But we should learn from those architects and engineers working in earthquake zones that buildings which are "supple like a tree in the wind" stand longer than rock-solid monuments. Being tolerant, open, supple, and ready to use what life brings, means we must also be free enough from our own ideas to be able to learn from other people and situations and to incorporate their wisdom into our own patterns of growth.

4.2 THE CLUSTER OF VIRTUES OF INTEGRITY

Just as the virtue clusters from Chapters 2 and 3 are much larger than the specific virtues discussed there, so integrity joins together many

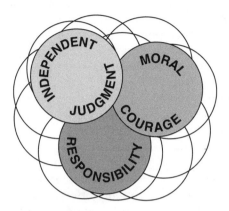

Exhibit 4.1   Cluster of Virtues of Integrity

more virtues than the ones described here. Three virtues, however, seem particularly central for acting with integrity: independent judgment, responsibility, and moral courage. (See Exhibit 4.1.) As you read, keep this question in mind: When you read through your autobiography several years from now, how would you like the page with today's date on it to read?

(a) Independent Judgment

I will start by describing at some length one of the most horrific examples of a lack of independent judgment that I have seen documented. Hannah Arendt's coverage of the Adolf Eichmann trial is well named: *Eichmann in Jerusalem: A Report on the Banality of Evil.* Arendt did not find Eichmann to be insane, nor was he a moral monster; instead, he was "banal," "commonplace, trivial."[17] During his trial in 1963, six psychiatrists examined him, and certified that he was "normal."[18] He related well to family and friends, and had all the normal concerns about doing his job conscientiously and advancing his career. After spending several years in sales, he joined the Nazi party, not out of ideological convictions, but because it provided good opportunities for advancing his own career. In 1938, he was appointed head of the "Center for Emigration of Austrian Jews," and was very successful at streamlining the emigration process. He found ways of processing paperwork efficiently, and he evidently had some international fund-raising skills, as he found ways to obtain funds from abroad to finance emigration for poorer Jews. A few years later he was promoted from "forced emigration" to "forced evacuation" and placed in charge of transportation. Processing paperwork, getting the right number of people on the right trains, and making sure the trains arrived on time at the right destinations were all tasks suitable for his organizational skills.[19]

How do we understand this thoroughly conventional man, who cared about his family, cared about his career, and cared about doing his job well—so well that he contributed to the deaths of eleven million people? Arendt concludes that the root of the problem was Eichmann's inability to imagine or understand other people's points of view.[20] About the notes Eichmann jotted down while in Argentina after the war, Arendt comments, "... every line of these scribblings shows his utter ignorance of everything that was not directly, technically and bureaucratically, connected with his job."[21]

Eichmann's inability to think beyond his own concerns showed up most clearly in his use of language. He spoke in clichés; he repeated stories using exactly the same words. Eichmann's speech clearly demonstrates the connection between language and thought: "The longer one listened to him, the more obvious it became that his inability to speak was closely connected with an inability to *think*, namely, to think from the standpoint of somebody else."[22]

We know that the Nazis were masters at manipulating language. The people who inscribed "Work Is Freedom" at the entrance to the concentration camps, and whose SS slogan was "My Honor Is My Loyalty,"[23] referred euphemistically to the gassing centers at Auschwitz and Treblinka as "Charitable Foundations for Institutional Care."[24]

Eichmann's story gives us rich material for understanding the dimensions of independent judgment. What he lacked were the two components of ethics as narrative: sympathetic understanding and attention to context. Eichmann thought he was helping the Jews by arranging for their expulsion from Nazi occupied territories. He lacked any understanding, sympathetic or otherwise, of how the Jews felt about how well he was doing his job.

Eichmann also lacked the ability to understand his daily activities within larger contexts. His job was transportation. He totally blocked out the larger questions of why the Jews were being transported, and what would happen to them after reaching their destinations so efficiently. As his lawyer was fond of saying, Eichmann was in transportation, not killing. His facility with language was so impoverished that he could do nothing but internalize and parrot the "officialese" of the Nazi party. Finally, and most tellingly, Arendt

observes, "As Eichmann told it, the most potent factor in the sooth-
ing of his own conscience was the simple fact that he could see no
one, no one at all, who actually was against the Final Solution."[25]
Surrounded by people who shared the same clichéd version of what
they were doing, it never occurred to him to think otherwise.

From this story, we can identify key components of independent
judgment. The first component is the ability to make connections by
placing a current idea or activity in the context of larger frameworks.
For fund raisers, this means asking, "How does this fund-raising
method fit in with other approaches we use and with the values we
stand for? How does it fit in with our organization's mission and the
larger values of philanthropy? The second component is to ask how
an idea or action affects other people and how they would interpret
it. "If I were the donor, the volunteer, the client, how would I think
about this idea or activity?"

It is critical that fund raisers exercise independent judgment in
this way and that they make these sorts of connections. It is dangerous for a fund raiser to accept without questioning when the chief
executive officer or a board member says, "Your job is just to raise
the money. Leave all the idea making and strategic planning to us."
This is dangerous, first, because it is ineffective. How can a fund
raiser possibly represent an organization to potential donors and
funding agencies, without understanding why an organization and
its projects are worth funding? But it is also dangerous to view your
job as "just raising the money." By just raising the money, you are as
implicated in carrying out the goals of the project as are the direct
planners. Much as Eichmann denied it, by being in transportation,
he was also in killing, and by not understanding this connection he
displayed a colossal lack of independent judgment.

We need to take our language and our vocabulary very seriously.
Eichmann could not think independently because he could not speak
except in the most perverted and perverse terms. We need to have
facility in describing our actions, our mission, and our commitments
in more than one way. When every decision becomes "strategic" and
every method assessed in terms of "efficiency," we become disconnected from explicitly philanthropic vocabularies and from the philanthropic sensitivities that we so desperately need to stay on course.
I am not suggesting a direct parallel here; I do not think that the
vocabulary of "strategy" and "efficiency" is perverted and perverse.
But when it exceeds its proper place, and replaces rather than sup-
plements explicitly philanthropic vocabulary, then it threatens to
become perverted and perverse. I get nervous when I hear people talk

about seeking "win–win" solutions. I get nervous, because the phrase does have a legitimate and morally praiseworthy intent; win–win solutions can be ways of enacting mutuality, cooperativeness, respect, and so on. But sometimes, there is a drift, a slippage. The moral content of mutuality and cooperation gets eased out. Win–win becomes a cover for "keeping everybody happy," where some party's happiness is based on morally unacceptable compromise.

Jane Addams tells a story of how she passed up an opportunity for a win–win solution. Hull House needed new facilities for the Jane Club, a cooperative boarding house for single young women. A trustee contacted a business owner, who agreed to give $20,000 to the project. But this generous donor "was notorious for underpaying the girls in his establishment and concerning whom there were even darker stories." Addams declined the offer. Hull House lost the money, the trustee was embarrassed, and the potential donor insulted.[26] Win–win solutions are wonderful for morally nonproblematic situations, but focusing single-mindedly on finding win–win solutions can cause us to turn off our moral sensors and blithefully ignore deep moral problems.

Finally, it is important to be thoughtfully engaged with people who do not share your own perception of the world, who do not share your assumptions, and who question what you do. This is not comfortable; it slows us down and makes our work inefficient. But it calls us into account, it forces us to think more broadly and independently, and it forces our unconscious assumptions out into the open. Chapter 9 discusses how the discomforts of diversity force us to think outside of conventional patterns and thus strengthen the independent judgment which is critical to integrity and to fund raisers' commitment to sustain the philanthropic gift economy.

(b) Responsibility

A second virtue of integrity is responsibility. In discussing this virtue, we will work with a definition drawn from the root of responsibility as *response*. Crucial dimensions of philanthropic work are done in response to needs, to suffering, to injustice, and to despair, and so Christian theologian H. Richard Niebuhr's analysis of responsibility in terms of responsiveness is particularly appropriate.[27]

Niebuhr understands responsibility as having three elements. Each of these elements will be illustrated here with wisdom from that most eloquent statement of responsibility, Martin Luther King's "Letter from a Birmingham Jail." In 1963, Martin Luther King was in Birmingham, Alabama, in his capacity as president of a philanthropic nonprofit, the Southern Christian Leadership Conference. He was in jail, quite simply, because he had broken the law. He had led a group of marchers through the city without a parade permit, in violation of a city ordinance. King wrote the letter in response to a statement by eight clergy members who sympathized with his ultimate goals but criticized his actions as "unwise and untimely."[28]

Niebuhr's first element of responsibility is "response to interpreted action upon us."[29] We and others with whom we empathize are acted upon. Our response is based on how we interpret those actions. Several years ago, I heard my son knock on the back door window, as he often did, but this time the knock was followed immediately by the sound of shattering glass. Running through the kitchen, I "interpreted" his action. He had knocked in joy, eagerly anticipating his after-school snack. I responded with concern and a good measure of humor. I interpreted the cause of the breakage, not as issuing from anger or impulsiveness, but as the result of his recent growth spurt, making his routine knock more forceful than before.

In explaining his response to the denied permit, King explains the particulars of the matter, but what is instructive for us is the way he places his response and his interpretation into a larger framework. Was the march unwise? King uses the virtue of mutuality and the way stories are embedded in larger stories to place the injustice of the denied permit into a wider perspective. "Injustice anywhere is a threat to justice everywhere. We are caught in an inescapable network of mutuality, tied in a single garment of destiny. Whatever affects one directly, affects all indirectly."[30]

Was the march "untimely?" The eight clergy members' memory time span was exceedingly short. King reminded them that Africans had been in America for over 340 years. He then eloquently personalized what all those years had felt like. "When you have seen vicious mobs lynch your mothers and fathers at will and drown your sisters and brothers at whim; ... when you suddenly find your tongue twisted and your speech stammering as you seek to explain to your six-year-old daughter why she can't go to the public amusement park, ... and see ominous clouds of inferiority beginning to form in her little mental sky ... when you are forever fighting a degenerating sense of "nobodiness" then you will understand why we find it difficult to wait."[31]

King took responsibility in the sense of interpreting the actions against him, placing those actions in the wider context of the history of his people's suffering, and then shaping his response to that inter-pretation. Here, response to interpreted action looks to the past, to understand what has happened.

The second element in responsibility that Niebuhr identifies is *accountability.* Here, accountability looks toward the future, by antic-ipating how others will respond to our responses.[32] King's response to injustice in Birmingham was to march. He anticipated how oth-ers would respond to the march, knowing that they would ask him: "How can you create justice by doing injustice, by breaking the law? How are you any different from ordinary criminals?"

In his letter, King gives a profound defense of civil disobedi-ence, and with great clarity distinguishes it from ordinary law-lessness. Placing himself in the natural law tradition of Augustine and Aquinas, he declares that "an unjust law is no law at all."[33] The city denied him a permit in order to support unjust laws of racial oppression.

King then goes on to detail the steps people should take in plan-ning acts of nonviolent civil disobedience. Taken from Gandhi, these steps instructed King and his colleagues to first gather the necessary facts to establish that injustice was in fact being done. The second step is to negotiate the disagreement, which King and others had tried with great patience, but to no avail. Third, they were to go through a process of self-purification, making sure that their motives were pure and that they were willing to suffer the legal consequences. Finally, an action of civil disobedience needs to be public and non-violent.[34] If these steps are followed, breaking the law is morally jus-tified. King's response showed accountability; he took into account how others would respond and had a thoughtful defense.

Niebuhr's third element in responsibility is social solidarity. Our actions, he says, are like lines in a dialogue; through our responsible actions we form a continuing community.[35] "Social solidarity?" the clergy ask. To them, an act of solidarity, a win–win solution, would be to wait, to go slow, to try negotiating again. But King knew that long-term solidarity sometimes depends on telling short-term rude truths.[36] He explained his painful realization that the greatest obsta-cles to justice were the white moderates. This included many Chris-tian and Jewish religious leaders who confused maintaining order with justice, and were willing to settle for "obnoxious negative peace" rather than striving for "substantive and positive peace."[37] King's ulti-mate vision was clearly that of social solidarity, as he concluded the letter with these words: "Let us all hope that the dark clouds of racial prejudice will soon pass away and the deep fog of misunderstanding will be lifted from our fear-drenched communities, and in some not too distant tomorrow the radiant stars of love and brotherhood will shine over our great nation with all their scintillating beauty."[38]

What can fund raisers learn from this analysis of responsibility? How can it help in answering the third question on the ethical decision-making chart, "In what ways does this alternative help or not help you develop into the person you want to become? How does it strengthen or weaken your own integrity?"

Several comments are germane here. First, in strengthening our own integrity, we should think of our actions as responses to larger needs. A common definition of philanthropy is "voluntary action for the public good." We need to evaluate every so often just what "the public good" is, and to be especially responsive to alleviating injustice and suffering. Second, our integrity includes accountability. We should act so that we can be held accountable, that is, we need to be able to give well-reasoned, value-based explanations of our actions to people who disagree with us. They may not be convinced, but we at least need to be prepared to give an answer. Finally, integrity includes a sense of responsibility for social solidarity, or in the language of this book, responsibility for sustaining the gift economy of philanthropy. Social solidarity can often be achieved through mutual cooperation, which is joyful for all. However, we also have to be ready for those times when achieving community in the longterm depends on being prickly in the short term. A colleague once said to me, "If you don't have at least three people mad at you at any given time, you aren't living right." I do not think that statement is always true, but it is often true, and knowing when to act to make it true requires that we use the three virtues in the integrity cluster: independent judgment, responsibility, and moral courage.

(c) Moral Courage

Many times we know what is the ethical thing to do. The difficulty is having the courage to act on that knowledge. It is hard to have the courage to act on your convictions if everyone else around you is cutting ethical corners. It is hard to have the courage to speak up if you know that you will be accused of not being a team player.

In the discussion on integrity as wholeness, Plato's understanding of courage was mentioned. Referring to the spirited part of the soul, Plato writes, "It is this part which causes us to call an individual brave, when his spirit preserves in the midst of pain and pleasure his belief in the declarations of reason as to what he should fear and what he should not."[39] Plato's definition brings out two dimensions of courage that are important for integrity. First, "his spirit preserves in the midst of pain and pleasure...." Courage is a matter of holding on, of persistence, of not giving up or giving in to easier paths. Courage is holding on, in spite of physical pain, social rejection, or loneliness. Second, courage is allied with reason. You remember the example from our discussion of Aristotle's understanding of courage. When Karen, the nonswimmer, rushes into the lake to rescue the child, she is foolhardy, rather than courageous. People who are just plain stubborn hold on, but if they do not have good reasons for holding on, they do not exhibit courage. Eichmann held on; he was very good at what he did, and he kept right on doing it, but he did not have moral courage. Martin Luther King gives us a splendid example of courage. His commitment to social justice was backed by a profound understanding of the history of injustice and the meaning of injustice, and of nonviolent methods of social change. He demonstrated this understanding repeatedly and with great courage. Here are examples of three ways of showing courage: courage to resist, courage to persist, and courage to change course.

The "Mothers of the Plaza de Mayo" of Argentina heroically displayed the courage to resist. In March 1976, the military overthrew the regime of Isabel Perón. People began to disappear. They were kidnapped, taken from their beds, off the street, out of the factories, and sometimes from behind the pulpit. They were never seen and never heard from again. No trace of their bodies remained, no knowledge of their fate. The military officials were thorough, as expressed chillingly by the governor of Buenos Aires province, "First we will kill all the subversives; then we will kill all their collaborators; then their sympathizers; then those who are indifferent; and finally, we will kill all those who are timid."[40] Enormous fear came into the hearts of those who loved the disappeared. People were afraid to comfort the families of the disappeared, fearing that even this gesture of sympathy might lead to their own disappearance. Between 1976 and 1983, over 30,000 Argentinians disappeared.[41]

One afternoon in 1976, a small organization of women gathered in the Plaza de Mayo, the main square of Buenos Aires, near the presidential palace and many government ministries. The "Mothers of the Plaza de Mayo" began to march. They wore white kerchiefs with the names of those who had disappeared embroidered on them. They carried photographs. They trained themselves not to be afraid, learning to stare at a police officer until they could see him as just a man and not an agent of terror. They circled around a police van until they could see it as simply another motorized vehicle.[42] These women displayed enormous courage of resistance. In this reign of terror in which "public silence became the only possible form of self-defense," every Thursday the women marched.[43] They resisted their own fear and the very real threat of their own potential disappearance, to keep vivid the memories of those who had disappeared and the knowledge of the grotesque injustice they had suffered. The women in the original nucleus of the group paid the ultimate price. On Christmas Eve, 1977, they were abducted from inside a church, tortured, and killed.[44]

Even if injustice is not at issue, we often need genuine courage to persist, to keep on responding to deep needs. The director of Saint Christopher's Hospice in London, Thomas West, explains the courage needed to persist: "It takes courage to go and talk to someone who you know is dying. It takes more courage to let them talk to you. It takes more courage still to sit in silence and not to fill that silence with idle chatter about the snow. And it takes the most courage of all to go back the next day and the next."[45] Sometimes, we need courage to battle injustice, but often we need courage to meet ordinary needs and to persist in meeting them day after day.

In his definition of courage, Plato talks about attending to what reason tells us to fear and not to fear. Sometimes, we make mistakes in judging what to fear and sometimes outside factors change, and with them, our reasons for what to fear and not fear. Having the courage to change course is a sign of courage's attachment to thoughtful moral judgment. Consider this case of changing course:

Ethics as Mop-Up: For the past 10 years, Mrs. Beneficent annually donated funds to your summer wilderness camp for urban youth to support scholarships in her deceased husband's name. You have just been given responsibility for administering the scholarships, and you are horrified to find that all the money had simply been put into an unrestricted, general fund. Mrs. Beneficent died a few months ago, and her grown children, who inherited her large estate, decided to honor your camping program with a large gift to endow the scholarships in memory of both of their parents. They had told the person who had been in charge of the scholarships before you that they wanted to place a plaque in the lobby of the main lodge with Mr. and Mrs. Beneficent's pictures and the names of all past Beneficent scholarship recipients. Your predecessor had told them that she would get the plaque made, but before doing so, she moved out of state. Now the muddle is in your lap. All of your colleagues in the office say you should just look through the files for students who had received general scholarship money and use their names, figuring the Beneficents' family would never know. What should you do?

This is a case in which you should have the courage to change course from the path your predecessor followed and your office colleagues recommend. If you do not act with moral courage, even if the Beneficents' family never finds out, the development office will be living a lie. Staff members will be in a state of "rotten trust," having to rely on each other not to reveal the secret. They may need to invent other lies to cover up the original lie, further diminishing the possibility of healthy trust.

It is time for you to exercise independent judgment and refuse to go along with this scheme. You should take responsibility and explain to your colleagues why you must refuse, and explain to the Beneficents' family why you cannot fulfill your predecessor's promise. They may be appalled and withdraw their financial support. But they might thank you for your honesty and continue to work with you, knowing that you have honesty and courage and so can be trusted. Either way, by having the courage to change course, you have maintained your own integrity. In the future, you will not have to look back at this page in your autobiography with shame.

4.3 HOLDING IT TOGETHER

We have traveled a long way in these first four chapters. We have accumulated quite a collection of conceptual tools to use in thinking through ethically troubling situations. Our toolbox is shown in Exhibit 4.2.

In Part II of this book, these conceptual tools will be used to think through particular topics in fund raising. At this point, you may be wondering, "How do I hold all of this together? In the press of on-the-job responsibilities, how can I manage to hold onto and use all of these tools at once?" Before turning to Part II two skills should be mentioned that should help you hold it all together. These are skills you already have, but naming them will help you to focus on them and develop them more finely. An auditory metaphor and a visual one will be used in naming these skills. We will call them "playing with polyrhythms" and "appreciating astigmatism."

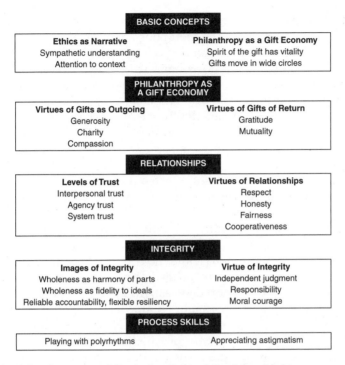

Exhibit 4.2   Conceptual Tools for Ethical Decision Making

(a) Playing with Polyrhythms

Traditional African music is typically polyrhythmic. This means that two or more quite different rhythms are layered together and played simultaneously. To someone who only listens to Western art music, polyrhythms sound chaotic on first hearing. But as one's ear gets accustomed to the sounds, the layerings make sense and the tensions among the various rhythms both challenge and delight the ear.

Remember the supermarket example in Chapter 1? There you were playing with polyrhythms. You kept up the rhythm of caring for the 4-year-old moment by moment, sometimes by calmly keeping your eye on him, sometimes by dashing madly to his rescue. On top of that rhythm, you layered the rhythm of attending to your friend, casually talking about guacamole while not so casually scanning her face to see if she was alright. We have many terms for dealing with these multiple layers of attention. Sometimes we call it balancing, juggling, or holding things in creative tension. I like "playing with polyrhythms" because of the metaphor's dynamism.

The ethical decision-making chart asks you to play with polyrhythms as you assess whether an alternative serves the organizational mission and philanthropic values, whether it builds trust among numerous professional relationships, and whether it strengthens your own integrity. Using the chart to work through the extra case studies in the book will also build your skills in playing with polyrhythms.

(b) Appreciating Astigmatism

Astigmatism, meant literally, is a defect. I have astigmatism. That means my eyes cannot pull the light rays into a single focal point. I am grateful to my optometrist and the people who make my eyeglass lenses for being able to correct this defect.

So why should we appreciate astigmatism if it prevents us from having clear vision? Think again about Maria Lugones. She appreciates astigmatism. She cannot pull into clear vision the two communities she cares about, both of which contribute importantly to her own identity. In her case, she could achieve clarity only by cutting off one of these communities, at great cost to her own self. In the future, her communities may change enough so that her Latina part and her lesbian part can achieve harmony. Appreciating astigmatism is a process skill that helps us hold onto disparate parts or disparate perspectives until clarity can be achieved.

Appreciating astigmatism is often needed to accompany sympathetic understanding. It is difficult to enter the frame of reference of someone who disagrees with you, and difficult to hold onto that frame side by side with your own. In the Beneficent family scholarship case, you as the fund raiser may not know what to do at first. Your colleagues probably are not calloused liars. They feel pulled by your predecessor's promise to the family, they want future students to benefit from the scholarships, and they want to fulfill their professional commitments to raise money for the institution. At the same time, as you keep your colleagues' perspectives in mind, you are concerned about the quality of trust in the office and with your own honesty and integrity. You feel pulled in both directions. Appreciating astigmatism is the ability to hold onto all of these things and not to force a clear resolution until you have thought things through. The *Tao* asks,

Do you have the patience to wait
Until your mud settles and the water is clear?[46]

Appreciating astigmatism is a way of having this patience, and holding on with sympathetic understanding to multiple, conflicting points of view. To resolve ethical difficulties thoughtfully, we need to hold onto all of these views and not seek easy, premature solutions. To do so risks ignoring genuine considerations and alienating others unnecessarily.

Let us try out the skills of playing with polyrhythms and appreciating astigmatism on this case:

> **Two Sides, One Mouth:** You are vice-president for development at Straight-Talk University. The director of alumni affairs shows you the latest issue of *Straight-Talk Today,* the school's alumni magazine. He is very excited about the issue's focus, "Making Straight-Talk More Inclusive for Women." There are several interviews with Straight-Talk alumna who have highly successful careers and an article on the new women's studies program. The issue's lead article is a piece by the president giving a glowing report on the school's efforts to hire more women in faculty and high administrative positions.
>
> As you read the president's column, you become increasingly agitated. As far as you are concerned, his commitment to women's concerns is negligible at best. Very few women have been hired into faculty and administrative positions recently; in fact, the president has just rejected a committee's recommendation of a highly qualified woman for chief financial officer in favor of a young, minimally qualified son of an old graduate school pal. The plans for the new women's studies program include very small budgets for library resources and secretarial help, and the Academic Affairs Committee just rejected a proposal for a course titled "Women in American History."
>
> You have been cultivating several wealthy alumni, who you know will be very impressed by the magazine. You are meeting next week with Dr. Equity, an alumna who heads a community women's task force, and who you think is close to making a major gift to the university. What should you say to her if she asks you what you think about the magazine's content?

You have several rhythms to play with here, and you feel considerable tension among them. You are committed to serving your institution loyally and working through its channels to further the university's mission. You are also committed to communicating honestly with prospective donors. Another rhythm layered into the mix is Dr. Equity's commitment to women's issues and her need for accurate information so that she can make wise decisions about her own philanthropic giving.

Astigmatism comes in as you try to decide how to think about Straight-Talk's commitment to women and what to convey to Dr. Equity. It could be that your impressions are right and that the magazine gives a misleading gloss to a dismal state of affairs. But there are other plausible interpretations. Universities, like all charitable institutions, are evolving, historical creatures (as are university presidents and academic affairs committees). Fifteen years ago, perhaps the president did not even realize that there was an equity problem on campus. Ten years from now, he may think back to the present and shake his head at how naive he was. Also, people equally committed to ameliorating the subordination of women can disagree about how a university should go about doing that. Should separate courses on women's history be offered, or should all history courses be reconceptualized to include women's contributions more extensively? Does the small budget reflect a lack of interest in women's studies, or are all budgets tight this year? Being loyal to the institution does not mean that you agree with everything the institution is doing right now, but that you are committed to its mission and its direction of growth.

As a fund raiser, you need to hold all these possible interpretations in mind as you think things through, even though the process may feel astigmatic. You should not mislead or lie to Dr. Equity. After reflecting carefully, if you decide that the school is committed to women's issues, but that the process of change just shares all the bumps typical in university proceedings, then you do not have to tell the donor that the magazine is misleading. However, if Dr. Equity asks your opinion, and after careful reflection you think that the magazine and the president's article are hypocritical, then you have to tell her what you think, being careful to make clear that this is your own interpretation of the situation. You are not being disloyal if your conclusion comes after careful reflection and fact gathering. Dr. Equity may decide that she is just the one to turn things around by endowing a chair in the women's studies program. She may also decide that her money would be better spent by the local battered women's shelter. Even if she chooses the latter, you have exercised the skills of playing with polyrhythms by keeping the rhythms of all your commitments on track, and you have appreciated astigmatism by not speaking too quickly or with unthoughtful bias.

We use the skills of playing with polyrhythms and appreciating astigmatism in our everyday lives as we manage multiple commitments and respond to a range of different people and circumstances. With practice, you will find that these skills are invaluable assets to ethical decision making.

DISCUSSION QUESTIONS

1. Some people may not agree with the claim made in this chapter that integrity as wholeness is a limited concept because it is not responsive enough to complexities in the social environment. They may think that in an environment characterized by moral disorder we should hold all the more tightly to integrity as wholeness, that is, as internal harmony and fidelity to ideals. Where do you stand on this issue? Do you think it is helpful to think about integrity as reliable accountability, sturdiness, and flexible resiliency rather than as inner coherence?

2. Reflect on Dewey's point that in making ourselves, we also make our world. Think of examples where personal acts of integrity were significant factors in shaping the work of a nonprofit organization.

3. What do you see as the principal barriers to acting with integrity in fund raising? How might these barriers be addressed?

4. To what extent do ethical codes of professional organizations and agencies support acting with integrity? How could this support be strengthened?

5. Imagine you are a fund-raising consultant to nonprofit organizations. Are there some organizations you would refuse to contract with as a matter of integrity? To what extent should consultants have to believe personally in an organization's mission before working with it?

6. The terms, "playing with polyrhythms" and "appreciating astigmatism" are new, but the skills they describe no doubt are already in your repertoire. Think of some ways in which you already exercise these skills in your fund-raising practice. Can you also identify other areas in which it would be helpful to apply these skills more extensively?

CASE STUDIES

Paying for Donations. An agency in your city is planning an auction and asks national celebrities to donate original drawings. The agency puts together a fabulous collection and projects that it should bring in at least $75,000. Unfortunately, before the event, the agency folds. Tom W., who has the collection stored in his garage, comes to you and offers it to you for a mere $10,000, to go to him personally. When you hesitate, he says, "I put a lot of time into collecting and storing this stuff. If you don't take it, I'm sure someone else will." What do you do?

Small Tokens, Really. Your organization purchases calculators with the agency logo on them to give out at the volunteer recognition dinner. The calculator company sends along a free clock radio with the calculators. The office doesn't need it. Is it alright for you (or someone else in the office) to keep it?

To Designate or Not to Designate. You are director of annual giving at a retirement community. Your annual fund campaign for unrestricted operating funds is approximately $11,000 short of its goal for the year and you are quite concerned because you will lose a $10,000 challenge grant if you do not make your goal. One afternoon, the daughter of one of your residents contacts you by phone and tells you she would like to make a $12,000 gift to the community for the purpose of building a gazebo for the garden. The community would enjoy a gazebo, but you want to include the gift in with your annual fund gifts. What should you do?

Reading the Will. You have been director of major gifts at the performing arts center for 15 years, during which time you have become personal friends with a number the center's faithful donors. Randall Actwell, one of these friends with whom you became particularly close, recently died. When his will was read, you were shocked to learn that he left you, personally, a piece of choice property worth about $80,000. After all of the individual beneficiaries are paid, the arts center's theater program is to receive the remainder, which is fairly small. What should you do?

Blanks in the Resume. Eight years ago, you worked for a small non-profit, but stayed only eight months. You found the office to be very disorganized and the executive director openly resented your skills and leadership abilities. The executive director is the type who holds grudges for a very long time, and although you have no evidence, you suspect that you lost a few job opportunities because of negative recommendations. Since that time, you have had positive work experiences with two different agencies. You are again looking for a new position. Is it ethical to omit that disastrous experience from your resume's employment history?

NOTES

1. Ralph Waldo Emerson, "Self-Reliance." *The Essays of Ralph Waldo Emerson* (1841) (Cambridge, MA: Harvard University Press, 1987), p. 30.
2. Plato, *Republic,* trans. by G.M.A. Grube (Indianapolis: Hackett, 1974), pp. 99–109; See also Julia Annas, *An Introduction to Plato's Republic* (New York: Oxford University Press, 1981), chapter 5.
3. Plato, *Republic,* trans. by G.M.A. Grube (Indianapolis: Hackett, 1974), p. 107.
4. Plato, *Phaedrus,* trans. by R. Hackforth, in Edith Hamilton and Huntington Cairns (eds.): *Plato: The Collected Dialogues* (Princeton, NJ: Princeton University Press, 1961), pp. 499–500.
5. R.C. Zaehner, trans. and ed., *Hindu Scriptures* (London: Everyman's Library, 1966), p. 197.
6. Plato, *Republic,* trans. by G.M.A. Grube (Indianapolis: Hackett, 1974), p. 106.
7. Walt Whitman, "Song of Myself." in Sculley Bradley and Harold W. Blodgett (eds.): *Leaves of Grass* (New York: W.W. Norton & Co., 1973), p. 88.
8. Maria Lugones, "Hispaneando y Lesbiando: On Sarah Hoagland's Lesbian Ethics." *Hypatia* vol. 5, no. 3 (Fall 1990), pp. 138–146.
9. Jane Addams, *Democracy and Social Ethics* (New York: Macmillan, 1907; reprint ed., Cambridge, MA: Harvard University Press, 1964), p. 275.
10. John Dewey, *Human Nature and Conduct* (1922); reprinted in Jo Ann Boydston (ed.): *John Dewey: The Middle Works, 1899–1924,* vol. 14 (Carbondale and Edwardsville: Southern Illinois University Press, 1988), p. 8.

11. Margaret Urban Walker, *Moral Understandings:A Feminist Study in Ethics* (New York: Routledge, 1998), pp. 106–115.
12. Cheshire Calhoun, "Standing For Something." *Journal of Philosophy,* vol. 92 no. 5 (May 1995), p. 260.
13. John Dewey, *Human Nature and Conduct* (1922); reprinted in Jo Ann Boydston (ed.): *John Dewey: The Middle Works, 1899–1924,* vol. 14 (Carbondale and Edwardsville: Southern Illinois University Press, 1988), p. 150.
14. John Dewey, *Individualism Old and New* (1930) (New York: G.P. Putnam & Sons, 1962), p. 171.
15. R.C. Zaehner, trans. and ed., *Hindu Scriptures* (London: Everyman's Library, 1966), p. 257.
16. Lao-tzu, *Tao te Ching,* trans. by Stephen Mitchell (New York: Harper & Row, 1988), #59.
17. Oxford English Dictionary.
18. Hannah Arendt, *Eichmann in Jerusalem: A Report on the Banality of Evil* (New York: Penguin, 1964), p. 25.
19. *Id.,* pp. 41ff.
20. *Id.,* pp. 47–48.
21. *Id.,* p. 54.
22. *Id.,* p. 49.
23. *Id.,* p. 105.
24. *Id.,* p. 109.
25. *Id.,* p. 116.
26. Jane Addams, *Twenty Years At Hull House* (New York: Macmillan, 1912; reprint ed., Urbana: University of Illinois Press, 1990), p. 82.
27. R. Richard Niebuhr, *The Responsible Self: An Essay in Christian Moral Philosophy* (New York: Harper & Row, 1963).
28. Martin Luther King, "Letter from a Birmingham Jail," http://www.msstate.edu/Archives/History/USA/Afro-Amer/birmingham.king, p. 1
29. R. Richard Niebuhr, *The Responsible Self: An Essay in Christian Moral Philosophy* (New York: Harper & Row, 1963), p. 61.
30. Martin Luther King, "Letter from a Birmingham Jail," http://www.msstate.edu/Archives/History/USA/Afro-Amer/birmingham.king, p. 2.
31. *Id.,* p. 4.
32. R. Richard Niebuhr, *The Responsible Self: An Essay in Christian Moral Philosophy* (New York: Harper & Row, 1963), p. 64.

33. Martin Luther King, "Letter from a Birmingham Jail," http://www.msstate.edu/Archives/History/USA/Afro-Amer/ birmingham.king, p. 5.

34. *Id.*,pp. 2–3.

35. R. Richard Niebuhr, *The Responsible Self: An Essay in Christian Moral Philosophy* (New York: Harper & Row, 1963), p. 65.

36. Emerson's statement merits reflection in spite of its self-righteous tone. "I ought to go upright and vital, and speak the rude truth in all ways." Further down the paragraph he adds, "Your goodness must have some edge to it-else it is none." Ralph Waldo Emerson, "Self-Reliance." *The Essays of Ralph Waldo Emerson* (1841) (Cambridge, MA: Harvard University Press, 1987), p. 30.

37. Martin Luther King, "Letter from a Birmingham Jail," http://www.msstate.edu/Archives/History/USA/Afro-Amer/ birmingham.king, p. 7.

38. *Id.*,p. 13. The letter can also be found in many anthologies.

39. Plato, *Republic,* trans. by G.M.A. Grube (Indianapolis: Hackett, 1974), p. 106.

40. Daniel Poneman, *Argentina: Democracy on Trial* (New York: Paragon House, 1987), p. 93.

41. Diana Taylor, "Spectacular Bodies: Gender, Terror, and Argentina's 'Dirty War.'" in Miriam Cooke and Angela Woollacott (eds.): *Gendering War Talk* (Princeton, NJ: Princeton University Press, 1993), p. 20.

42. Sara Ruddick, *Maternal Thinking: Toward a Politics of Peace* (New York: Ballantine, 1989), pp. 225–227.

43. Femenía, Nora Amalia, "Argentina's Mothers of the Plaza de Mayo: The Mourning Process from Junta to Democracy." *Feminist Studies,* vol. 13, no. 1 (Spring 1987), pp. 10, 13.

44. Horacio Verbitsky, *The Flight: Confessions of an Argentine Dirty Warrior* (New York: The New Press, 1996), p. 4.

45. Joan Flanagan, "Horizon Hospice: From Zero to $2.7 Million a Year," in Michael Seltzer (ed.): *Fundraising Matters, True Stories of How Raising Funds Fulfills Dreams. New Directions for Philanthropic Fundraising,* no. 1 (San Francisco: Jossey-Bass, Fall 1993), p. 124.

46. Lao-tzu, *Tao te Ching,* trans. by Stephen Mitchell (New York: Harper & Row, 1988), p. 15.

TOPICS IN ETHICS AND FUND RAISING

Relations with Philanthropic Givers: Donors and Volunteers

Donors and volunteers are at the heart of the philanthropic gift economy. Jon Van Til makes this explicit: "Philanthropy is, first, an intentional process of voluntary action, voluntary service, and voluntary giving aimed at advancing the public good."[1] In this chapter, we will think about relationships between fund raisers and donors, and between fund raisers and volunteers. It makes sense to talk about donors and volunteers together. Donors and volunteers are both philanthropic participants in nonprofit organizations. They differ simply in the form their gifts take. Donors and volunteers are often the very same people, supporting a nonprofit's work with time, skills, and money simultaneously. If we move beyond the question of who is giving right now to a specific nonprofit and think in terms of life spans and the philanthropic gift economy as a whole, the overlap between donors and volunteers is even greater. For example, Ranjoo currently contributes to the annual fund of the Cancer Society. She will conduct sing-alongs at the nursing home as a service volunteer next year and will be a board member of the Society for the Preservation of Traditional Korean Music three years from now. She will leave charitable bequests to all three of these organizations.

In this chapter, we will talk about donors and volunteers together in order to emphasize the shared voluntary nature of their contributions to the philanthropic gift economy. We should think of "donor" and "volunteer" as two distinguishable roles that people can fill, but not as labels for two distinct groups of people.

Let us refocus for a moment and restate just who the players are and what roles they have in the philanthropic gift economy. Formally incorporated nonprofit organizations have many ancestors. There have always been gift economies. People have always placed time, skill, and money in circulation among families, extended kin groups, and tribes. Gifts need some channels or social structures through which to flow. These structures, be they family networks, kin groups, or formal nonprofits, are transfer stations, moving gifts from givers to beneficiaries, and on around. We can think of nonprofit organizations as transfer points, transforming gifts of time, skill, and money into services that benefit the commuity. By helping to keep the gifts moving, fund raisers are facilitators of these transfers. They are also educators by helping people to understand how the philanthropic gift economy works and how they can participate.

5.1 MILL, DE TOCQUEVILLE, AND VOLUNTEERING

We know that giving serves others, but why is it important to donors and volunteers *themselves* that they give of their time, skill, and money to serve others? One of the most eloquent spokespersons for how voluntary giving is valuable both for society and the volunteers themselves was nineteenth century British philosopher John Stuart Mill. Mill was deeply concerned with education in the broadest sense. How to educate people so they can lead full and vigorous lives within a flourishing and harmonious society was his central question. While he did worry about governmental coercion, he was more concerned about mental passivity and the corrosive effects of social custom. Education can counteract this, but here formal instruction is only one component. It is equally essential that people develop their mental capacities and exercise their talents through active engagement within their society.[2]

Mill's little book, *On Liberty*, is a magnificent statement connecting freely chosen voluntary activity with mental and emotional development. "He who lets the world, or his own portion of it, choose his plan of life for him has no need of any other faculty than the ape-like one of imitation. He who chooses his plan for himself employs all his faculties. He must use observation to see, reasoning and judgment to foresee, activity to gather materials for decision, discrimination to decide, and when he has decided, firmness and self-control to hold to his deliberate decision.... It really is of importance, not only what men do, but also what manner of men they are that do it."[3]

Mill does not propose a society of disconnected, free-thinking, vigorous individualists. His ultimate aim is a vigorous society, in which social harmony is created through active cooperation and vibrant ties of affection. He places engagement in philanthropic voluntary associations on his list of ways in which these ties of connection could be established. As people cooperate together in collective endeavors, their goals and feelings become identified with others. "He comes, as though instinctively, to be conscious of himself as a being who *of course* pays regard to others. The good of others becomes to him a thing naturally and necessarily to be attended to, like any of the physical conditions of our existence."[4]

Mill would have appreciated how David Rosen used philanthropy creatively to connect together parts of himself, and then knit that into the larger frame of community needs. A rabbi in New York, Rosen wanted to find a way to combine his Jewish faith with his concern for urban poverty. He founded Avodah, the Jewish Service Corps, as an avenue for integrating social and spiritual concerns. Through Avodah, Jewish young people participate in a year-long community service program. They combine study of their Jewish heritage with service through nonprofit organizations addressing such needs as illiteracy, homelessness, and community organizing.[5]

In discussions of the value of voluntary associations, Alexis de Tocqueville's name almost invariably comes up. The French aristocrat visited the United States and in 1835 published his observations in *Democracy in America*. It may sound odd to claim that voluntary associations can perform some of the valuable functions of an aristocracy, but that was de Tocqueville's argument. De Tocqueville valued how an aristocracy provided lines of connection binding people together. The social hierarchy was admittedly fixed; people could not move up and down, but they did have a sense of responsibility to and for others in the chain. In fact, de Tocqueville claimed that an aristocrat was "the head of a permanent and compulsory association."[6] If things needed to be done, the aristocrat had the human and material resources to carry out the task. But in America, aristocratic ties were rejected. De Tocqueville saw people retreating into individualism, feeling neither responsible for nor dependent on others. Although the virtues of equality and individualism are often praised, de Tocqueville worried about their dark side. He saw in America that connections with ancestors, contemporaries, and descendants were often ignored, and he worried that individualism would lead to a lonely, confining solitude.[7] De Tocqueville saw Americans' predilection for forming voluntary associations as a way out of this isolation. Associations could perform the same functions as an aristocracy, both in attending to social needs and in providing a setting for interdependence and fellow-feeling. "Feelings and opinions are recruited, the heart is enlarged, and the human mind is developed by no other means than by the reciprocal influence of men upon each other. I have shown that these influences are almost null in democratic countries; they must therefore be artificially created, and this can only be accomplished by associations."[8]

Both Mill and de Tocqueville understood how critical it is that people have social structures available to them that lead them out of a narrow self-interest and into mutual engagement with and affection for others. Voluntary associations can do much to provide these settings.

5.2 MODELS OF RELATIONSHIPS AMONG NONPROFITS, FUND RAISERS, DONORS, AND VOLUNTEERS

In this section, we will take out the conceptual tool box and use its concepts and virtue clusters to think about what the relationships between fund raisers and donors, and fund raisers and volunteers should be like. We will begin with two descriptions or models from the fund-raising literature. The first is Kathleen Kelly's description in terms of the "two-way symmetrical model," described in *Effective Fund-Raising Management.*[9] The second is Kay Sprinkel Grace's notion of a donor–investor, described in *Beyond Fund Raising.*[10] These will be examined in detail because both conceptions of the relationship strongly support the concepts and virtue clusters developed in earlier chapters. Also, in both books, the authors do a particularly fine job of integrating ethical concerns into the structure of their theories and they raise ethical concerns consistently throughout their books.

(a) Two-Way Symmetrical Model

Kelly gives a history of professional fund raising in the United States and adapts models from public relations theory to identify four models of the relationship between a nonprofit organization and its donors, which emerged historically. The first three models, press agentry, public information, and two-way asymmetrical, are all based on asymmetrical relationships between fund raisers and donors, with fund raisers using various techniques to persuade, cajole, or convince donors to contribute to their cause. Press agentry aims for emotional appeal, theatrically staging campaigns and events to pull on people's heartstrings. The public information model uses truthful information, hoping to give people reasons that convince them to donate. The two-way asymmetrical model uses scientific research to identify the most persuasive forms of appeal, colloquially referred to as *hot buttons*. Kelly finds these three models inappropriate. In each one the donor is considered to be fairly passive and the agency's role is dangerously close to manipulation.

The fourth model, which Kelly advocates, is the two-way symmetrical model. Here, the goal is mutual understanding. The fund raiser tries to identify donors who share the organization's mission and would like to participate in the nonprofit's projects as a way of fulfilling their shared commitment to the common good. Donors give, but not because they have been convinced, persuaded, or hot buttoned into the nonprofit's camp. They give for their own reasons; some of these reasons may be self-interested, for example, to enhance their own social status or to meet community or corporate expectations. But some of the donors' reasons are those expressed in the nonprofit's mission statement. The relationship is characterized by mutuality, fairness, honesty, and collaboration.[11] Based on her research, Kelly concludes that while some fund raisers and organizations practice the two-way symmetrical model, many fund raisers use a mix of the four models, with press agentry being the most predominant.[12]

(b) Donor–Investors

Grace's model of the donor–investor is in many respects similar to Kelly's two-way symmetrical model. Grace rejects the image of donors as essentially passive, waiting for fund raisers to rattle the tin cup loudly enough, or persistently enough, or close enough to their ears until they throw in some coins to meet the agency's needs. Instead, Grace sees donor–investors as dynamic participants with nonprofit organizations. In themselves, nonprofit do not have needs, but they function as conduits through which donors can address the needs and enhance the quality of life in their communities. The relationship is centered on shared values. The emotional connection between nonprofits and donors grows out of their shared commitment to using philanthropy to address community concerns.[13]

There are many points of connection among these models, the ideas of Mill and de Tocqueville, and the concepts and virtues in the conceptual toolbox. Philanthropic intent, that is, serving the community through nonprofits as conduits, is at the heart of both models. The nonprofit is not an entity unto itself, but a "channel through which people's moral energy can flow," to recall Addams's apt phrase. The virtue of mutuality characterizes this relationship because the donors' and nonprofits' values about public good and purposes are truly shared. The virtues of relationships define how nonprofits and donors interact. Respect and honesty are paramount in order to avoid manipulation and inappropriate control. "Give me the money now" attitudes are replaced by a desire for long-term relationships. These are fostered through continuous cultivation and involvement, characterized by cooperation and associated efforts. This establishes a context for growth on both sides. The virtues of integrity are also evident, with each party respecting the integrity of the other. Because information is honestly and respectfully shared, both parties can exercise independent judgment—whether to make a gift or be involved as a volunteer in a given way, and whether to accept a gift of time, skill, or money for a given purpose. Responsibility, defined in terms of responsiveness, accountability, and solidarity, can be exercised throughout.

Here, it is crucial to stress that the relationship of the nonprofit to the donor or volunteer is *not* a dyadic one. Kelly and Grace both understand this well; it is clear in their texts, although it may not be immediately apparent in their terms *two-way symmetrical* and *donor–investor*. The relationship is not *between* the nonprofit or the fund raiser and the donor or volunteer. The relationship is *among* the donor or volunteer, the nonprofit as a transfer point, and the community, or the gift economy of philanthropy.

With these models, we can identify the fund raiser's role as educator and facilitator. By providing information about the nonprofit and how it proposes to use philanthropy to address community concerns, fund raisers educate potential donors about the nonprofit's values and its particular proposals to act on those values. There is no manipulation, so potential donors and volunteers can use independent judgment to assess whether a given nonprofit shares their values. If the donor or volunteer determines that it is a good match, fund raisers can then facilitate all parties acting together on these mutually shared values to accomplish mutually shared goals.

Using the two-way symmetrical model and the donor–investor model, let us examine some situations in which fund raisers sometimes find themselves. This will illustrate how to use some of the virtues in the virtue clusters to think through concrete situations.

(i) Charitable Intent

Shared values and mutual understandings are built on shared commitment to achieving public purposes through philanthropy. Even if money is raised and projects successfully completed, if philanthropic intent is not at the center of the fund raiser's relationship with a donor or volunteer, the gift economy of philanthropy is damaged. Some planned giving practices give us an example. In the United States, when the stock market performs well, many people find planned giving with charities financially attractive. Many commercial financial advisors recommend planned giving instruments such as charitable remainder trusts to their clients, without mentioning charitable intent. Nonprofits need to be careful not to imitate these methods, because they treat shared values and mutual understandings as if they were irrelevant. The nonprofit is simply treated as a means to the donors' private financial advantage, rather than as a collaborative partner. This breaks the cycle of giving, as would become obvious were tax laws to change or stock market performance to diminish.[14] It is fine for charities to benefit from the stock market and tax regulations, but charitable intent must be a central part of the donors' transactions. When nonprofits and fund raisers think of and treat major donors primarily as partners who share a commitment to the organizational mission, charitable intent will remain central to the relationship.

(ii) Honesty

An important consideration in both Kelly's and Grace's models is that nonprofits and fund raisers not manipulate donors and volunteers. This means that decisions to give time and money to nonprofits must be freely made, based on sufficient and accurate information. Several provisions in the "Donor Bill of Rights" speak to this issue, including donors' rights to know who is on the board and how gifts will be used, to have access to nonprofits' financial statements, and to receive truthful and forthright answers to their questions. The Red Cross's "Ten Principles of Volunteerism" states that "Volunteers and the organizations they serve must meet each other's expectations." If expectations are not clearly and honestly spelled out, disappointments and disagreeable outcomes are likely.

In March 1998, the *Chicago Tribune* published a special report on how several international child sponsorship agencies used false and misleading information in their fund raising efforts. One story told how investigative reporter Lisa Anderson traveled to Mali to visit Kortoumou Kone, the child she had been sponsoring through the Save the Children Federation, only to find the child had died two years earlier. The extensive news report also described how Childreach, in its direct mail appeals, sent photos of Miguel, Lilia, and other children, along with vivid descriptions of their sad, impoverished lives. The photos elicited emotional responses far more effectively than paragraphs of statistics ever could. Unfortunately, the photos were selected at random out of the agency's archives; the descriptions were fictional composites.[15]

Emotions are powerful connectors, and we want to encourage emotional ties among donors, volunteers, and clients or recipients. Both Mill and de Tocqueville stress how emotional ties of affection can serve as antidotes to narrow self-interest. But emotional appeals based on twisted distortions of the truth deny donors the right to assess the programs and agencies with which they might want to collaborate. The truth is heart-rending enough and need not be tampered with just to create sensational appeals.

Consider another case involving honesty:

> **Challenge Grant:** "Thirty minutes for $300," the announcer's voice declares from the public radio station. "If we get enough callers in the next 30 minutes to donate just $300, we will match an anonymous $1,000 challenge grant."

Have you ever wondered whether people who offer challenge grants donate their money anyway, even if the challenge is not met? Used honestly and appropriately, challenge grants can add sparkle and intensity to the admittedly difficult job of radio fund raising. Spontaneous decisions to just phone in and donate are sometimes fine. But it is disrespectful and manipulative to use this technique if the person or company offering the challenge in fact plans to donate the money whether it is matched or not.[16]

(c) Collaborative Partnerships

(i) Special Events

Opinions vary on the wisdom of special events. Many special events are memorable occasions. For example, that occasion on which King George stood up during the "Hallelujah Chorus" was a fund-raising special event. The first performance of Handel's *Messiah* took place in Dublin in 1742 for "relief of the prisoners in several gaols, and for the support of Mercer's Hospital in Stephen's Street, and for the Charitable Infirmary on the Inn's Quay." The performance raised £400.[17]

Some argue that special events net relatively little money compared to the enormous amounts of time and energy they take.[18] Others find them beneficial for several reasons apart from the amount of money actually raised. Consider the following case:

> **Dedicated Volunteers:** A dedicated group of older volunteers has been doing an annual gala benefit for years. Many of them have lost spouses, and their children have grown and moved away. They have become a tight-knit support group for each other; doing the benefit gives focus and meaning to their lives. Your nonprofit has a new, young, and dynamic chief executive officer (CEO) with a brand new masters degree in nonprofit management. She wrote a paper for one of her graduate classes on how inefficient and out of date special events actually are. She is convinced that the volunteers' annual benefit should be discontinued. Since you have worked with this volunteer group for years, she asks your advice on how to tell the volunteers that time is up. How do you reply?

Several things need to be considered as you formulate a response. First, this group of volunteers has a long history of engagement with the organization, far longer than the new CEO's. Simply to tell them that time is up would be disrespectful and would be contrary to the collaborative partnership the nonprofit has had with them. Second, there are many possible responses to this situation. If the benefit does not take up too much staff time, then it could be continued until the volunteers decide they want to stop. Alternatively, the volunteers could be encouraged to substitute other forms of service to the organization as a replacement. Finally, the CEO could spend some time with the volunteers herself to get a sense of the history of their commitment to the organization. But to cut them off simply because their style of volunteer work is out-dated disregards the spirit of collaborative partnership which should be a part of nonprofit-volunteer relations.

(ii) Campaigns and Volunteers

The wisdom of organizing fund-raising efforts around campaigns is also debated.[19] Wise or not, all sides agree they are exhausting. How would you handle this case?

Tired Volunteers: Your capital campaign is approximately three quarters completed and almost on target with four months to go. You have a tremendous volunteer staff that is motivated but getting very tired. A well-known member of the community calls you and says that because the stock market has been so good to him, he wants to double the size of his original pledge. With this gift, you are within 5 percent of attaining your goal. The donor specifies that you may announce the gift any time you wish. You have a choice: You can announce the gift now, but you are afraid that would de-energize your volunteers with the thought, "We made it. No need to push beyond another 5 percent." If you hold the announcement until the campaign is almost over and if your volunteers keep up their pace, you will able to announce that you achieved 120 percent of your goal. What should you do?

Your volunteers have busy lives, with demanding responsibilities apart from your campaign. Withholding this information is a form of manipulation, because the volunteers' continued efforts would be based on false impressions of the state of the campaign. To withhold this information would break the collaborative partnership and treat the volunteers as subordinates who do not deserve the truth. This is disrespectful and likely to damage the trust you have already established with them.

5.3 STEWARDSHIP

Stewardship is a term nonprofits often use to describe their programs for showing appreciation to donors and giving donors various forms of recognition for their gifts. Kelly and Grace stress the importance of responsible stewardship and integrate it deeply into the entire cultivation process, broadening the concept beyond donor appreciation and recognition. Before looking directly at their ideas about stewardship, it will be fruitful to examine some of the philosophical and religious roots of the concept of stewardship. This will give a context for understanding why it is important to define stewardship more broadly than with the traditional categories of donor appreciation and recognition.

(a) Religious and Philosophical Conceptions

Stewardship as used in mainstream U.S. philanthropy comes from the Christian religious tradition. Stewards have a role in several of

Jesus's parables, in which a steward is a person responsible for managing the property of another. The relationship involves trust and calls for discretion as well as wise management decisions. A passage from the *Wisdom of Solomon* beautifully expresses the ethical and religious context of stewardship. "God of our fathers, merciful Lord, who hast made all things by thy word, and in thy wisdom hast fashioned man, to be the master of thy whole creation, and to be steward of the world in holiness and righteousness, and to administer justice with an upright heart, give me wisdom, who sits beside thy throne, and do not refuse me a place among thy servants."[20] In his letters, Paul refers often to stewardship, as this passage typifies: "Like good stewards of the manifold grace of God, serve one another with whatever gift each of you has received."[21]

Western philosophers into the modern era preserved this notion of stewardship even as they constructed theories justifying private ownership of property. The most famous of these theories was published in 1690 by John Locke in England. He wrote his *Second Treatise of Government* as an argument against the divine right of kings to govern with absolute power. Arguing for rights of private property was his way of supporting the English parliament's claim to share power with the monarch. Locke begins with the theological claim that God has given the earth in common to all humankind for their support and comfort. He concludes his argument for individual private property rights with the claim that resources appropriated by individuals must not be wasted and there must be "enough and as good" left for others.[22] The concept of stewardship toward natural resources is preserved throughout his theory.

The underlying theme of Christian stewardship is that talents, natural resources, and wealth belong to God and are entrusted to people to use wisely and responsibly. In this tradition, giving time, skills, and money to nonprofits is one form that stewardship can take.

Although the term *stewardship* has Christian roots, the idea that talents and resources are entrusted for wise use is found in other religious traditions. The same theme is found in Islam. God gives the earth and its bounty to the people as a divine trust. They are to care for it as God's agents and on God's behalf.[23]

There are two forms of charity from the Qur'anic tradition. *Ṣadaqa* is voluntary charity; people are to give it freely and frequently. *Zakāt* refers to almsgiving, which is one of the five pillars of Islam. From the individual Muslim's point of view, *zakāt* is not voluntary, but a sacred obligation. Through *zakāt* Muslims simultaneously worship God and serve the community. Muslims should give 2½ percent of their wealth and assets (not just income) annually to fulfill this obligation. A secondary meaning of *zakāt* is "purity." To give purifies one's wealth; if one neglects this obligation, one's property is unclean. The *Qur'an* gives explicit instructions on how alms are to be used: "Alms are for the poor and the needy, and those employed to administer the (funds); for those whose hearts have been (recently) reconciled (to the truth); for those in bondage and in debt; in the cause of Allah; and for the wayfarer: (thus is it) ordained by Allah, and Allah is full of knowledge and wisdom."[24]

Almsgiving has played a prominent and continuous role in Islamic history. Muslims have fulfilled their stewardship obligations of *ṣadaqa* and *zakāt* in many ways, from giving alms directly and informally to the poor, to highly formalized, institutional forms of giving such as the Islamic foundations, or *waqf*.[25]

The concept of a steward contains within it a hierarchical model of subordinates caring for what belongs to their superior. This fits in well with the monotheistic religions of Christianity and Islam, but does not lend itself easily to other traditions of giving. The fundamental cosmology of Native American tribes, for example, contrasts with Christian and Islamic traditions. The earth itself, plants, animals, and humans are all interconnected in a sacred, ecological whole. Just as a tree functions by taking in carbon dioxide and giving out oxygen, so the cycle of life is based on continuous patterns of giving and receiving. Don Coyhis of the Mohican tribe explains these connections: "If you look at the principle of functioning in harmony with Creation, there is what I would call an ecology of giving. ... If we function in harmony with the principal laws and values, we would be able, like a tree, to give and to receive in the understanding that we participate in a spiritually interconnected system."[26]

Native American cosmology gives an ecological rather than a hierarchical understanding of sacred connectedness. But what Christian, Islamic, and Native American traditions share is the understanding that participating in a gift economy is deeply rooted in the fundamental relationship that humans have with the cosmos. In light of this, what is peculiar, and a minority opinion on the world historical stage, is the idea that one's wealth is one's own, to use and misuse as one pleases.

From this discussion of the philosophical and religious backgrounds of responsibilities for giving, we see that donors and volunteers have historical and cultural resources providing them with reasons to give, beyond narrowly defined self-interest. Fund raisers do not need to manufacture reasons for giving and somehow foist them on potential donors and volunteers to make them give. Kelly and Grace talk about development as based on mutual understanding and shared values. Stewardship, ecological conceptions of giving, and equivalent understandings from other traditions give donors and volunteers profound values on which mutual understanding and shared values can be based.

(b) Stewardship and Donor Relations

Both Kelly's and Grace's models of donor relations envision stewardship more broadly than donor appreciation and recognition. To them, stewardship is an integral component of donor cultivation, resonating through all stages of the development process. Because many donors give repeatedly, Kelly sees stewardship as an essential step in keeping donor cultivation as a continuous loop. Kelly places responsible gift use as a central part of stewardship, and underscores the importance of keeping donors informed about how their gifts are being used. Continuously nurturing the relationship is also a part of stewardship, offering donors options of ways to stay involved with the organization.[27]

Many of the points Grace emphasizes in her discussion of stewardship overlap with Kelly's. Grace also stresses that responsible gift use is a key component of stewardship. She places stewardship within the long-term frame, writing, "Increasingly, stewardship has come to mean the essential function by which organizations develop lasting relationships with their donor–investors. This *includes* the ethical management and care of all human and financial resources."[28]

We can describe this expanded view of stewardship using the concepts of the philanthropic gift economy and the virtue clusters. From the donors' and volunteers' point of view, stewardship expresses the belief that one's talents and material wealth are not one's own but are to be shared with the community. From the nonprofit's perspective as a transfer station in the gift economy of philanthropy, gifts given to the nonprofit are not *its* own, either, but are to be passed on and kept in motion.

Kelly and Grace rightly emphasize that using gifts wisely and responsibly belongs within the concept of stewardship. The notion of philanthropy as a gift economy underscores this point, and if anything, places wise use of the gift at the core of stewardship. Those practices that usually define stewardship (e.g., thank you notes, letters of appreciation, and other forms of donor recognition) are of course decent, expected, and obligatory. But these practices are forms of stewardship only in a secondary sense. Remember that the relationship of nonprofits and donors or volunteers is not dyadic, it is not *between* the donor or volunteer and the nonprofit agency. The relationship is between the donor or volunteer and the public purposes for which the gift is intended, with the nonprofit as the transfer agent, or intermediary. Nonprofits provide the links within the community through which volunteers can donate their time and skills and through which donors' money can be transformed into public goods.

Within this perspective, many of Kelly's and Grace's concrete suggestions about stewardship make eminent sense. For example, Grace suggests letting major donors select the level and type of recognition they want. To show that relationships are for the long term, she stresses maintaining relationships during periods when other financial pressures decrease donors' ability to give. She also offers the valuable suggestion that nonprofits should focus on intangible rather than tangible benefits as forms of donor recognition. This way, the focus remains on shared values, realizing that the most genuine form of donor benefit is furthering the mission of the nonprofit, rather than tokens of appreciation to the donor.[29]

So the critical relationship is *among* donors and volunteers, nonprofits and fund raisers, and the gift economy of philanthropy. This places wise use at the center of stewardship. We can still say more about the direct relationship between a nonprofit or fund raiser and donors or volunteers and explain why donor appreciation and recognition are important. Recall the discussion of professional relationships from Chapter 3. As in all professional relationships, the goal is to sustain healthy, long-term, well-warranted trust between the donor or volunteer and the nonprofit. Showing appreciation, sharing information, tailoring involvement, and being responsive to a donor's or volunteer's concerns all fit well into that pattern of trust sustained through the virtue cluster of relationships: respect, honesty, fairness, and cooperativeness.

5.4 DONOR CONTROL AND NONPROFIT COMPETITION

Reflecting on the models of donor and volunteer relationships discussed so far, we can anticipate two questions arising at this point— one about donor control and the other about competition among nonprofits.

This question may well come up: "How far should responsiveness toward donors and volunteers go? If the nonprofit is the steward of donors' gifts, shouldn't nonprofits do just what the donors want? Sometimes, it seems that nonprofits go too far in trying to keep donors happy. When does keeping donors happy turn into inappropriate donor control?"

This is a good question and a difficult issue. As with so many questions, no general answer can be given that makes decisions about specific situations simple. Judgments about where to draw particular lines will have to be made in each case. Keeping three points in mind may help.

1. In light of the above discussion about the philosophical and religious roots of stewardship, both donors and nonprofits are stewards, and so neither can claim rights to absolute control. In Christian and Muslim traditions, donors hold what is theirs as trustees of God's gifts; Native Americans view themselves as nodal points within ecological chains of giving. From these perspectives, donors themselves are transfer points, analogous to the way nonprofits are.
2. Giving money and volunteering time are collaborative acts. The nonprofit should not give up its legitimate collaborative role just to keep an influential donor or volunteer happy.
3. The gift is a *gift*. It is not the outcome of a purely marketplace contractual transaction.

From Chapter 1, recall that gifts pass out of a giver's control. The giver trusts that the gift will be wisely used, but trusting includes giving something up to another's discretion. Gifts can be designated for restricted use, and with large, complex gifts the arrangements may look like and read like contracts, and they certainly contain many contractual elements. But they are not, and should not, be market transactions. If they are, they are no longer gifts. The Donor Bill of Rights is correct in saying that donors have the right "to be assured that their gifts will be used for the purposes for which they were given." At the same time, donor restrictions should not be permitted if they negate the nonprofit's prerogatives as collaborating partners and as keepers of the public trust. Consider this case:

Controversial Film: A college student organization plans to show a controversial film at its annual film festival, which is always a successful fund raiser for the scholarship fund. The students have taken the appropriate steps to obtain permission from the university authorities to screen the film. Publicity materials have been printed and distributed. Four days before the festival, you, as vice-president for development, get a phone call from Mr. Poseidon who has given the largest one-time gift to your college. He is extremely upset about the scheduled showing of this "piece of filth" film at *his* university. He wants to know how his college could condone such a presentation. He closes by saying that if the film is shown, he will cut all ties with the university, including the gift agreed upon last month to build much-needed classroom space. What should you do?

Two factors are important here. First, academic freedom is a well-established, honored tradition on college campuses. Donors should not be able to usurp the judgment of faculty and administrators over political differences. Acceding to Mr. Poseidon would set a dangerous precedent. Second, the students went through established procedures to set up the film festival, and pulling the film at this point would break the trust relationship that faculty and administrators had established with them.

There may be ways to acknowledge Mr. Poseidon's concerns without withdrawing the film. For example, the college could offer one or more sessions concurrently with the film festival on topics such as art and morality, constitutional issues regarding freedom of expression, and so on. This may or may not satisfy Mr. Poseidon, but his demand is contrary to the mission of the university to promote free and open inquiry, and so should be refused.

Not all attempts at inappropriate control come from the donor's side. Collaborative partnership is the goal, but sometimes the equation tips too far the other way. Some fund raisers feel caught between their responsibilities to honor donor intent and boards or CEOs who simply want to take the money and redirect it to other purposes. This is disrespectful to donors and violates their basis for trusting the nonprofit. Handling these situations is always difficult; fund raisers may even believe that their integrity is on the line and their job security threatened. Moral courage, one of the virtues of integrity, is a most needed virtue at these times.

Have you heard this version of this concern? "All of this talk about nonprofits being transfer points in the larger philanthropic gift economy and about relations with donors and volunteers being based on shared understandings and mutual respect sounds lovely in theory, but in the real world there is a lot of competition among non-profits for donors' money and volunteers' talents. There are more nonprofits needing more money than there are donors with money; there are more slots for committed, active volunteer board members and service providers than there are people to fill those slots. A lot of donors and volunteers have mutual understandings and shared values with many more nonprofits than they have time or money to support. My nonprofit has to use aggressive fund raising tactics to stay ahead of the rest of them."

There are no magic answers to this one. The tensions this person describes are polyrhythms that we will be playing with for a long time. This problem will persist as long as there are unmet needs, and as long as there are imaginative people who use nonprofit organizations to express their creativity. We need to recognize these tensions without losing our focus on the entire gift economy of philanthropy and without abandoning our ethical responsibilities. Here are a few points to keep in mind.

First, we must be careful not to think of nonprofit competition as analogous to market competition. The aim is *not* to drive other nonprofits out of business. (Whether some nonprofits should go out of business because of ill-conceived missions or poor management is a separate issue). The press agentry model of nonprofit–donor relations that Kelly rejects, with its emphasis on overly emotional appeals, encourages this kind of unhelpful, competitive attitude. Employing the two-way symmetrical model or the donor–investor model may mitigate the sense of competition somewhat.

Second, communities have multiple needs and functions, so thinking about communities holistically may help us play more successfully with these polyrhythms. People in the arts want community members' basic needs for food, shelter, health care, and job training to be met. Nonprofits working with the homeless and the hungry want communities with strong cultural resources, so they will be available when those now homeless and hungry are able to focus on other aspects of their lives. There are many good suggestions in the nonprofit literature for alleviating some of the tensions from nonprofit competition through collaboration and partnerships.

Third, it may be that some of the competition could be mitigated through collaboration among nonprofits. When competition is connected to duplication of services or to agencies and nonprofit leaders' desires for status and prestige, then it is time to assess whether the competition for funding is really necessary. There may be more cooperative ways to fulfill organizational missions and serve the community.

Finally, I end on a somber note, one that paradoxically gives me patience based on understanding, while simultaneously increasing my sense of frustration at the enormity of the problem. These competitive tensions arise from sources outside of and much larger than the particular nonprofits with which a fund raiser may feel competitive. Several writers have pointed out that because people give to causes they care about and which they themselves often use, funding patterns reflect the overall distribution of wealth in the society, and thus mirror inequities in its distribution. Teresa Odendahl concludes from her study of wealthy donors that donations from the wealthy primarily go to fund elite education, elite cultural institutions, and elite health care facilities from which they themselves benefit. Thus, philanthropy in the United States reinforces the maldistribution of wealth and power in this country, rather than mitigating it.[30] This is a serious and disturbing charge. Nonprofits that address basic survival needs lack sufficient funding to meet these needs in part because many of the people with the most expendable wealth choose to place their donations elsewhere. However, this is only a part of the analysis. When government policies and economic forces generate and perpetuate inequitable access to wealth, education, health care, and culture, the gift economy of philanthropy is simply not equipped to turn this around. The competition that nonprofits feel among themselves is in large part the result of social forces outside of themselves. This analysis is not comforting, but it does place the problem into a wider perspective.

Playing with these polyrhythms is just one of many complexities involved in nonprofit relations with donors and volunteers. But ethical tensions in these relations can be eased and the benefits of voluntary association so clearly envisioned by Mill and de Tocqueville can be realized when these relationships are based on mutual understanding and shared values and then developed as collaborative partnerships.

DISCUSSION QUESTIONS

1. Nonprofits and fund raising are becoming increasingly professionalized. In what ways is this of positive value? Are there any drawbacks (in terms of value implications) to professionalization? Does professionalization do a disservice to volunteerism in any way? Are there ways to keep the professionalization, while not losing important values of volunteerism?

2. How serious do you think the concern is about commercial financial advisors recommending forms of planned giving to their clients without discussing charitable intent? How might fund raisers, non-profits, and fund-raising associations address this issue?

3. In what ways or to what extent do the two-way symmetrical and the donor-investor models describe your agency's relations with its donors? Examine literature and forms of direct communication you use with donors. Do these foster mutual understanding and shared values or are they manipulative or misleading in some respects?

4. This chapter's section on stewardship discusses religious and philosophical traditions which hold that one's wealth and talents are not entirely one's own and so should be used to benefit society. Are these traditions of stewardship still meaningful for donors and potential donors? How widespread is the belief that "my money, my time, and my skills are completely my own?"

CASE STUDIES

Recognition Categories. You are director of development for a retirement community that is sponsored by several churches in town. The Mennonite Church, with their tradition of quiet giving, has been a strong supporter. However, support is increasing from another denomination, whose members feel strongly that big donors deserve public, hearty thanks. You are worried that you cannot simply cater to each group, but that a clash is brewing. What do you do?

Hot Meals. Your organization delivers meals to elderly people in their homes. One client, who has Alzheimer's, calls you and says her diamond necklace is missing, and she thinks your volunteer took it. You know the volunteer fairly well and do not think she would take it. She is volunteering as part of her community service requirement for a legal offense, so you hesitate to bring it up with her without having at least some evidence to go on. How would you deal with this charge?

Verbal Avoidance. Your agency runs a "reading to the blind" program. One of your volunteer readers comes to you with a troubled look in his eyes. He has been a steady, responsible, and committed volunteer for the past two years, so you are immediately concerned.

He says he has recently undergone a dramatic religious conversion and has taken stock of his life. Although he understands your agency's policy that the readers are to read every word of the text, he says he can no longer read words that he finds blasphemous. He says that he wants to continue serving God through his volunteer work with your agency. What do you do?

High School Help. You are having a disagreement with the executive director of your organization, who happens to be married to the local school superintendent. The high school in your community has just adopted a service requirement; students are required to volunteer for a minimum of 40 hours at a nonprofit organization before graduating. However, no funds have been made available to train or supervise the volunteers. Your executive director wants you to find funds right away for accommodating these volunteers; you are concerned that anything the students could do would be "make work." Even if funds were found, it would divert time and staff resources away from the mission of the organization. How could you try to resolve this?

Politics and Pledges. With spectacular desert scenery, chronic water shortages, and a troubled mining history in your area, your environmental studies department is an important—and sometimes controversial—program in Southwestern Community College's curriculum. Concern for environmental ethics is integrated into every aspect of the program. Glanford Glowing, owner of Glowing Uranium Works, is politically tight with the county commissioners; everyone in town knows he wants to be appointed to the college's board of trustees. He has just offered a very generous gift to support the mining technology component of the environmental studies department. Given his mine's history of environmental law violations and anti-union tactics, you are worried that his involvement with the college will "tone down" the stress on environmental ethics in the program. What do you do?

Multiple Disasters: You are executive director of a national emergency relief program. Within one month, three disasters occur in the United States—an earthquake on the West Coast, a tornado in the Midwest, and a flood in Texas. Because of the severity of the disasters and the thorough, constant media coverage, donations have been pouring in. Most gifts are designated to either the earthquake or tornado victims; however, there are many people in Texas who have lost their homes and are in desperate need of help. As time passes, you see that the relief needs of the West and Midwest will be easily met by 60 percent of the relief money coming in. Yet, more than 95 percent is designated for those specific areas, leaving you with insufficient funds to meet the needs in Texas. What should you do?

Special Event? As executive director of a hospital foundation, you have planned a major fund-raising event, a gala dinner and ball, for the publicized purpose of raising dollars for a new psychiatric wing. One week before the event, the hospital board of trustees decides that the wing should not be built. Given recent cuts in HMO payments, they decide that all expansion programs should be terminated for the foreseeable future. Your foundation has already received more than $50,000 designated for the wing from enthusiastic and loyal donors. What should you do?

Recent Restrictions. You are the executive director of a city-wide foundation, which has just received an unrestricted $100,000 grant from Mercy Industries, Inc. for inner-city school projects. Your disbursement committee has met and decided to allocate 33 percent of the grant to the vocational development program, 33 percent to the program for children with special needs, and 34 percent to the music program. Before the funds are actually disbursed, however, you receive a call from Ava Mercy, the founder and owner of Mercy Industries, telling you not to disburse any money to the inner-city music program. Later, you find out that she had resigned in a huff from the board of the music program because the board voted, against her wishes, to invite a celebrity rap artist to come and work with the children. Ms. Mercy is well known for both her generosity and her mercurial temper. What should you do?

NOTES

1. Jon Van Til and Associates, *Critical Issues in American Philanthropy* (San Francisco: Jossey-Bass, 1990), p. 33.
2. John Stuart Mill, *Principles of Political Economy* (1848) (reprint ed., New York: Augustus M. Kelley, 1965), p. 948.
3. John Stuart Mill, *On Liberty* (1859) (reprint ed., Indianapolis: Hackett, 1978), p. 56.
4. John Stuart Mill, *Utilitarianism* (1861) (reprint ed., Indianapolis: Bobbs-Merrill, 1957), p. 41.

5. Marina Dundjerski, "Rabbi Nurtures Young Jews' Quest for Faith and Service." *The Chronicle of Philanthropy*, vol. 11, no. 6 (January 14, 1999), pp. 15–16.

6. Alexis de Tocqueville, *Democracy in America*, vol. II (1835) (New York: Schocken Books, 1961), p. 129.

7. *Id.*, p. 118–120.

8. *Id.*, p. 131.

9. Kathleen Kelly, *Effective Fund Raising Management* (Mahwah, NJ: Lawrence Erlbaum Associates, 1998).

10. Kay Sprinkel Grace, *Beyond Fund Raising* (New York: John Wiley & Sons, 1997).

11. Kathleen Kelly, *Effective Fund Raising Management* (Mahwah, NJ: Lawrence Erlbaum Associates, 1998), pp. 155–172.

12. *Id.*, pp. 179–184.

13. Kay Sprinkel Grace, *Beyond Fund Raising* (New York: John Wiley & Sons, 1997), pp. 28–35, 88.

14. Kathleen Kelly, *Effective Fund Raising Management* (Mahwah, NJ: Lawrence Erlbaum Associates, 1998), pp. 511–512.

15. Lisa Anderson, "Charity's Probe Finds Sponsors Funded at Least 24 Dead Children." *Chicago Tribune*, Sunday March 15, 1998, Section Two, Special Report, pp. 1, 13.

16. Kathleen Kelly, *Effective Fund Raising Management* (Mahwah, NJ: Lawrence Erlbaum Associates, 1998), pp. 459–460.

17. Peter Jacobi, *The Messiah Book* (New York: St. Martin's, 1982), p. 37; cited in Joan Flanagan, *Successful Fundraising: A Complete Handbook for Volunteers and Professionals* (Chicago: Contemporary Books, 1993), pp. 54–55.

18. Michael Page Miller, "Nine and a Half Theses about Fundraising Benefits: Rationalizations, Indulgences, and Opportunity Costs." in Dwight F. Burlingame & Warren F. Ilchman (eds.): *Alternative Revenue Sources: Prospects, Requirements, and Concerns for Nonprofits. New Directions for Philanthropic Fundraising*, no. 12 (San Francisco: Jossey-Bass, Summer 1996), pp. 109–117.

19. Kathleen Kelly, *Effective Fund Raising Management* (Mahwah, NJ: Lawrence Erlbaum Associates, 1998), pp. 551–563.

20. *Wisdom of Solomon* 9:1–4; an apocryphal book, noncanonical for Jews and Protestants, canonical for Roman Catholics.

21. *First Peter* 4:10, New Revised Standard Version.

22. John Locke, *The Second Treatise of Government* (1690) (Indianapolis: Bobbs-Merrill, 1952). See chapter 5, "On Property", pp. 16–30.

23. *Qur'an* 2:30, 33:72, 35:39.
24. *Qur'an* 9:60. See also John L. Esposito, *Islam, the Straight Path* (New York: Oxford University Press, 1988), pp. 30, 34, 92; and Frederick M. Denny, *An Introduction to Islam*, 2nd ed. (New York: Macmillan, 1994), pp. 124–125.
25. Said Amir Arjomand, "Philanthropy, the Law, and Public Policy in the Islamic World before the Modern Era." in Warren F. Ilchman, Stanley N. Katz, and Edward L. Queen, (eds.): *Philanthropy in the World's Traditions* (Bloomington: Indiana University Press, 1998), pp. 109–132; and Gregory C. Kozlowski, "Religious Authority, Reform, and Philanthropy in the Contemporary Muslim World." in Warren F. Ilchman, Stanley N. Katz, and Edward L. Queen, (eds.): *Philanthropy in the World's Traditions* (Bloomington: Indiana University Press, 1998), pp. 279–308.
26. Ronald Austin Wells, *The Honor of Giving: Philanthropy in Native America* (Indianapolis: Indiana University Center on Philanthropy, 1998), p. 59.
27. Kathleen Kelly, *Effective Fund Raising Management* (Mahwah, NJ: Lawrence Erlbaum Associates, 1998), pp. 433–442.
28. Kay Sprinkel Grace, *Beyond Fund Raising* (New York: John Wiley & Sons, 1997), p. 163.
29. *Id.,* pp. 84–85, 171–172.
30. Teresa Odendahl, *Charity Begins at Home: Generosity and Self-Interest among the Philanthropic Elite* (New York: Basic Books, 1990), pp. 3–4.

6 ▼ Privacy and Confidentiality

Privacy and confidentiality are highly valued and explicitly protected in fund-raising codes of ethics. The NSFRE Standards of Professional Practice are unequivocal, "Members shall not disclose privileged information to unauthorized parties," and "Members shall keep constituent information confidential." The ethics code for the Association of Professional Researchers for Advancement (APRA) begins not with a pledge to find the finest quality and greatest quantity of information obtainable, but with a commitment that "members shall support and further the individual's fundamental right to privacy and protect the confidential information of their institutions." The Council for the Advancement and Support of Education (CASE) and the Association for Healthcare Philanthropy (AHP) have equally explicit commitments in their codes of ethics. We value our own individual privacy and the privacy involved in friendships and family relations, as well as privacy in professional relationships. Because privacy is so important, it is helpful to take some time and spell out just what privacy and confidentiality are and why they matter so much. It is helpful to be explicit about just what it is that these fund-raising associations' codes of ethics require their members to protect. This chapter will first discuss what privacy and confidentiality are and how they function, and then relate them specifically to nonprofits and philanthropy as a gift economy. The final section will look at specific aspects of development work in which questions of privacy and confidentiality are particularly germane.

6.1 DEFINITIONS OF PRIVACY AND CONFIDENTIALITY

"Get out of my room! I want my privacy!" your preadolescent screams, slamming her bedroom door. You smile, remembering how just a few years ago she shared everything with you and could not understand why you sometimes muttered under your breath, "Can't you leave me alone for just five minutes?"

We often associate privacy with being left alone. The United States Supreme Court has defined the right to privacy in terms of being left alone. The United States Constitution does not name a right to privacy explicitly. Privacy as a right entered judicial law in 1965 when the Supreme Court overturned a Connecticut law that banned the use or dissemination of contraceptive devices, even for married couples. Justice Douglas, writing for the majority, argued that a right to privacy emerges in the "penumbra" of rights named in the Bill of Rights such as the right to associate, the right to be secure in one's dwelling, and so on. Privacy gives "life and substance" to these enumerated rights. The sanctity of marital and family relations, he wrote, deserves to be protected by a right to privacy protecting them from governmental intrusion.[1] This articulation of a constitutionally protected right to privacy became the basis for subsequent decisions that overturned laws prohibiting contraceptive use between unmarried people, interracial marriage, and abortion.

Privacy in the sense of being left alone, either by oneself or with selected others, is one of several forms that privacy can take. There are other forms; we want to control who has access to our thoughts and feelings, to our bodies, and to various pieces of information about us. The root notion of privacy underlying all these forms is being able to control other people's access to various aspects of oneself. Confidentiality is the guardian that protects these forms of privacy. A child tells you a secret, perhaps about how she is giving her brother a daisy chain for his birthday. You promise not to tell, and so keep her secret safe.

While Supreme Court decisions speak of a right to privacy as something people as individuals possess, it is more helpful for our purposes to think of privacy as an aspect of our relationships with others. Philosophers are fond of expressing abstract ideas in quasi-algebraic formulas. George G. Brenkert describes the relational quality of privacy using three variables: "To say that something is rightfully private is to say that A may withhold from or not share something, X, with Z. Thus, to know whether some information, X, about a person or institution, A, is, or ought be, treated as rightfully private, we must ask about the relationship in which A stands to Z, another person or institution."[2] Ferdinand D. Schoeman thinks that six variables are needed in the definition: "A privacy attribution pertains to certain subjects (S), is about certain matters (M), is relative to certain people (P), in certain roles (R), in certain contexts (C), and typically for certain associational objectives (O)."[3]

Writing about privacy this way makes for slow reading, but these formulas capture something important. Privacy is not a single or a simple thing. Privacy has to do with complex relationships among various people and groups, about various subjects, in various contexts, and for various purposes. We can make this variability clear by describing some of the forms and functions of privacy. The following story will be useful for understanding the dimensions and complexities of privacy.

> Frank and Gina are sitting in a quiet corner of Grantville's new cybercafe, sipping gourmet coffee.
>
> "I'm so nervous, I can hardly stand it," Frank whispers so softly Gina can hardly hear him above the click of the keyboard six tables away. "Tomorrow I'm going with one of our trustees to meet with Mrs. Higginsbotham. I've heard such strange stories about her."
>
> Gina sighs, "Yes, she's eccentric, alright. When I met with her, I failed her Greek mythology test by putting the wrong people inside the Trojan horse. She wouldn't give my agency a thing. Do you know Ezra at the art museum? He majored in classics in college, and she gave him half a million for their Islamic architecture exhibit."
>
> "Then I'm finished. That's the end of my career at the history museum," replied Frank. My CEO wants to ask her to make the lead gift for our proposed excavation of that Native American village outside town. In this town, without her money, a nonprofit might just as well forget about big ticket projects."
>
> That night Frank stopped by the library, checked out the Cliff notes on *Iliad* and *Odyssey*, and had a brilliant and successful visit with Mrs. Higginsbotham the next day.

The preceding story illustrates a number of forms that privacy can take.

(a) Physical Privacy

Even though Frank and Gina are in a public place, they use spatial distance from others and a soft tone of voice to protect the contents of their conversation. The computer keyboardist or a server would violate their privacy by straining to overhear them.

A need for physical privacy is common among animals as well as people. Studies show that most species have a sense of individual distance and at times animals seek to be alone or exclusively with a small, intimate group. Animals in a field and birds on bushes or telephone wires establish species-specific distances between themselves. As demonstrated by overcrowding rats in laboratory cages, when animals cannot have this distance, they become disoriented and aggressive. While privacy norms among cultures vary enormously, humans share with animals a basic need for times alone and for ways of creating distance from others. We are social beings who must participate in association with others, but we also need separateness at times.[4]

(b) Psychological Privacy

Frank wants to share his nervousness with Gina, but he also wants to keep it private from his CEO and especially from Mrs. Higginsbotham. His nervousness is close to his psychological core, reflecting his desire to do a good job and his fear of failure and embarrassment. He feels safe sharing this with Gina because they have been friends for a long time, and he feels sure that she will keep his confidence. Also, Frank and Gina know that they both share an appreciation of Mrs. Higginsbotham's financial acumen and her sensitive reading of the town's philanthropic priorities. With each other, they can fuss about how nervous her eccentricities make them feel. With others around, they would make sure to give a more balanced view.

The point of psychological privacy here is not to keep one's fears all bottled up as secrets from everyone, but to control selectively who has access to this information. Frank did not ask Gina explicitly to keep his nervousness confidential. That is understood, since part of their friendship is an implicit pact to show good judgment about what to keep confidential. It could well be that talking with Gina was the very thing that helped Frank to work through his nervousness.

Norms about psychological privacy also vary widely among cultures. In Java, there are villages in which people have almost no physical privacy, but they compensate with extensive norms of politeness, emotional restraint, and a lack of candor, which are equally applicable inside and outside the household.[5] Among the Tuareg, a nomadic, Muslim people of North Africa, men wear a turban and veil, which cover all but their eyes. They are almost always veiled, even with close family members, while eating and sometimes while sleeping. The veil creates a sense of psychological distance and enables the men to deal with ambiguity and ambivalence in relationships when they cannot withdraw physically.[6]

(c) Informational Privacy

Frank mentioned the project his agency was going to ask Mrs. Higginsbotham to fund, but he did not give Gina particular details. Gina is a very good friend, and although Frank will admit embarrassing psychological fears to her, he will not divulge certain details about donors' gifts or other information confidential to the agency. His organization entrusts him with private information about donors and agency matters because he needs to know these things to do his work. Keeping this information confidential from anyone who does not need to know it is essential for maintaining trust within the agency.

(d) Privacy of Social Personae

Frank is many things to many people. He is willing to appear nervous before Gina, but not before Mrs. Higginsbotham or his CEO. To both of them, he wants to appear competent and professional. Frank really *is* competent and professional, but even professionals have their doubts and days when they question their abilities.

For Frank to be able to navigate successfully through all of these roles—as a doubting, growing, worried, yet resourceful person; as a good friend to Gina; as a loyal employee to his CEO; and as a competent development officer with Mrs. Higginsbotham—he needs to be able to control access to information about himself in order to shape the various kinds of relationships he has with various people.

This is not a matter of being deceitful or lacking integrity. Different people or different organizations need different parts of us. To play these multiple roles, we need to be able to design and enact an appropriate persona for each one. In some settings, privacy in the sense of being able to keep these roles separate may even be a matter of survival. When Sara Moore aimed a gun at President Ford in 1975, Oliver Sipple stepped out of the crowd and knocked it out of her hand. Newspapers quickly vaulted him into hero status. Sipple was a gay rights activist in San Francisco, but he could not tell his family in Detroit about his sexual orientation. The news stories led to such estrangement between him and his family that he suffered serious psychological problems and later committed suicide.[7] For many gays and lesbians working and living in settings hostile to homosexuality, being able to control access to information about them is a matter of life and death.

We can now summarize the functions that privacy serves. Privacy about certain aspects of our lives enables us to protect ourselves from embarrassment or shame in front of those who might not understand or accept them. It also creates the physical and psychological space needed for working through difficult and ambiguous concerns so that we can mature and grow. Privacy also enables us to develop intimacy with some people and relations of professional propriety with others. Finally, privacy enables organizations to share sensitive information only with those who need it and restrict access by others. Guarding privacy is confidentiality, where people privy to confidences have the responsibility and the integrity to preserve others' needs for privacy.[8]

6.2 PRIVACY AND PHILANTHROPIC NONPROFITS

Concepts and virtue clusters from our conceptual toolbox can be used to explain specifically why protecting privacy and respecting confidentiality are crucial in philanthropy and in philanthropic nonprofits. Privacy and confidentiality are aspects of relationships, so let us start with trust, the oxygen supply of healthy professional relationships. In a relationship based on healthy trust, the parties have good reason to believe in each other's goodwill. They are willing to make themselves vulnerable to each other and rely on the other's discretion to make good judgments about the things they consider most valuable. In Chapter 3, three levels of trust were discussed: interpersonal trust, agency trust, and system trust. Here, we will look at how privacy and confidentiality are important for maintaining trust at each of these three levels.

(a) Interpersonal Trust and Respect

The first virtue of relationships discussed in Chapter 3 is respect, with recognition of fundamental moral worth, attention to particularity, and generosity in judgment as its aspects. Respecting others' fundamental moral worth includes respecting their prerogative to establish boundaries for themselves regarding what they value and how they want to use privacy to protect those boundaries. By admitting his nervousness, Frank made himself vulnerable to Gina. She could, after all, phone his CEO and Mrs. Higginsbotham and tell them how nervous Frank felt. Being able to work through his fears with Gina, and then being able to present himself as the competent professional that he is, are important to Frank's sense of dignity and self-worth. If Gina breaks his confidence with her in this way, she would violate his sense of dignity and damage his trust in her.

A second feature of respect is attention to particularity. Here, respecting privacy entails sensitivity to cultural variations in what various groups hold to be private. Asking a Tuareg man to remove his veil when he enters the room as if it were an English gentleman's hat would show disrespectful inattention to particularity.

Within a culture there are personal variations in terms of what people value most closely and in how much they want to keep those things private. Some people who care deeply about religion may discuss their views freely with anyone who comes along. They would be proud to have their donor files saturated with information about their religious commitments. Other people, equally devout, want to keep their religious commitments private. This is not necessarily out of embarrassment or shame. As Schoeman explains, "Innermost aspects of self are supercharged with emotional color. One is defiled if part of this self is wrenched out and exposed as if it were just an ordinary bit of information that means nothing to the world."[9] Respect as attention to particularities means letting the individual make the decision about what to reveal and what to protect.

(b) Privacy and Agency Trust

Privacy and confidentiality have significant roles in creating and sustaining agency trust. If an individual fund raiser treats donors' confidential information casually, those donors may hesitate to continue their relationships with the agency even after the fund raiser at fault is replaced. Other donors or potential donors may hesitate to entrust the agency with the personal information involved in arranging any more than token gifts. Annette Baier notes perceptively, "Trust is a notoriously vulnerable good, easily wounded and not at all easily healed."[10] Frank, his CEO, and the staff and volunteers at his museum need to hold private information regarding donors in confidence if the agency is to fulfill its mission. Schoeman explains the connection between privacy and associations clearly. "The point of the restrictions on access is in large part not to isolate people but to enable them to relate intimately or in looser associations that serve personal and group goals. Characteristically, privacy is engaged as a social category not just to preclude a wider influence but to enshroud with respect an association of people that is meaningful in its own terms."[11]

Maintaining respectful and trusting relationships among the various constituencies of an organization can get complicated when different people have different ideas about what sorts of things should be kept private. Consider this case:

> **Camp Pictures:** You are thrilled. Your organization, Ecology Camps for Urban Kids, has just met its long-time goal of being able to support 50 percent of the children attending next season with need-based scholarships. A major donor and board member, Ms. Alvarez, reminds you that board members and donors will be attending the grand finale program the last day of camp. Wanting to honor your donors, she suggests, "Why don't you match up each donor with some of the scholarship kids, take their pictures, and then make a poster and display it in the camp lodge lobby for the final program?" What do you reply?

To maintain trust among your various constituents, you need to respect the privacy of each one. Since the mission of the organization is to use the ecology camp to foster growth in all areas of the children's lives, including social interactions among children of different economic classes, you worry that the poster could cause embarrassment and friction among the children, and possibly among their parents. By simply refusing Ms. Alvarez's request, you risk alienating your dedicated, enthusiastic donor, and possibly other donors who support her idea. You want to think of a way to honor the donors and make them feel personally involved in the camp without violating anyone's privacy.

There are many ways of accommodating all of these concerns. One possible solution would be to explain to all the campers that the camp is supported by generous donors. A picture of all the children and donors who wanted to participate could be taken and placed on the poster. Another idea would be to ask each camper to write a letter to a specific donor, describing his or her camping experience, and then display some of the letters in the lodge lobby.

There is an additional aspect of respecting privacy that is important for agency trust. That has to do with how staff and volunteers respect the boundaries of their professional roles. In nonprofit agencies, we often work with people whom we do not particularly like and may disagree with strongly regarding aspects of their personal lives. What joins us is our shared commitment to the organization's mission and the larger purposes of philanthropy. Respecting others' privacy regarding their roles outside the workplace helps us to maintain our focus.

We now have two angles from which to appreciate the importance of privacy for nonprofit agencies. First, privacy protects and enables individuals to define themselves as individuals and to work out important relationships. Second, privacy and confidentiality make associational life possible. They protect those chains of information on which fulfilling the mission depends, and they help us to shape our professional relationships so that we focus on shared commitments rather than irrelevant points of disagreement.

(c) Privacy and System Trust

Gifts move through the entire gift economy of philanthropy with individual nonprofits as transfer points. Unhealthy trust within or among individual nonprofits can have repercussions throughout the philanthropic gift economy as well. In Chapter 3, we discussed how trust is the warranty of philanthropic relationships. This has implications for how we think about privacy and confidentiality in the gift economy of philanthropy. Sometimes, people use the metaphor of a balancing scale and talk about balancing the needs of the agency with individuals' rights to privacy. I am sure that people who use this metaphor mean well and are trying to say that a donor's privacy cannot be violated for trivial reasons or for the sake of expediency. But the image of a balance scale suggests that if an agency's needs are great enough, then violating privacy rights is justified. We need to examine this claim carefully.

Let us start with cases about which there is widespread agreement that violations of privacy are justified. Cases in medicine include a physician's obligation to report gunshot wounds to law enforcement. Here, the reasoning goes, public safety, that is, the public's interest in catching the shooter, outweighs the privacy rights of the person who was shot. In business ethics, drug testing as a condition of employment is vigorously debated because of ways in which testing can compromise privacy. However, there is substantial agreement that such testing is justified for people in occupations in which public safety is at risk, for example, airline pilots and air traffic controllers. In criminal investigations, law enforcement personnel sometimes use surveillance or other methods that violate privacy, but they are required to adhere to safeguards such as obtaining search warrants and court orders. In each of these examples, what tips the balance to outweigh privacy rights are serious threats to public safety and not just a desire to improve social well-being. With the law enforcement case in mind, we can say that public trust in government rests on government's respect for privacy rights except for those cases in which public safety is threatened in a serious way.

Do analogous threats ever arise in fund raising? How often is public safety threatened if fund raisers do not reveal confidential information about a donor? Violating privacy rights in the name of the greater good makes sense only in the context of governmental authority to preserve the peace and enforce the law, and then, only with extraordinarily scrupulous attention to safeguards. Notice that nothing is said here about balancing the needs of a nonprofit agency. When we are talking about the needs of the agency versus donors' rights to privacy, *balancing* is the wrong metaphor. The needs of an agency cannot be put in the opposite side of the balancing scale against rights to privacy. There is nothing here to balance.

Unless philanthropic fund raisers somehow find themselves in positions of protecting public safety from serious threat, I do not see any justifications for violating rights of privacy. Maintaining agency trust and system trust in the gift economy of philanthropy depend on protecting privacy and respecting confidences scrupulously. Without this careful attention, trust as the warranty of philanthropy is seriously diminished.

6.3 COLLECTING INFORMATION AND KEEPING IT SAFE

The preceding sections on privacy and philanthropy provide a theoretical understanding of why privacy and confidentiality are such significant moral issues. Applying these theoretical considerations to concrete cases is sometimes difficult, especially when we look at the informational context in which nonprofit work takes place. At least in the United States, an enormous amount of information about people is readily available and frequently swapped and sold.

Much of the public is unaware of how all this is done. There has not been sufficient public debate on these issues, in part because so many informational transactions are hidden from public view. This is a case in which technology has outstripped public awareness and debate. Many of the people in the major gift category are savvy enough to know what information about them is available, and they feel insulted if your office does not do enough background work. At the same time, many people are appalled at the very idea of prospect researchers using news clipping services and going through financial reports.

I do not have all the answers. This is one of those issues about which we need to appreciate astigmatism by holding onto our worries while not drawing premature conclusions. Technology's impact on privacy and confidentiality merits vigorous discussion and we should reflect deeply on how to respond. In this section, three specific areas about privacy of concern for nonprofit organizations will be addressed: what information should be sought, what methods should be used, and how information should be recorded and safeguarded.

There are two questions that follow from the first part of this chapter, which can serve as guidelines for thinking about information and privacy:

1. Do our methods respect people's ability to control access to information about themselves that *they* may consider to be sensitive?
2. Is the information sought or the methods used consistent with maintaining healthy levels of interpersonal trust, agency trust, and system trust?

(a) What Information to Gather

The APRA code gives some explicit guidelines here. The key guidelines are relevance and accuracy: "Prospect researchers shall seek and record only information that is relevant and appropriate to the fund raising effort of the institutions that employ them," and "Prospect researchers shall record all data accurately. Such information shall include attribution. Analysis and products of data analysis should be without personal prejudices or biases."

Deciding what information is relevant is not always immediately apparent. Some might argue that every detail of a person's life is potentially relevant, since most details have some bearing on a person's financial status (Mr. Midas just won big money at the slot machines during his Vegas vacation!) or on their personal interests and emotional attachments (Mr. Midas just bought a tank full of exotic tropical fish for his grandchild! A perfect prospect for the aquarium!).

In deciding relevance, it is important to keep the goal clearly in mind. That way, irrelevant information that infringes on privacy will not be a problem. For major gift prospects, an agency needs enough information to identify the projects a prospect might be interested in funding, the level of support it is appropriate to seek, and which staff members and volunteers should do the asking.[12]

Beverly Goodwin takes the familiar question about how much information is needed and gives it a thoughtful twist. She suggests, "Perhaps we should try thinking more in terms of how little we need to know in order to make a successful request for a gift." Although volunteer solicitors need some information about the prospective donor, Goodwin emphasizes that what is most important is that the volunteer know solid current information about the organization and about what funding possibilities exist. She also reminds us, "The solicitor needs to know that enthusiasm and commitment are catching (most major donors give for the joy of it). He needs to let the donor know that he can make a difference."[13]

Let me suggest a "privacy safety checklist." If pieces of information pass this checklist, you can be confident that the prospect or donor's privacy is being respected.

(i) Does the Information Come from a Publicly Available Reference Source?

Some researchers say that if information is a matter of public record, then it is acceptable to seek it out. This criterion needs to be fine-tuned to distinguish between information in standard reference sources such as *Who's Who, Standard and Poor's,* and newspaper clipping services on the one hand, and public records of wills and divorce decrees on the other. When dealing with information that is a matter of public record, we need to ask in what sense and for what reason that information is public. The reason wills, divorce records, and many other legal documents are matters of public record is to ensure the integrity of the judicial system. In light of the life-and-death power of the state, openness is important. This does not justify curious parties taking a look when they have reasons of their own for wanting the information. Much that is legally permissible is morally insensitive and not conducive to fostering long-term, cooperative relationships. Goodwin expresses this well: "Having reputations as high-tech supersleuths may be nice, but it does not do much for cultivating mutual trust."[14]

(ii) In a Face-to-Face Interview, Would the Prospect or Donor Give You That Information Willingly?

When people freely give you information about themselves, you know that they do not think that their privacy is violated when you have it. If you cannot conduct an actual interview, try running an imaginary interview in your mind.

(iii) Are Your Donor Files Open for Donor Inspection?

If donors may examine their own files, that is an excellent check on the propriety of their contents. If you are not willing to have a donor or prospect be fully knowledgeable about the contents of the file, that is a flag that privacy concerns may be an issue.

Let us look at a test case:

> **Personal Skeleton:** You do prospect research for a conservative religious college. Through a loose-lipped (though reliable) personal friend, you learn that Mr. Tisdale, a prominent, wealthy citizen and college trustee, has a skeleton in his closet. He lost a paternity suit, and a good portion of his wealth goes to maintaining a severely retarded child in an institution. President Straightarrow wants to ask Mr. Tisdale to head a capital campaign and make the lead gift. The president asks you for relevant information to decide how much to ask Mr. Tisdale to contribute. Dr. Straightarrow has a general policy of wanting all information in hard copy. What do you do?

The college has two concerns here. First, Dr. Straightarrow wants to avoid the embarrassing situation of asking Mr. Tisdale for more money than he can afford. Second, some of the college's supporters may think Mr. Tisdale's skeleton raises issues about his character.

This case does not meet any of the three guidelines given above, so I do not think anything should be done to follow up this rumor. Since knowledge of this situation exists only at the rumor level, and cannot be confirmed by a publicly available reference source it is undignified to dig into it any further. It is doubtful that Mr. Tisdale would be willing to offer the information in a face-to-face interview and he would probably be unhappy to find it in his donor file. If Mr. Tisdale has been a faithful trustee and community member, does the college really want a character test so stringent that past mistakes, responsibly cared for, are treated as impermissible blots? If Mr. Tisdale is putting considerable wealth toward the child's care, then that wealth is not going into real estate, stock transactions, and so on. The development office can determine an appropriate gift amount by using standard methods.

(b) Methods of Obtaining Information

The APRA code of ethics has a section that gives ethical guidelines for collecting information. Honesty, accountability, and accuracy are the guiding principles. Information should be collected lawfully and in keeping with agency policies; data should be verified and attributed. Researchers should identify themselves as representing their agencies and make payments through their agencies whenever possible.[15] These are all good and important guidelines to follow. They provide checks on methods that donors might find objectionable and that might undermine trust in the philanthropic gift economy.

Consider this case:

> **Inside Information:** Your struggling drug rehabilitation agency is overjoyed that Achilles, Inc., a large manufacturing company, is relocating its corporate headquarters in your economically depressed Midwestern city. Many of its top-level people are moving to town. Your neighbor has just been named director of personnel services at Achilles and has access to information on all employees' salaries, pension plans, stock options, and so on. Several years ago, her son went through your rehabilitation program and credits your agency with turning his life around. She offers to give you any information you might find useful, on the condition you do not in anyway attribute the information to her as the source. What do you do?

This case is full of potential disasters. First, you should not accept your neighbor's request that the information not be attributed to her as the source. Without attribution, you and others at the rehabilitation center have no way of certifying that the information is accurate. Second, much of the information is private in nature, justified to reside in Achilles' records because of the relationship the company has with its employees. Your relationship with these people as potential donors is decidedly different. It is unlikely that Achilles' employees would approve of this type of information transfer. Finally, you would be participating in and benefitting from your neighbor's acts of violating privacy. As an employee of Achilles with access to sensitive information, she has a responsibility to the company and its employees to protect their privacy. You should not benefit from someone else's wrongdoing.

It sounds as if your neighbor is well intentioned. She is grateful for the help your agency gave her son and wants to show her gratitude by giving your agency something in return. You might suggest other ways by which she could show her gratitude, such as volunteering at the drug rehabilitation center or answering calls on a hotline. By explaining why you cannot accept her offer you would be serving in the role of fund raiser as educator, informing your neighbor about the importance of privacy on her own job as well as being explicit about the importance of privacy and confidentiality in philanthropy.

(c) What to Record and What to Keep

Confidential information needs to be protected. Appropriate information, appropriately obtained, still needs to be kept secure so that only the appropriate people have access to it. The following measures are frequently suggested: Researchers shall record facts objectively and distinguish facts from analysis so that their work is not misinterpreted by others. All materials shall be stored securely so that only authorized people have access to them. Paper files need to be stamped as confidential and locked, with care that only authorized people have access to keys. Data stored electronically should be protected by passwords, which are frequently changed. When documents are no longer needed, they should be disposed of in a secure manner, for example, by shredding rather than simply tossing.[16]

These guidelines are important for maintaining interpersonal trust, agency trust, and system trust. The question sometimes arises whether potentially embarrassing information should ever be kept in a donor's file. Is this a justified exception?

Warning in the File: Mr. Dorsey has long been a faithful supporter of your agency. He donates significant amounts to the annual fund, and has begun working with you on a planned gift annuity. Four years ago, Alicia, the previous planned giving officer, came back in tears from a luncheon meeting with him. "That old goat. He sure has trouble keeping his hands on his own side of the table. He may have money, but he is disgusting. Please jot down in his file something, anything, so people like me don't have to meet with him anymore."

This scenario comes in many versions, with racial bias, discomfort with people with obvious disabilities, and so on, substituting for sexual harassment. We have sympathy for the fund raiser's discomfort, and it is natural to want to protect staff members from this sort of treatment. However, there are a number of moral objections to putting anything in the donor's file that implies prejudicial behavior. The first test is simple: Would you feel free to show Mr. Dorsey the file if he requested it? Even if he never sees the file, there are still reasons not to record behaviors or preferences like this. One of the aspects of respect from the conceptual toolbox is to show generosity in judgment. People can change, and they sometimes reevaluate aspects of their own behavior. Since his meeting with Alicia four years ago, Mr. Dorsey may have participated in workplace training programs on diversity and sexual harassment. His wife or daughter may have experienced harassment and he may have learned from their pain.

You also need to ask whether a note in the file would serve its intended function of protecting staff and volunteer solicitors from unwelcome advances. Such "protections" are double-edged; the history of women's subordination is laced through and through with protections that had the effect of keeping women away from career opportunities as much as protecting them from threats. Such protections are also of negligible effect; a note in this donor's file will not protect fund raisers from other prospects or donors with similar behaviors. It is far better to give staff and volunteers training in how to respond to incidences like this and to equip them to handle them, rather than trying to protect them.

Trying to protect staff from embarrassment and discomfort of this sort is also problematic because it essentially gives official sanction to donors' discriminatory prejudices. If you accommodate a donor who is uncomfortable around people of a different ethnic background or finds it more appealing to deal with attractive, young people than with older, graying ones, you are in essence certifying as acceptable what is in fact disrespectful behavior. This goes against the promise found in fund-raising codes of ethics to treat all persons, including staff members, with dignity and respect.

Sometimes highly trustworthy, though private, information just falls in your lap. Do you act on it? Consider this case:

Family Tragedy: For the past several years, Charles Chadwick, a very wealthy corporate tax attorney, has contributed minor amounts of money to the social service agency where you are director of development. Your executive director asks you for financial information on Mr. Chadwick, as well as any personal information that might be useful for encouraging Mr. Chadwick to increase his contributions substantially. Your daughter, Celia, has been a friend and classmate of Mr. Chadwick's estranged daughter, Sarah, for years. Celia tells you that Sarah's infant son has AIDS. Your agency is planning to start an AIDS hotline in the next few months if a source of major funds can be found. What do you do with this sensitive information?

A number of relationships are involved here, and acting on this information could damage current or potential trust within these relationships. You treasure the open, uncensored communication you have with your daughter, Celia. When she told you about Sarah, she was concerned for her friend, and she confided in you in your role as her parent. It is unlikely that your daughter was trying to feed you donor information for your professional role as development officer. Respecting confidentiality between yourself as parent and Celia is important for maintaining trust within your relationship.

You do not know what the nature of the estrangement is between Mr. Chadwick and Sarah, but it certainly involves matters that are private between them. Assuming you are not a close personal friend of Mr. Chadwick, you are not in a position to heal the breach. You do not want to act in a way that might further damage the relationship between them. You should proceed with your executive director's request as if you knew nothing about the matter. Because Mr. Chadwick is currently a donor, he should be receiving your newsletter and other agency literature about the proposed hotline. He could then choose to donate to the hotline, but he should be treated like any other donor in this regard.

6.4 MISPLACED SECRECY

Sometimes, secrecy is misplaced. To avoid embarrassment, we sometimes keep matters private that need to be aired publicly. Consider this case that a prospect researcher told me about:

Private Job Title: Anissa has just been hired to do prospect research for a major medical center foundation in a large city, and has been given the latest technology and software with which to research prospective donors. The medical center has a long history of large gifts from many wealthy families and adds regularly to that list. The board of trustees reads like a "Who's Who" in the city. The vice-president for development worries that the trustees and potential major donors would feel nervous if they realized what information Anissa has access to. Her official job title is "Information Analyst," and she is told to keep quiet about what it is that she really does. Anissa feels uncomfortable about the secrecy and the pressure to be evasive, if not deceptive. What should she do?

Anissa should discuss her discomfort with the vice-president for development; however, the problem belongs to the medical center foundation, not to her. In trying to avoid embarrassment, the development office is failing to communicate crucial information to the board about how development work is done. It is disrespectful to trustees to ask them to assume major leadership positions in a nonprofit without knowing exactly how the nonprofit functions. Long-term trust in a nonprofit is built on honesty and adequate levels of communication. This is a case of jeopardizing long-term trust to avoid short-term embarrassment.

The above comments have wider implications regarding the educational responsibilities of fund-raising professionals and fund-raising associations. Public trust in nonprofits needs to rest on a straightforward, honest understanding of how development work is done. Although privacy and confidentiality must be respected, we must not use secrecy as a cover for how the development process in general is carried out. Trust in the philanthropic gift economy depends on openness about the methods used to keep the spirit of the gift alive and circulating well.

DISCUSSION QUESTIONS

1. There is a loose end from the story about Frank and Gina, although it does not pertain to privacy per se. What do you think about Frank's brushing up on Homer? Was he:

a. Being respectful of Mrs. Higginsbotham, by becoming conversant in what she cared about?

b. Being disrespectful by being manipulative? Frank doesn't care about Homer, he just wants to play her game to get her money.

c. Being appropriately professional? He may not care about Homer, but he does care about his agency and his commitment to it. Brushing up on Homer is a morally acceptable part of the job.

How do you tell which of these options is the correct interpretation? Does it matter?

2. In this chapter, reasons were given why obtaining court records of divorces could violate privacy, even though they are matters of public record. Would it make any difference if the terms of the divorce are splashed all over the newspapers? Should those clippings be part of the file? Suppose the news stories are splashed all over the tabloids?

3. Nonprofit organizations are now required to have their 990s (informational tax returns) readily available. Some board members, with good reason, are very concerned about having their names and addresses so publicly available. For example, people associated with family planning agencies do not want anti-abortion zealots picketing outside their homes or places of employment. Should provisions be made in the law to protect people in this position? Do you think this legal requirement will make it difficult for some agencies to find new board members?

4. Some nonprofit organizations rent out or sell their donor lists to other organizations. What privacy issues are involved here? The Donor Bill of Rights says that donors should "have the opportunity for their names to be deleted from mailing lists that an organization intends to share." Do you agree with this position? Does it protect privacy in an important way or do you think it extends rights to privacy farther than they should go?

CASE STUDIES

What's Relevant? Since any information can be potentially helpful, your executive director asks you to put everything you find on Harvey Changeover, a highly regarded member of your community, into his file. What do you do with the following bits of information?

a. Mr. Changeover has a bit of a drinking problem, so it is not wise to call him before noon.

b. Twenty years ago, he dabbled with a right-wing militia group, but left it as soon as he realized what he was getting involved with.

c. Twelve years ago, he was expelled from a graduate program for cheating on an exam.

d. Mr. Changeover, who divorced 5 years ago, is currently intimate with Lydia Davidson, president of Davidson Electronics, a corporation your organization is soliciting.

e. He is an avid golfer and has memberships in several clubs that do not admit women or people of color.

Scholarship Dilemma. As the new development officer at the local community college you learn that one of your primary duties is raising money for scholarships. Two days after you begin your new job, the vice-president for institutional advancement gives you the name and phone number of Mr. Meanwell as someone who "wants to set up a scholarship." When you reach Mr. Meanwell on the phone, he seems embarrassed, but tells you that 20 years ago he ran away from town, leaving behind his 17-year-old, pregnant girlfriend. Through a cousin, he has kept track of the child, but has never made contact or had the resources to help out in any way. He knows that the child would like to go to your college but cannot afford to. "Could I just send you the money to pay for his college costs, and you tell him it's a scholarship, but don't connect it with me in any way? His mother still hates me and would never accept the money, but I figure this is one way I could make up for what I did."

What ethical issues are involved in this kind of scholarship? What do you do?

Private Relations. Along with a number of very welcome checks from new donors, your mail pile for the day included this letter: "Dear Money Grubber," it begins, "I deeply resent your overbearing solicitation of my all too precious, all too fixed income. I've never even been to your outfit and certainly will never give you a penny after you so flagrantly violated my privacy." As director of development for a retirement community, it is your practice to send solicitation letters (carefully and respectfully worded, of course) to people listed as "closest living relative" in residents' files. You discover that the letter is from the brother of a new resident, and that cantankerous disagreement has been a standard feature of their relationship since childhood.

How should you respond to the letter? Did a violation of privacy occur? Should you change your policy?

No Longer Benign. One of your long-time donors at the university is a scientist who runs a laboratory doing medical experiments on animals. Your university is currently experiencing a rise in student activism to a level that has not been seen since the 1960s. Last week, students marched about human rights violations in prisons; last month's protest was about pesticides in agricultural runoff. Although all the posters and the protests can be annoying, people in your office, along with the faculty and administrators, are generally pleased that the students are taking these issues so seriously. But you are worried. The animal rights group is particularly vocal, and like so many of today's college students, some of its members have superb computer skills. One member has a work study job in your office. Getting through ordinary password safeguards is no problem. The members' commitment to their cause tends to outweigh their sensitivity to rights of privacy. You have heard of other animal researchers being harassed in their homes. Should you remove normally benign information from your files, such as the scientist's home address and telephone number and any information about his family?

Analogous cases could involve abortion providers, or politicians, judges or other people of prominence in countries with active guerilla movements, and so on.

Friendly Relations. As executive director of an arts organization, you receive a phone call from a major donor who has always requested anonymity for his gifts. He is angry because he was approached by a young financial advisor in the community who is the son of a member of your board of trustees. Apparently, the financial advisor has access to your agency's major donor mailing list. What should you do?

Channeling Clients. The wait at the drop-in clinic can get long and tiring. A volunteer at the desk cannot help but overhear some of the clients' conversations as they begin to reveal personal information. On more than one occasion the volunteer has joined the conversations and, sensing the clients' emotional vulnerability, has invited them to sessions at her New Age channeling center. She is merely trying to help, she says, and does not understand why you are not sympathetic. How do you respond?

NOTES

1. *Griswold v. Connecticut*, 381 US 479 (1965), U.S. Supreme Court, excerpted in David M. Adams (ed.), *Philosophical Problems in the Law* (Belmont, CA: Wadsworth, 1992), pp. 160–165.
2. George G. Brenkert, "Privacy, Polygraphs, and Work." *Business and Professional Ethics Journal*, vol. 1, no. 1 (1981), p. 23.
3. Ferdinand D. Schoeman, *Privacy and Social Freedom* (New York: Cambridge University Press, 1992), pp. 106–107.
4. Alan F. Westin, *Privacy and Freedom* (New York: Atheneum, 1970), pp. 8–11.
5. Clifford Geertz cited in Alan F. Westin, *Privacy and Freedom* (New York: Atheneum, 1970), pp. 16–17.
6. Robert F. Murphy, "Social Distance and the Veil." in Ferdinand D. Schoeman (ed.): *Philosophical Dimensions of Privacy: An Anthology* (New York: Cambridge University Press, 1984), pp. 34–55.
7. The story is recounted in Ferdinand, D. Schoeman, *Privacy and Social Freedom* (New York: Cambridge University Press, 1992), pp. 154–155.
8. For a clear description of the various functions of privacy see Manuel G. Velasquez, *Business Ethics: Concepts and Cases*, 4th ed. (Upper Saddle River, NJ: Prentice Hall, 1998), pp. 449–453.
9. Ferdinand D. Schoeman, *Privacy and Social Freedom* (New York: Cambridge University Press, 1992), p. 20. Schoeman's book is extremely helpful in clarifying the dimensions and importance of privacy.
10. Annette C. Baier, *Moral Prejudices* (Cambridge, MA: Harvard University Press, 1995), p. 130.
11. Ferdinand D. Schoeman, *Privacy and Social Freedom* (New York: Cambridge University Press, 1992), p. 21.
12. Laura J. Avery and John L. Gliha, "Computer-assisted Prospect Management and Research." in James D. Miller and Deborah Strauss (eds.): *Improving Fundraising with Technology. New Directions in Philanthropic Fundraising*, vol. 11 (San Francisco: Jossey-Bass, Spring 1996), p. 86.
13. Beverly Goodwin, "Ethics in the Research Office." in Marianne G. Briscoe (ed.): *Ethics in Fundraising: Putting Values into Practice. New Directions in Philanthropic Fundraising*, vol. 6 (San Francisco: Jossey-Bass, Winter 1994), pp. 99, 100.
14. *Id.,* p. 104.

15. Kay Sprinkel Grace has an excellent discussion of maintaining confidentiality through silent prospecting. Kay Sprinkel Grace, *Beyond Fund Raising* (New York: John Wiley & Sons, 1997), pp. 66–69.
16. APRA code, also Vanessa Hack, *Targeting the Powerful: International Prospect Research* (London: Association for Information Management, 1997), p. 46.

7 ▼ Conflicts of Interest and Other Tensions on the Job

When I was a child, the holiday season was a lovely time at my house. All through December, packages would arrive from names and places I did not know, containing boxes of candy, fruit, hams, jams, and cheeses, and an occasional barometer. My father worked for a publishing company; his job was to contract with commercial typesetters and printers to get the work done. His contacts were very generous to our family during the holidays. Then, at some point during my adolescence, the packages stopped coming. My father's workplace had adopted a conflict of interest policy, stating that employees could no longer accept gifts from outside contractors. The decision makers there were concerned about two things: that the ability of people like my father to make good decisions on behalf of the company not be compromised, and that trust among colleagues in the office, many of whom worked equally hard but lacked outside contacts, not be diminished by jealousy or resentment. Concern over potential conflicts of interest led to a change in policy.

7.1 "CONFLICTS OF INTEREST" AND "CONFLICTING RESPONSIBILITIES"

The NSFRE code of ethics refers directly to conflicts of interest and states that NSFRE members shall "disclose all relationships which might constitute, or appear to constitute, conflicts of interest." Similar statements appear in the ethics codes of the Council for the

Advancement and Support of Education (CASE) and the National Committee on Planned Giving (NCPG).

Black's Law Dictionary, referring to public officials, defines a conflict of interest as "a clash between public interest and the private pecuniary interest of the individual involved."[1] In the case of employees of nonprofit or for-profit organizations, a conflict of interest arises when employees' private material benefit has the tendency to interfere with their ability to exercise good judgment on behalf of their organization's mission. If a second-rate typesetter gave my father a first-rate box of chocolates during the holidays, and that threatened to distort my father's ability to make good judgments on his company's behalf, that would be a conflict of interest.

Before dealing in detail with specific conflicts of interest, we need to distinguish between conflicts of interest and conflicting responsibilities. We want to avoid conflicts of interest if we can. By contrast, conflicts of responsibilities are inherent in our jobs and in our complicated lives; they are the complex polyrhythms with which we must play. Think about an engineer who contracts with a client to build a trash incinerator. Her client wants a high-quality design for a competitive price. The firm that employs her wants good work done, but at a profitable rate. As a member of an engineering professional association and as a responsible human being, she also has a responsibility to care for the public's safety. These three sources of responsibilities do not represent conflicts of interest, although they do come into conflict at times. Likewise, fund raisers have multiple professional responsibilities that sometimes conflict. They are responsible to further the mission, to serve larger philanthropic purposes, to strengthen long-term relationships, and to preserve their own personal integrity. All of these responsibilities are involved in every interaction with donors, volunteers, and colleagues. Since these responsibilities are not matters of individual benefit to the fund raiser per se, conflicts among them are not conflicts of interest. Instead, we can think of these as the polyrhythms with which fund raisers must play.

Section 7.2 will examine various conflicts of interest that fund raisers sometimes face and use the three basic value commitments from the ethical decision-making chart to explain why they are ethically problematic. Section 7.3 will look at tensions that can arise when fund raisers move to a new job, but remain in the same geographic area. These are not conflicts of interest because a fund raiser's personal benefit is not involved. However, these issues are troubling, so some analysis of the ethical issues involved will be helpful.

7.2 CONFLICTS OF INTEREST

For professionals, a conflict of interest may interfere with their ability to make good, professional judgments on their clients' behalf and to serve their clients' interests without compromise. Therefore, our first task is to identify precisely who the fund raisers' clients are. Our initial tendency is to think of donors and potential donors as the clients, because they are the people with whom fund raisers are principally concerned. But since, by definition, the client is the person whose interests a professional serves, donors cannot be a fund raiser's clients. Although fund raisers want to treat donors fairly and decently, they do not work to further the donor's own interests. This is clear if we think in terms of the two-way symmetrical model or the donor–investor model from Chapter 5. On these models, what the fund raiser does is find people who share the values of the nonprofit; fund raisers serve only those interests of the donors that are identified by and identical to the values expressed in the nonprofit's mission. The relationship between fund raisers and donors is a partnership, not a professional–client relationship. Fund raisers in partnership with donors serve the mission of the organization and, through that, the philanthropic gift economy. If anyone can be identified as the fund raiser's clients, it would be the organization's clients: the patrons of the theater for example, or the people using the nonprofit's services for job training, counseling, or education. So for fund raisers, conflicts of interest are conflicts in which their own personal concerns interfere with their ability to use good judgment on behalf of their organization and the public purposes of philanthropy, as personified by the organization's clients. It is hard to remember this, since in terms of day-to-day work, many fund raisers spend much more time concerned with donors than they do with their organizations' clients. For example, a university fund raiser may rarely interact directly with students and a health care fund raiser may rarely see patients. Nonetheless, the central consideration in identifying conflicts of interest is whether fund raisers' personal interests interfere with their ability to make good professional judgments on behalf of their organizations' mission and clients.

(a) Commission-Based Pay

With this background, we can now see why commission-based pay is a classic conflict of interest for fund raisers. The conflict of interest is that if fund raisers' own personal income is correlated with the size of the gift, it takes their attention off of the organizational mission and refocuses it onto their own personal financial well-being. Fund raisers' ability to exercise good judgment on behalf of the nonprofit's mission may be compromised.

Let us run through a particular case to see the dimensions of the potential conflict.

> **Commission-Based Pay:** "Vim and Vigor," a summer day camp for children with spinal cord injuries, has been funded for a number of years by very large annual contributions from three local donors. Unfortunately, the three funding sources are on the verge of drying up. One donor sold his business, which funded his contributions; another retired to Florida; and the third has Alzheimer's and has become quite capricious in her giving. The organization has no full-time fund raiser, and Gita Sen, the executive director, does not have time to fund raise on a large enough scale to ensure the organization's future. The board tells her to go ahead and hire Theo, one of their dedicated volunteers, as a full-time fund raiser and grant writer. The board says they can budget $15,000 toward Theo's salary and he can keep 8 percent of any donations and funded grants. Should the executive director hire Theo on this commission basis?

Major fund-raising professional associations state clearly that this arrangement is unethical. The NSFRE code states that members shall be compensated by salary or set fee, and not by percentage-based compensation or commission. The National Committee on Planned Giving ethics code is equally explicit. The reasons for this position become clear as we examine commission-based pay from the perspective the the three basic value commitments on the ethical decision-making chart.

(i) Organizational Mission

The organization's mission is to provide camping experiences that enhance the children's physical, social, and emotional well-being. With his income dependent on commissions, Theo may be tempted to put his fund-raising efforts into grants and potential donors based on the income they bring him, rather than on how closely they share the organization's mission. The mission may begin to drift. Donors may seek to attach unreasonable demands to their gifts, for example, that a wealthy donor's blind niece be allowed to go to the camp, although they are not prepared to serve her needs. Since Theo's livelihood depends on this income, it will be hard for him to resist such offers. Theo will also be tempted to seek gifts that are immediately forthcoming rather than cultivating a wide donor base, whose members are not presently able to give large gifts. Theo may be tempted to sacrifice the organization's long-term financial stability for his own short-term gain.

(ii) Relationships and Trust

In Chapter 3, we discussed how trust is the atmosphere of healthy relationships, the oxygen supply that sustains them. Let us start with interpersonal trust between donors and the fund raiser. Donors, too, need to be able to exercise good, independent judgment. Theo, like all fund raisers, possesses knowledge upon which donors rely in making their own decisions about charitable giving. The "Vim and Vigor" organization carefully works through what specific programs will best serve the children with spinal injuries; what medical, educational, and recreational staff will best serve the camp; how to contact and enroll potential campers; and so on. Potential donors trust Theo, as a representative of the agency, that this work has been done and that their donations will be put to good use. In order for donors to make good decisions, they need to know, or at least have access to, any information that might affect their decision. Knowing that a percentage of their donation goes directly into Theo's salary is quite likely to diminish their trust in Theo and in the veracity of the information he shares with them. It could also diminish their trust in the agency itself, when donors question the agency's judgment in sanctioning such an arrangement.

Now consider trust among Theo, the rest of the staff, and board members at "Vim and Vigor." Many staff members besides Theo contribute to successful fund raising; other staff members may feel that they deserve a percentage of the gifts as well. If the agency had a large fund-raising staff, fund raisers working on the annual fund and prospect research might well resent the income opportunities available to those in planned giving and major gifts. Keeping accounts straight can also be problematic. Who gets the commission for an unannounced bequest that was set up before any of the current fund raisers joined the staff? Voluntary board members who participate in fund raising may find the contrast between their uncompensated efforts and Theo's percentage a little hard to bear. Those who would rather not fund raise at all may decide this is just the excuse they need: Let Theo do all the fund-raising work, since he is the one receiving the commissions.[2]

(iii) Integrity

Finally, commission-based pay puts Theo in a position in which preserving his own integrity is severely tested with every call. I know a dieter who keeps plenty of candy around the house just to test her willpower. You can imagine the results. Theo might feel the same way, except the "candy" in his case translates into food, housing, and other necessities. If Theo were completely forthright with donors, he would, in effect, have to say to them, "Please increase your gift this year so I can afford winter clothing for my children." Donors understand (or they should) that nonprofits have operating costs and salaries to pay. But it is not fair to put Theo in a position in which being completely forthright would bruise his own sense of dignity and embarrass potential donors.

Many nonprofit missions are worthy; it is understandable why a board might be tempted to hire a fund raiser on commission so that the mission can be furthered. But if a board cannot find enough money to pay a fund raiser a decent salary, they should not hire one. Otherwise, they are putting the fund raiser in a position in which it is extremely difficult to stay focused on the organization's mission and not be swayed from its path. It is unfair to put people in situations in which conflicts of interest are bound to come up. Fund raisers are dedicated to serving the public good, but with few exceptions, vows of poverty are not in their job descriptions. Fund raisers have financial responsibilities for themselves and their families and they should be able to fulfill them in a dignified way. Because many new board members and new fund raisers come from the business world where commissions are standard, these ethical concerns need to be explained clearly in board and staff training sessions.

The NSFRE code does permit members to accept performance incentives and bonuses if certain provisos are kept. Among these is the provision that fund raisers' performance be assessed in terms of multiple measures besides the amount of money brought in, such as total cultivation efforts, teamwork, mentoring other fund raisers, and so on. No mention of a percentage of funds raised is permissible.

Some people in philanthropic fund raising are not comfortable with the practice of giving bonuses and incentives, worrying that it encourages fund raisers to move their focus from the mission over to their own financial advantage. This is a significant concern and instructs us to monitor bonus and incentive programs to see what effects they will have.

(b) Finders' Fees

We have worked through several reasons why fund raisers themselves should not receive commission-based compensation. But what of other people in for-profit businesses who assist fund raisers in some way? Is it ethical to pay them on a commission basis? Consider this scenario:

Finder's Fees: Sonia Sorkin is the new executive director of a large arts organization. The board has asked her to develop a planned giving program. As luck would have it, during her first week on the job, an attorney, Trevor Trueblood, calls her and tells her that one of his clients is interested in making a $2 million planned gift to the organization. He also indicates that he expects a finder's fee, just like last time. Sonia discovers that several planned gifts have been received by the organization in the past year, and that local financial advisors, including Trevor Trueblood, were paid finders' fees for them. Sonia sets up a meeting with the board's finance committee and discovers that two of the board members are thoroughly in favor of paying the fees. They explain that such fees are expected by financial professionals and are absolutely necessary to the financial health of the organization. They tell Sonia that if she refuses to pay them, the fund-raising burden on the board will be more than they are willing to undertake. What should Sonia do?

NSFRE and the two planned giving associations, the National Committee on Planned Giving (NCPG) and American Council of Gift Annuities (ACGA), forbid their members to pay or accept finders' fees and direct their members to discourage their organizations from participating in this practice. If Sonia is a member of one of these associations, she must either refuse to pay the fees or discontinue her membership. However, there are ethical reasons for refusing to pay the fees, regardless of membership. When outside financial advisors seek finders' fees, it is unlikely that "shared values" and "mutual understanding" are at the center of concern. Trevor Trueblood may well be searching for the nonprofit that will give him the most financial benefit from the planned gift. Whether the donor supports the organization's mission or wants to participate in sustaining the philanthropic gift economy is a secondary consideration, at best.[3]

Agency and system trust are at risk here. It must seem hypocritical to donors when fund raisers approach them with talk of shared philanthropic values and then turn around and "buy" gifts from commercial financial advisors seeking to line their own pockets. The public trust in nonprofits as truly committed to the gift economy of philanthropy will surely be weakened by this practice.

There is one other caution involving good judgment and planned giving, although "conflict of interest" is not quite the right category for it. The planned giving associations strongly recommend that their members encourage donors to have their own legal and financial advisors review their planned gift arrangements. This is not a conflict of interest as defined earlier, because fund raisers' own personal financial advantage is not an issue. But fund raisers' objectivity could be questioned, because they are raising money on behalf of their agencies. Retirement and estate planning involves many financial and value considerations: How much do I need to live on for the unknown duration of the rest of my life? How much do I want to pass on to family members and how much shall I leave to other causes? Because of the complexity and serious nature of these decisions, it is wise to bring in an independent advisor to review the entire plan. Also, family members could raise questions about the arrangement after the donor dies and is no longer able to explain the plan's rationale. Input from independent advisors helps to protect nonprofits from unhappy family members.[4]

(c) Volunteers Funding Themselves

Fund raisers are creative folks. Fund raising lends itself to imaginative thinking, but we must assess new concepts to make sure that conflicts of interest are not lurking in the background. Here is one example of a fund-raising method that initially sounds appealing.

A number of nonprofits have used the current interest in physical fitness and adventure travel in creative ways to recruit fundraising volunteers and raise money for their organizations.[5] Here is how it works. The National Name-a-Disease Association (fill in with your favorite) picks a fitness event, say, a marathon, a mountain climbing expedition, or white water rafting. If potential runners, climbers, or rafters raise a given amount, then Name-a-Disease will arrange the event. For example, the nonprofit reserves slots in a marathon race, a coveted commodity in some marathons, and may engage a trainer for its runners.

On the face of it, this sounds like a win-win situation. The athletes get great opportunities to participate in events and the nonprofit gets funds and the athletes as supporters, plus a lot of publicity for their organization. Just think of all those other marathon runners and watchers reading "National Name-a-Disease Association" on all those T-shirts streaking by.

This funding project can be set up in a number of different ways. I do not see any ethical problems if the volunteers raise a specified amount for the nonprofit and then pay their own expenses out of their own pockets. It is also not a problem if the event itself carries out the organizational mission. "Vim and Vigor," for example, could sponsor some of its clients with spinal cord injuries in a marathon's wheelchair division and have them raise some additional donations as well. But the third way does raise ethical concerns that bear an uncomfortable resemblance to the problems raised by commission-based pay and paying volunteers.

Consider Sidney and Sam, both perfectly healthy volunteers. Each one raises $5,000 for the National Name-a-Disease Association, $3,000 of which goes toward paying their expenses for a hiking trip in the Andes. Now if Sidney and Sam were fund-raising staff members, this arrangement would give them the equivalent of a 60 percent commission for their work. Although Sidney and Sam are volunteers, the arrangement makes them "paid" volunteers, with payment in the form of a travel opportunity.

A philanthropic nonprofit is not a travel agency. There are plenty of fine commercial travel companies, some specializing in adventure travel, that people can use if traveling is their goal. (We need to distinguish this situation from nonprofits that run travel tours for their members. In these cases, the members pay their own way, and the cost of the trip can include a charitable donation. Also, the trip is planned to fit in with the mission of the nonprofit, such as art tours sponsored by art museums and educational tours sponsored by universities.)

The three basic values of the ethical decision-making chart can be used to explain what is wrong here. First, the mission of the nonprofit is diluted. Sidney and Sam cannot say straight out to a potential donor, "I am raising $5,000 for Name-a-Disease." To be fully honest, Sidney and Sam should say, "We are raising money, some for Name-a-Disease and some to send us hiking in the Andes." Sending healthy people on an adventure hike is not in Name-a-Disease's mission statement. Second, this arrangement can damage relationships. The relationship between donor and nonprofit should be centered on how both parties are committed to the mission, with donors being able to trust that the nonprofit will use their dollars to fulfill the mission. Now, honesty is one of the virtues of relationships, and it is doubtful that donors' trust in the nonprofit will be strengthened if they know that some of their donations will go toward non–mission-related adventure travel for volunteer fund raisers.

Finally, asking Sidney and Sam to raise funds, some of which will benefit them personally, places them in a position in which they need to raise questions about their own integrity. It is very awkward for healthy people to ask other people for charitable donations so they can enjoy a hiking trip. Two virtues in the virtues of integrity cluster are at risk here: independent judgment and responsibility. Components of independent judgment include sympathetic understanding and attention to larger contexts. Sidney and Sam should ask themselves, "How would people suffering from name-a-disease and their caretakers view this arrangement? Would they feel gratified that an agency whose mission it is to serve them took money collected on their behalf and used it to send healthy people on a hiking trip?" The larger context question for Sidney and Sam is about what it means to volunteer for a nonprofit organization. When they raise money for themselves and for the nonprofit simultaneously, the meaning of *volunteer* gets muddied in their minds, making it more difficult for them to understand and appreciate just how the gift economy of philanthropy functions.

Also, responsibility, another virtue of integrity, is involved here. Recall Niebuhr's analysis of responsibility as involving response, giving account, and social solidarity. Giving account links directly with honesty. For their own integrity, Sidney and Sam (and Name-a-Disease) need to be able to give account to potential donors. They need to be able to face donors and tell them directly that a given percentage of their donations will be used to fund the hiking trip. If Sidney and Sam feel that they need to keep this point hidden, their own integrity is at stake.

This is a conflict-of-interest situation in which the volunteers' self-interest in taking the trip obscures what should be a clear focus on the mission, and may well damage donors' trust in the nonprofit organization while compromising the participants' own integrity.

(d) Unavoidable Conflicts

Not all conflicts of interest can or should be avoided. In the United States, for example, real estate transactions have conflicts of interest right at their center. The real estate agent who represents the buyer is paid a commission by the seller; thus, the buyer's desire for the lowest possible price is directly at odds with the agent's desire for a high commission. The only way real estate agents can avoid this conflict is by changing professions. We need not debate here whether this is a reasonable way to structure a profession. What makes it tolerable is the fact that all parties know that this is the way real estate transactions take place; nothing is hidden and there is no deception.[6]

In fund raising, there are times when it is impossible or unwise to avoid conflicts of interest. Consider this case:

Conflicting Relations: Your small historical society is soliciting bids for restoring an old Spanish mission. You are the society's fund raiser, and you have more historical and archeological knowledge about missions in the area than anyone else in the organization. One of the three firms submitting bids is owned by your brother-in-law. What should you do?

This is a conflict of interest for you, and it would be advisable if someone with experience equivalent to yours could take your place on the selection committee. But this is not always feasible, especially for small organizations in relatively unpopulated areas. If you think the decision process would be harmed by your withdrawal, you should make sure that everyone involved in the decision is aware of your conflict of interest and agrees that you should continue to participate. That way, they can evaluate what you say in light of this conflict. You may be able to think of ways to mitigate the conflict; for example, you could participate in all discussions, but not cast a vote.

7.3 NEW JOB, SAME TOWN

Many tensions that arise from changing to a new job in the same geographical area are not conflicts of interest, but they can involve troubling conflicts and deserve some reflection. You move from one job to another, but because so much of what fund raisers do is out in the community, many aspects of the new job overlap with the old. You continue to deal with the same local businesses, the same group of "volunteer for everything" people (you know, the ones who are on a minimum of four boards while dreaming up at least seven new projects all at the same time), and the same NSFRE chapter members. The NSFRE ethics code is clear that donor and prospect information belongs to the agency, not to the fund raiser, and so must stay with the agency. Tempting though it might be, bringing a copy of your donor disk along to the new job is a form of theft. The code states, "Members shall adhere to the principle that all donor and prospect information created by, or on behalf of, an institution is the property of that institution and shall not be transferred or utilized except on behalf of that institution." But what do you do with knowledge you carry in your head? What do you do with relationships you have established with community donors and volunteers? No delete key can wipe all of that from your brain, yet you want to be fair to the nonprofits you worked for in the past. Let's think through a couple of cases; more are included at the end of the chapter.

> **Whose Knowledge?** You have moved from being director of corporate relations at Icarus College to holding the equivalent position at Orville and Wilbur University, a more well-endowed university in town. You know that Icarus is planning to develop its rather small aeronautical engineering program, and from working there, you know which corporations would be particularly receptive to requests for donations. You also know that Icarus plans to approach these corporations with proposals within the next month. After arriving at Orville and Wilbur, you learn that they, too, plan to strengthen their widely respected aeronautical engineering program. Your boss asks you to come up with a list of corporate contacts and a timetable for when to contact them. What do you do with your knowledge about Icarus?

Let's begin with the NSFRE ethics code. The code prohibits taking donor lists or files. Those remain with Icarus. The guidelines for the code state that this prohibition applies only to "information unique to a specific organization," not to "publicly available information." Information about corporate funding guidelines, which are available to any nonprofit that inquires, is not considered proprietary.

Some fund raisers would not be comfortable moving from one position to another where so much of what they learned in the first would invariably apply to the second. Others would not see the job change as a problem, but might ask their supervisor not to give them this particular assignment. If you do accept the assignment, here is one pattern for thinking it through.

Using the three fundamental value commitments from the ethical decision-making chart, we can work through this case in terms of mission, relationships, and your own integrity. Because both organizations are universities, there will be considerable overlap in their missions. But you still need to check the mission of Orville and Wilbur University and the goals of their aeronautical engineering program. The publicly available corporate information that you learned at Icarus may not fit the programs at Orville and Wilbur quite so well.

While at Icarus, you established relationships with the same corporate funders that you now want to approach for the Orville and Wilbur program. If the funders already consider you a trustworthy person, you will not erase that when you move to Orville and Wilbur, nor should you have to. But remember the discussion of social personae from Chapter 6. When you worked at Icarus, corporate funders had a relationship with "you in the role of fund raiser for Icarus College." Even though you as an individual are still the same person, corporations will now be relating to "you in the role of fund raiser for Orville and Wilbur University." The corporate funders may have different relationships with and impressions of the two universities. Both you and the corporate funders will in a sense have to construct your relationship anew. Being sure you act in a way that respects Icarus and is appropriately loyal to Orville and Wilbur is important in recasting relationships.

Part of showing respect to Icarus is not taking advantage of your insider's knowledge of their cultivation timetable. The knowledge may be in your head and not on a disk, but in this case the best thing to do is proceed with your assignment at Orville and Wilbur as if you had no knowledge of the timetable. You should not rush certain proposals to make sure corporate funders see them before Icarus's proposals arrive.

The other dimension of relationships here has to do with your continuing contacts with people working at Icarus and the relationship between the two universities. People can move away, but universities rarely do, so acting in ways that sustain long-term, healthy relationships between the two universities is important for the community as a whole. Engineering programs are expensive, and there may be ways the two universities can collaborate. You want to be in a position in which you could facilitate this kind of partnership and not damage the trust such collaboration requires.

In terms of the virtues of integrity cluster, following the above suggestions should preserve your independent judgment and sense of responsibility. You may need to draw on moral courage if people at Orville and Wilbur want you to take advantage of your insider's knowledge of information from Icarus, which rightfully should stay there.

Another kind of dilemma arises when a fund raiser leaves a job under less than amicable circumstances. Consider this case:

Domineering Boss. Gwenna has just moved to a new development job in the same city. She left her previous position because of serious difficulties with Henry, the executive director. She felt that Henry was domineering and demeaning and that he stifled initiative and creativity among the staff. Manuel, a fellow NSFRE member who is looking for a new position, asks Gwenna about her previous job and wants to know why she left. What should she say to him?

Gwenna is in a difficult position. She is an honest person; it is part of her own sense of integrity, and she has found that being honest is essential to developing relationships of trust. Manuel is relying on her for help as he makes a very significant decision, and Gwenna does not want to give him false or misleading information. At the same time, in spite of her experiences with her former boss, she wants to respect the privacy of her former agency and not make personal grievances public.

Chapter 6 discussed how the confidentiality of information varies with the nature of the particular relationship. Very intimate friends can be privy to Gwenna's anger and exasperation about her former boss; with them, a strong sense of confidentiality would already exist and they would know how to place Gwenna's anger in perspective. It is likely that Manuel is not this sort of an intimate friend of Gwenna's; if he were, he probably would have received blow-by-blow accounts of her frustration all along.

Potential relationships of trust are most at stake here. Gwenna wants to preserve Manuel's trust in her without damaging his ability to develop a good workplace relationship with Henry. Gwenna should first of all be very careful to place her difficulties within the context of her own relationship with Henry; others may be able to work well with him. She should judge very carefully what and how much to say about the ways in which they did not get along. She might suggest certain things for Manuel to check on during his interview. She might also name some people who get along well with Henry and suggest that Manuel talk to them.

What and how much to say is also a question of integrity for Gwenna. A good test is whether she would be willing to say directly to Henry everything that she says to Manuel. Although she should be concerned about issues of confidentiality, privacy should not function as a form of protection. Henry's relationship with Gwenna was not a private relationship between Gwenna and himself. It was a professional relationship between Henry as executive director and Gwenna as fund raiser, and Henry is responsible for how he treats his professional colleagues. People with power need to be held accountable for the ways in which they exercise that power. Not being a gossip is part of Gwenna's sense of integrity; however, she should also refuse to let her own silence function as a shield for others' bad behavior.

Tensions are an inevitable part of a fund raiser's job. It is important to reflect on these tensions to determine whether they arise from conflicts of interest or conflicting responsibilities. If conflicts of interest are involved, the conflicts needs to be discussed openly and avoided if possible. If the tensions arise from conflicting responsibilities, they need to be understood and dealt with, with sensitivity to their ethical dimensions.

DISCUSSION QUESTIONS

1. Can you think of other examples besides the historical society case in which conflicts of interest cannot be avoided or in which it would be unwise to avoid them?

2. The wildlife painting case, used to explain the ethical decision-making chart in Chapter 1 (see Exhibit 1.3), involves a conflict of interest. There, the conflict is that by accepting the artist's painting as a personal gift, the fund raiser's ability to use sound professional judgment on the college's behalf may be compromised, and trust among her office colleagues may be diminished. Is it always wrong for fund raisers to accept personal gifts from donors or vendors? What sorts of guidelines would you propose?

3. People often serve many nonprofit organizations simultaneously. In addition to a paid position, fund raisers may want to be involved with religious groups, parents' organizations for their children's school-related activities, civic organizations, boards of other non-profits, and so on. What guidelines should they use in selecting their own volunteering activities to avoid conflicts of interest with their principal employer?

4. Is it ethical for nonprofit organizations to pay commercial tele-marketing firms a percentage of what they raise for the nonprofit?

CASE STUDIES

Freelance Commission. Money is tight at your agency and you do not have the time to write a specific grant proposal. Your chief executive officer (CEO) asks you to contact a highly skilled, freelance grant writer in town. She only charges if a grant is funded, but then she asks for a percentage of the grant as her fee. How do you respond to the CEO?

Personal and Professional Conflict of Interest. You work for a religiously affiliated nonprofit. You also serve on the board of your local church and are placed on the finance committee. The finance committee chairperson asks you if you know any people who are inclined to give to organizations that share your church's religious values, and they ask you to write solicitation letters to them. Would complying with the request conflict with your workplace loyalties?

Hush about the Money? In its drive to raise annual operating funds, your nonprofit performing arts group receives a gift of $5,000 from the county in which you reside. You, as development director, would like to recognize this gift and other gifts in a newspaper press release. Your board of trustees, however, insists that the gift not be publicized because "strings were pulled to get it." On further investigation, you discover that the sister-in-law of one of your board members is a county administrator who has authority to disperse up to $5,000 without county board approval. Your performing arts organization is one of three arts organizations struggling for funds in the same city. What should you do?

Trust Revoked. In your old job with a highly regarded, financially stable organization, you developed a close working relationship with an elderly couple who set up a revocable trust with the organization. You recently moved to a new organization whose financial situation is somewhat shaky. The couple comes to you and says that because they have such confidence in your ability to look after their interests, they want to revoke the original trust and set up a new one through you with your new organization. What should you do?

Whose Volunteers? In your position with a disaster relief agency, you worked hard to develop a group of active, committed volunteers. In November, you changed jobs and started working for a shelter for the homeless. Your new boss wants you to develop a strong volunteer group in a hurry, as forecasters predict an unusually severe winter. Do you call on your committed volunteers from disaster relief?

Prospect or Not? As development director of an art museum, you are in the thick of planning for a capital campaign. Your husband is also volunteering his services in fund raising as chair of the new building campaign at your church. One evening, while talking with your husband at home, you learn that an older gentleman in your congregation, Mr. Stayquiet, has anonymously pledged the lead gift ($750,000) for the church building fund and is the major shareholder in a large corporation. Your husband knows that Mr. Stayquiet appreciates fine art, but he has never been involved with your art museum.

You are tempted to approach him for a gift but worry about violating his privacy. What should you do?

NOTES

1. *Black's Law Dictionary*, 5th ed. (St. Paul, MN: West, 1979).
2. James M. Greenfield, "Professional Compensation." *NSFRE Journal* (Summer 1990), pp. 35–39.
3. Kathleen Kelly, *Effective Fund Raising Management* (Mahwah, NJ: Lawrence Erlbaum Associates, 1998), pp. 509–512; Holly Hall, "Two Fund-Raising Groups Denounce Commission Payments to Gift-Annuity Advisors." *The Chronicle of Philanthropy*, vol. 11, no. 5 (December 17, 1998), p. 30.
4. Kathleen Kelly, *Effective Fund Raising Management* (Mahwah, NJ: Lawrence Erlbaum Associates, 1998), p. 510.
5. Debra E. Blum, "Raising Funds over the Long Run." *The Chronicle of Philanthropy*, vol. 11, no. 8 (February 11, 1999), pp. 23–26.
6. Larry May, *The Socially Responsive Self: Social Theory and Professional Ethics* (Chicago: University of Chicago Press, 1996), pp. 125–127, 133.

8 ▼ Corporations and Philanthropy

Through partnerships with nonprofit organizations, corporations have contributed in many ways to enhancing the quality of life in our communities. In this chapter we will examine these partnerships, spelling out ethical responsibilities which both types of organizations share, as well as acknowledging distinctive differences between them. Since joint ventures, especially cause-related marketing and sponsorship, are such prominent forms of partnership between nonprofits and businesses, we will analyze the ethical dimensions of these relationships in some detail.

8.1 HISTORY OF CORPORATE GIVING IN THE UNITED STATES

Prior to the 1950s, business involvement in philanthropy was minimal, limited for the most part to contributions to community chests, donations to relief agencies during wartime, and the like. Of course, business leaders as individuals were certainly involved in philanthropy and many gave generously out of their own wealth. Names like Carnegie, Rockefeller, and Morgan come to mind. Corporate charters often excluded use of corporate funds for nonbusiness purposes. In the early twentieth century, railroad companies justified their donations to the Young Men's Christian Association (YMCA) on the grounds that their own workers stayed in YMCAs along the routes.[1] Until the 1950s, the law was ambiguous; it was not clear whether corporate giving was legally permissible.[2]

The legal test case came when manufacturer A. P. Smith Company gave $1,500 to Princeton University. The company's president testified in court that the donation was in the company's interest: It would generate goodwill from the community, contribute to educating competent future employees, and help create a favorable business environment. The court agreed that corporate contributions not directly tied to the corporation's own advantage were legitimate. The court reasoned that corporate philanthropic giving contributed to the survival of the free enterprise system and of democracy itself and represented one way of discharging the duties of good citizenship.[3] During the 1960s and 1970s, with issues such as the Vietnam war, civil rights demonstrations, and emerging environmental concerns, so prominent in the press businesses felt that their legitimacy was under attack. *Social responsibility* became the buzzword. Louis Lundborg, then head of the Bank of America, explained the idea this way: "Those in corporate life are going to be expected to do things for the good of society, just to earn their franchise, their corporate right to exist."[4] While contributing to nonprofits was seen as one way of fulfilling corporate social responsibility, the concept was also used to address internal corporate practices. For example, corporate responsibilities to address racial and gender segregation in the work force and to alter polluting manufacturing processes were debated under the rubric of *corporate social responsibility.*

During the 1980s, as the political environment became more conservative under the Reagan administration, the tenor of the social responsibility debate also became more conservative. Merger frenzy characterized the business environment. The Reagan administration was cutting social programs; nonprofit requests to corporations to help make up the difference were increasing.[5] *Enlightened self-interest* rather than *corporate social responsibility* became the vocabulary of choice.

At first glance, this vocabulary shift may seem to indicate a change from an outward focus ("What is a corporation's responsibility *to* society?") to an inward focus ("How can serving society benefit the corporation?"). However, many business executives defined enlightened self-interest broadly, seeking to create and preserve a mutually supportive relationship between the corporation and the community. After all, a corporation benefits when the people who are its customers, employees, and the teachers of employees' children are healthy, literate, and have access to cultural amenities. The underlying idea is that of corporate citizenship. The corporation has the responsibility to be a good citizen in the community. In the long run, what is good for the community will benefit business, so businesses should be willing to look beyond short-term, bottom-line benefits to accomplish these larger purposes. Hence, self-interest is enlightened, rather than narrowly focused.

During the 1990s, the vocabulary of the debate shifted again. *Strategic philanthropy* and *corporate social investing* entered the debate. These terms suggest tighter links between a corporation's community involvement and the corporation's own interests. For example, print media companies might focus their giving on literacy, sporting goods manufacturers on children's recreation programs, software manufacturers on educational technology programs, and so on. Corporations look on nonprofits as partners that can serve corporate purposes while addressing community needs at the same time. Curt Weeden, author of *Corporate Social Investing*, describes the relationship this way: "Corporate profits make corporate social investing possible. *And in turn,* social investing uses charity to create conditions that are conducive to making a profit"[6] Many corporations have begun asking how their marketing, advertising, and human relations departments, as well as the corporate philanthropy office, might be involved in partnership with philanthropic nonprofits.[7] Weeden explains, "Identify a significant business reason for every corporate social investment and obtain as much business value from social investments as is allowable and practical."[8]

Scholars debate whether the shift from corporate social responsibility to enlightened self-interest to corporate social investing represents a loss in philanthropic intent and whether corporate contributions have diminished accordingly. Some argue that with corporate social investing, a short-term focus on the bottom line has replaced the broader, long-term perspective.[9] These critics remind us that many nonprofits fulfill their missions by chipping away at difficult, deeply embedded, and recurring social needs. A new crop of children who need to learn to read keep appearing with great regularity; adolescent anger manifesting itself in destructive ways keeps recurring, and the vulnerabilities that come with living in aging bodies visit us all. These are not problems to be solved in the sense of putting them on a timetable, finishing them off, and closing the file drawer.

Others defend the vocabulary shift, contending that corporate giving has always been self-interested, and that vocabulary shifts reflect responses to changing political and economic conditions rather than changes in underlying corporate purposes. They claim that strategic philanthropy, if done well, can accomplish more in addressing social needs and building strong communities than the old-fashioned perspective of corporate charitable work.[10] This is an important debate and it will be interesting to follow empirical studies investigating it.

8.2 CONCEPTUALIZING CORPORATE–NONPROFIT RELATIONSHIPS

How corporations envision their responsibilities toward community well-being and how they define their relationships with nonprofits are important questions, ones that members of the business community should reflect on deeply and often. However, the focus of this book is from the nonprofit perspective. Nonprofit organizations need to consider both what they share and how they differ from for-profit corporations and then construct their relationships with these factors in mind. Let us review each of these considerations.

(a) What Corporations and Nonprofits Share

At a most fundamental level, nonprofit organizations and for-profit businesses share many ethical responsibilities and goals. It is commonplace for people to say that philanthropic nonprofits are held and should be held to a higher ethical standard than for-profit businesses. The reasoning goes that nonprofits are dedicated to accomplishing lofty public purposes, rather than pursuing private gain, so their ethical standards should parallel the loftiness of their mission. Although I appreciate the sentiment that nonprofits should embody high ethical ideals, stating this point by way of contrast with marketplace profit motivation makes me uncomfortable.

This line of thinking overglorifies charitable nonprofits and it sets ethical expectations for for-profit businesses too low. For-profit manufacturers of pacemakers, ambulances, and infant baby formula are in the business of saving and sustaining lives, just as much as many nonprofits. Even businesses whose products and services sound less directly humanitarian, say stapler manufacturers, dry cleaners, and tool and die makers, still exist to enhance the quality of life and the well-being of the community. The point of a free enterprise system is not to make profits per se; the point is to improve social well being and to use the for-profit business organizational form to do that. Many businesspeople know this and run their businesses accordingly.

This is an important point that goes right to the heart of the capitalist system, so I want to dwell on it a bit. We should go directly to

Adam Smith's *Wealth of Nations,* often called the bible of capitalism. (I tell my students that its publication was *the* big event of 1776.) One paragraph in the book has become the obligatory quotation for Economics 101 textbooks: "It is not from the benevolence of the butcher, the brewer, or the baker that we expect our dinner, but from their regard to their own interest. We address ourselves, not to their humanity but to their self-love ..."[11] What these textbooks leave out is *everything else* Adam Smith said. Smith did think that self-interest was a powerful motivator for economic exchange, but he never intended for people to think of it as the sole motivator or as the sole criterion for corporate operations. Smith, who was Professor of Moral Philosophy at the University of Glasgow, was deeply concerned with moral issues. In his book, *Theory of Moral Sentiments,* he writes, "Humanity, justice, generosity, and public spirit, are the qualities most useful to others."[12] Amartya Sen, 1998 Nobel Prize winner in Economics, explains that Smith thought self-interest was an appropriate motivator for the *exchange* aspect of an economic system, but this is hardly the whole of it. Production and the background social conditions in which exchanges take place should be regulated by all sorts of ethical considerations. Sen stresses that maintaining relationships based on warranted trust is foundational in business. An economic system that uses self-interest as a motivator for exchange only makes sense against the backdrop of a high level of institutional trust.[13]

The point here is that both for-profit and nonprofit organizations exist fundamentally to serve the public good. Of course, there is as much variability in how businesses define public good as there is among nonprofit definitions. Stated missions and organizational forms differ, but the underlying, most fundamental justification for the existence of both nonprofits and businesses rests on societal well-being. Both share the fundamental moral responsibility to act in ways which justify high levels of institutional trust. These include being honest and fair in their dealings, treating all persons with dignity and respect, and contributing to community sustenance. Nonprofits should set high ethical standards for themselves and should expect the same from their corporate partners.

(b) Distinctive Foci

In explaining the concept of a gift economy, Chapter 1 discussed how gift economy elements are present in for-profit businesses. Many people use the for-profit organizational form to provide life-enhancing services to clients. I know a firm of for-profit financial planners who begin every session by doing a values assessment with their clients. Many of their clients are so-called "displaced homemakers," elementary school teachers, and others who need the firm's services precisely because they have so little money to play around with. The firm quite deliberately focuses on clients such as these. Although a for-profit firm, by pouring their intelligence and commitment into this work, the partners mix together gift economy and market economy elements every day.

Market economy elements are also present in nonprofit operations. Very few nonprofits could exist on philanthropic contributions alone.[14] To the extent that nonprofits are funded by fees, ticket sales, and tuition, they function with market *quid pro quo* mechanisms. This is not ethically problematic. By relying in part on these sources of income, and by entering into partnerships with government agencies and corporations, nonprofits have accomplished a great deal in fulfillment of their missions. But in working with corporate partners, nonprofits should take care to remain true to what makes them distinctive. Again, drawing from Chapter 1, what makes nonprofits distinctive are those features that create the gift economy of philanthropy: first, the mission statement as explicitly serving public purposes, and second, nonprofit reliance on volunteers. These include people who give unremunerated time as board members, nonboard volunteer fund raisers, and service volunteers, as well as donors who give money as gifts toward serving the mission.

In assessing the ethics of relationships between nonprofits and corporations, all of the usual concerns come into play: honesty, fairness, trust, integrity, and so on. These virtues apply equally to nonprofits and corporations alike. In addition, we should also make sure that the distinctive character of nonprofits as participants in the philanthropic gift economy not be compromised. A nonprofit's focus on its mission should always be sparklingly clear. Just as nonprofits and donors should work on the basis of shared values, so in nonprofit projects with corporations the shared value of carrying out the nonprofit's mission should be at the center. If in doing this, corporate goals are also furthered, that is fine. The danger to watch out for is "mission drift." In the excitement of forming nonprofit–corporate partnerships, the nonprofit mission should not become distorted. Also, nonprofits should remember that sustaining the gift economy of philanthropy through voluntary action is their fundamental purpose, and they should be careful not to neglect their responsibilities to foster the virtues of the philanthropic gift economy: generosity, charity, compassion, gratitude, and mutuality.

(c) For-Profit Missions and Nonprofit Missions

Chapter 5 discussed donor–nonprofit relations in terms of the two-way symmetrical model and the donor–investor model. These models stress that donors and nonprofits should work from a basis of mutual understanding and shared values. Individual donors and corporate donors are analogous to a degree; individuals, nonprofits, and corporations can all share values such as improving literacy, perpetuating bluegrass music, or stopping domestic violence. In other ways, individual donors and corporate donors are not alike. There may be some individuals who build their lives around a mission statement and then dedicate every waking moment to carrying it out. People training for the Olympics and concertizing violinists come to mind. But most of us have many missions on which we work and we also spend some of our time in activities that do not correlate with any of them. (Parent to adolescent: "What have you been doing?" Universal, all-purpose adolescent response: "Messing around.")

Corporations have mission statements. Corporations stand for something in a way not paralleled by most individuals. Assessing the compatibility between a nonprofit's mission and a corporate mission is an important first step in dealing with corporate donors. This is especially true when dealing with those corporations that produce products of debated social value. The clearest case of conflict is between tobacco companies and health-related organizations. Timothy Smith, Executive Director of the Interfaith Center on Corporate Responsibility, explains the contradiction vividly: "A health-care organization that serves people who are ravaged by cancer caused by smoking is in a living contradiction if it seeks grants from tobacco companies that are responsible for the sickness and death of literally millions of people around the world. What hypocrisy for a cancer hospital to ally itself with the tobacco industry while treating the industry's victims every day."[15] But many potential conflicts are not so clear. Consider this case:

> **Dollars from Dionysus:** A brewery, Dionysus, Inc., wants to fund several scholarships at the local community college. Although the college appreciates the offer, they do not want the scholarship arrangement to be viewed as support for student drinking, nor do they want the company to make the offer simply to polish its public image. Is it consistent with the college's mission to accept this funding?

This is a complex question. Beer is a legal product, and for many people it is an appropriate part of social life. Assuming the college is not a private college with an explicit policy excluding alcohol, it is consistent with the college's educational goals to help students to learn how to use the product responsibly. The development officer and the college officials might ask themselves questions such as the following:

- Does the college have problems with excessive use of alcohol, especially among students younger than the legal drinking age?
- Are a significant number of students above the legal drinking age?
- Are the college's alcohol policies in good order regarding when and where drinking is acceptable and how violations are handled?
- Does the company have responsible drinking programs as part of their marketing?
- Could the company sponsor some alcohol awareness programs or events at the college?

This may be one of those cases in which ethics resides in the details and contextual factors determine what should be done. But thinking through all these details is of paramount importance.

This has not been an easy day for the community college development office. Right after the Dionysus, Inc., representative leaves, Ms. Delphi appears.

Corporate Pressure: Ms. Delphi, of Datalink, Inc., a long-time, important corporate donor to your college, approaches you and says she wants to fund two computer technology scholarships. She wants it understood that upon graduation, the recipients will work for the company for two years. However, she insists that there be no legal documentation of this agreement, as it skirts the Internal Revenue Service's *quid pro quo* regulations. (If any conditions are attached that would bring benefit to the corporation, the gift cannot qualify as a charitable deduction.) When you discuss this matter with the vice-president for advancement, she basically tells you to hush up. This has happened before, and you are to proceed as the donor wants. What should you do?

If your stomach turns at the vice-president's response, there are good reasons. Ms. Delphi wants to claim the charitable deduction, but she also wants the direct benefits of the donation. She wants the scholarship recipients to give her gift right back to the company in the form of skilled labor. This is not philanthropy or gift giving. The circle of giving is too small; the exchange is too direct.

Think through this case in light of honesty, one of the virtues of relationships. Remember Al-Ghazálí's advice: "If you want to know the foulness of lying for yourself, consider the lying of someone else and how you shun it...."[16] Now trace the dishonesty involved in this arrangement. Ms. Delphi's offer is not a "gift," yet to "hush up" as instructed, you would need to represent it as such to colleagues and college officials, and to all the people, including auditors and IRS personnel, who review your record-keeping accounts. Imagine yourself in the place of any of these individuals; you would undoubtedly consider the practice "foul."

Also, what would you say to the students? If they think they are receiving genuine scholarships, they may well plan their futures quite differently than if they knew they were contractually committed to work for the donor's company. If they know they are to work there, they will have to compound the lying when they explain to family and friends why they "freely choose" to work at the company. It is unfair to the students to involve them in this kind of an arrangement.

Finally, you need to worry about your own integrity. In the same passage, Al-Ghalází writes, "If you come to be known as a liar, your uprightness becomes worthless, your word is not accepted, and (men's) eyes scorn and despise you."[17] By participating in this scheme, your own trustworthiness is compromised.

Ms. Delphi needs to think through what it is she wants, as there are legitimate alternative courses of action. If she wants her company to receive the benefits of the education the company funds, she could offer tuition reimbursement to her own employees to continue their education. Also, she could fund some scholarships as legitimate philanthropic donations and then offer internships to students in the program as a way of presenting her business as an attractive workplace.

8.3 JOINT VENTURES BETWEEN CORPORATIONS AND NONPROFIT ORGANIZATIONS

The preceding analysis applies to forms of corporate giving that come out of corporate philanthropy budgets. This section focuses on the joint ventures, principally cause-related marketing and sponsorships. Weeden and others advocate them with enthusiasm, seeing them as "win–win" solutions, with the corporation getting sales, an enhanced image, and publicity, while the nonprofit receives funding.[18] In stark contrast, Kathleen Kelly calls joint ventures "pseudo philanthropy."[19] Patricia Martin says flat out, "Corporate sponsorship is not philanthropy."[20] Maurice Gurin says that cause-related marketing "commercializes and degrades so much of what is altruistic and priceless in the voluntary sector."[21] This controversy merits some ethical analysis, but first we should define cause-related marketing and sponsorships, two principal forms that joint ventures take. Cause-related marketing is a marketing arrangement between a corporation and a nonprofit organization in which the corporation uses its association with the nonprofit as a way of attracting sales for its products. In return for the use of its name, the nonprofit receives contributions from the corporation, generally calibrated to the level of sales generated.[22]

Cause-related marketing arrangements became common in the 1990s. The first highly public arrangement was between American Express and the Statue of Liberty renovation project in the 1980s. American Express gave the restoration committee one cent each time a cardholder used the card and gave one dollar for every new card application that was approved. This arrangement generated $1.7 million for the renovation.[23] The Arthritis Foundation's association with Johnson & Johnson is also well known. The product line of Arthritis Foundation Pain Relievers, a brand name for over-the-counter pain relievers, provides the Arthritis Foundation with at least $1 million a year toward research. Package inserts provide educational information and offer a free membership in the Foundation.[24] Boys and Girls Clubs and Coca-Cola have a 10-year, $60 million dollar marketing agreement, which includes several cause-related marketing promotions. For example, one summer in selected markets Coke included discount bowling coupons with its products. For each coupon redeemed at an AMF bowling alley, one dollar went to Boys and Girls Clubs. Coke has also featured artwork by Boys and Girls Clubs members with some of its products, and sent a percentage of resulting sales to local clubs.[25] IEG Network, a consulting company specializing in sponsorships, estimated that in 1999, North American corporations would spend $1 billion on cause-related marketing arrangements.[26] Generally, companies spend two to four times as much money publicizing the arrangement as they actually send to the nonprofit.[27]

A second major form of joint ventures is corporate sponsorships. Here, corporations agree to fund events, exhibits, concerts, and so on in exchange for publicity. An IEG estimate placed corporate sponsorships in 1999 at $7.6 billion. Some research shows that money spent on sponsorships has greater advertising impact than an equivalent amount spent on direct advertising.[28]

To think through the ethics of joint ventures and to evaluate critics' claims that cause-related marketing and sponsorships are "phony philanthropy," let us separate out three questions:

1. Are joint ventures forms of philanthropy?
2. If not, what sorts of ethical concerns are raised by joint venture arrangements?
3. Even if joint ventures taken singly are morally unobjectionable, are there larger ethical concerns about their use?

(a) Are Joint Ventures Forms of Philanthropy?

In a 1989 article in *Foundation News,* Maurice Gurin was unsparing in his criticism: "I see companies, in the guise of giving charitable assistance, exploiting philanthropic causes for their own financial profit, commercializing the causes and threatening their traditional sources of longterm support. In my view, the marketers are taking literally the ironic observation made more than two centuries ago by Sir Thomas Browne—that the intent of charity is to ameliorate the condition of the benefactor."[29] Instead of calling them "win–win," Gurin would probably call joint ventures "corporations win by using nonprofits for their own advantage."

Gurin identifies several ways in which joint ventures do not fit our understanding of philanthropy. The "donations" they generate are not tax-deductible contributions, and there are explicit strings attached.[30] With cause-related marketing, the *quid pro quo* is measurable, with the amount of funding for the nonprofit directly dependent on sales. I think the critics are correct here. Joint ventures are not philanthropic gifts. They are better understood as forms of marketing whereby the nonprofit's name is used to attract consumers to purchase a product. The most direct analogy would be corporate use of celebrity sports figures' names in advertising. When consumers purchase a product linked to a nonprofit organization, they are not giving a philanthropic gift to the nonprofit via the corporation. Instead, they are funding the corporation's marketing department, just as they do with every other purchase. The corporation then reimburses the nonprofit for use of its name, just as it would reimburse celebrity sports figures for using their names in marketing campaigns.

If joint ventures are not philanthropy per se, does that automatically make them ethically suspect? Let us put them in perspective with the fuller picture of how nonprofit organizations receive financial support. I see joint ventures as revenue generators, more analogous to ticket prices and fees for service than to philanthropic contributions. Ticket prices and fees for service are not "phony philanthropy"—they are not forms of philanthropy at all. No one questions their ethical legitimacy, and they provide crucial support for many nonprofits. Likewise, joint ventures are nonphilanthropic ways of generating income. With fees for service, there are ethical concerns in setting parameters on their use. For example, we should ask whether the fees represent a fair exchange for the services provided and whether they are explained to clients before payment in a clear, informative manner. We should also ask whether the fees should be waived or reduced for those who cannot afford them. On this line of analysis, joint ventures can be legitimate revenue generators as long as the parameters are set carefully. In the next section, what these parameters are will be discussed.

(b) Ethical Parameters for Joint Ventures

In considering whether to enter into cause-related marketing agreements and sponsorships, the three basic value commitments from the ethical decision-making chart are applicable, so this section will be organized around them.

(i) Organizational Mission
The first question to ask is whether the corporation's mission and the particular features of the joint venture are compatible with the nonprofit's mission. Some incompatibilities are obvious. Amnesty International, for example, does not accept money from arms manufacturers because it publicly criticizes selling arms to countries with records of human rights violations.[31] Children's health services and recreation programs are incompatible with tobacco, alcohol, and "adult" media companies. In some cases, it is more difficult to decide if product and mission are compatible. For example, if the manufacturer of Barbie dolls wanted to sponsor Girl Scout events, one can imagine the ensuing debate over how much Barbie has contributed to girls' obsession with glamour and body size, with less attention

going to acquiring skills and competencies. Some may even ask if Barbie has contributed to young women's problems with anorexia.[32] Just as the relationship between individual donors and nonprofits should be based on mutual understanding and shared values, so joint ventures should reflect shared values and mutual commitment to the organizational mission.

(ii) Relationships

All of the ethical considerations regarding relationships between non-profit organizations and donors from Chapters 3 and 5 apply to corporate partners in joint ventures as well. Maintaining an atmosphere of healthy trust among the nonprofit, the corporation, and the public is paramount. In joint ventures, corporations obviously are acting in their own self-interest. Just as individual donors often give for a variety of reasons, so we should not object if corporate self-interest is *one* of a corporation's motivations. As long as the nonprofit's mission is not distorted by the joint venture, its reputation for integrity is not harmed, and genuine community well-being is enhanced, then simultaneous corporate benefit is not a problem. However, it is sometimes difficult to assess just what benefits the corporation has in mind. It is worrisome if a corporation tries to use nonprofit collaboration to give a cover of legitimacy to ethically questionable behavior. Consider this case:

> **Sympathy Money.** Board member David Dedicated is ecstatic. After months of careful cultivation, he is confident that Profitable Plastics, Inc. is on the verge of agreeing to sponsor an expensive touring art exhibit at your museum. However, through contacts close to state government, you have just learned that Profitable Plastics has been violating state environmental standards for years and may face indictment. (But then, the state environmental agency is notoriously inefficient.) You are concerned that the company's principal motive is to gain public sympathy before the story hits the press. You want the exhibit, but worry that the museum is being "used." What do you do?

If Profitable Plastics wants to use the museum sponsorship to bolster its shaky credibility, then it is not respecting the museum's need to maintain its own credibility as an institution of integrity. The museum should be very cautious if it suspects the corporation's concern with its own self-interest overrides its respect for the museum's reputation as an ethical organization.

A principal concern regarding joint ventures and trust centers on the virtue of honesty. At a recent NSFRE chapter meeting, members of our ethics education committee took a quick survey of those attending. We asked them, "Would typical donors to your nonprofit think that if a nonprofit logo is on a product, that means the nonprofit endorses the product? Would they think that they are being philanthropic if they buy a product and the producer says a percentage of the profits go to a charity? Would they think that if an over-the-counter drug is endorsed by a health-related nonprofit, then that drug is superior to other brands?" Virtually all those attending agreed with each statement. Admittedly, this was not a scientifically designed, statistically significant survey. What is troubling is that each statement is based on false impressions about joint ventures. If these responses are not simply idiosyncratic to the Ohio Miami Valley, then I am very concerned about the ethics of joint ventures.

Even if joint ventures, and particularly cause-related marketing, per se are ethically benign, a nagging worry about deception remains. If the success of cause-related marketing rests on consumers' false impressions, then consumer trust is misplaced and agency and system trust potentially damaged. Customers of a corporation and potential donors to nonprofits deserve to know just what the terms of the arrangement are. They deserve to know if a cause-related marketing arrangement generates a lot of media splash but relatively little income for the nonprofit. They deserve to know when use of a nonprofit logo does not constitute an endorsement or indicate that the product is superior over its competitors, and whether the nonprofit has signed any sort of exclusive agreement with the corporation. For maintaining trust with the public, we should use the same criterion as for individual donors: If knowledge of anything about the arrangement would alter a potential donor's or customer's decision about whether to participate, then the potential donor or customer is entitled to that information. Anything less is manipulative and contrary to honesty and continuing trust.[33]

It is helpful to distinguish different senses in which we can support nonprofit organizations. I make a point to buy gas from a nearby service station. The people there do a nice job of servicing my car and, as I watch similar small service stations close up shop, I think it is important to support the one in my neighborhood. I am supporting the station, but my support is not philanthropic. Similarly, when I attend a nonprofit theater, I support the theater by buying a ticket and filling a seat, but these are not modes of philanthropic support in the way a voluntary contribution of time or money would be. Likewise, when some of my purchase price for a market good goes to a nonprofit organization, I have contributed to its support, but not philanthropically. I have supported the nonprofit in the same way that I support celebrity athletes who endorse products that I buy. This is an important distinction, and one that should be made known to the public. It is misleading and dishonest for either a corporation or a nonprofit to foster the impression that purchases are instances of voluntary, philanthropic donations.

(iii) Integrity

One component of integrity is maintaining one's own independent judgment. Joint ventures become ethically problematic when they diminish or threaten to diminish the nonprofit's ability to act with independent judgment. This is all the more true when maintining intellectual objectivity is part of the mission of the institution. An example comes from 1997, when the Alyeska Pipeline Services Company sponsored the Smithsonian Institution's National Museum of American History's exhibit on the Trans-Alaska pipeline. The company contributed $300,000 and items for the exhibit to the Smithsonian. Officials at the museum claim that the company did not interfere in any way with the curators' work in designing the exhibit. However, critics contend that the exhibit gives only brief mention to the Exxon *Valdez* oil spill. A representative of the environmental group, the Alaska Wilderness League, claims the exhibit was unbalanced in "celebrating this engineering marvel without showing the risks."[34] Because presenting exhibits with intellectual objectivity is at the heart of a historical museum's mission and its public credibility rests upon faithfulness to this mission, entering into sponsorship arrangements such as this are fraught with difficulties and require great caution and careful consideration.

8.4 LARGER FRAMEWORK CONCERNS: BLURRING THE LINES

One of Gurin's criteria for assessing whether a fund-raising technique is philanthropic asks, "Could the offer blur the public's understanding of the difference between philanthropy and business? That distinction is essential if philanthropic support of voluntary organizations is to continue."[35] Our society is increasingly commercialized.

More and more personal interactions take place through contractual arrangements rather than through giftlike ties of family, friendship, or Buddhist-like universal compassion. In advertising, nonmarket values are ubiquitous, suggesting that if you buy the right products, friendship, sexual allure, love, and wisdom will all be yours.[36] As non-profits enter partnerships with corporations, and especially when the available vocabulary for describing these partnerships is the vocabulary of commerce, nonprofits need to be exceedingly careful that they define themselves, talk about their work, and act primarily as sustainers of the gift economy of philanthropy. Although both corporations and nonprofits have giftlike and marketlike elements, gifts economies and market economies are distinct, and we must take care not to blur the lines. "Consumer" and "donor" are two distinct roles, located in two distinct types of economies. If people think they are being philanthropic when the breakfast cereal company sends a few pennies to a nonprofit, and begin to think that this is an acceptable substitute for donating to the annual fund, then the gift economy is undermined.

In an article for the *Nonprofit Times,* Jon Van Til reflected on a conference he attended on collaborations among nonprofits, government, and business. Sometimes, the most important thing to notice is what is not said. Van Til mused, "There was no discussion of why one might want to collaborate–just a lot of management school advice on how to do it." In all the talk about stragetic plans and mutual advantage, there was precious little assessment of whether all this partnering will "achieve genuine accomplishments in a humane way."[37] Corporations and nonprofit organizations have done enormous good by joining their energies and their economic resources in addressing social needs and creating vibrant communities. Corporate–nonprofit partnerships have revived ailing neighborhoods and city centers, improved education and health care, and sustained artistic excellence. Corporate personnel give invaluable service to nonprofits as board members and service volunteers. In corporate–nonprofit collaborations, however, nonprofits and fund raisers need to remember their responsibilities as educators and facilitators of the gift economy of philanthropy. The spirit of the gift must be kept vital. This vitality is fed by the virtues of the gift economy: generosity, charity, compassion, gratitude, and mutuality, If these virtues stop informing our participation in nonprofits, if they are transmuted into "investments," then the gift economy becomes a parody of market exchanges.

DISCUSSION QUESTIONS

1. Reflect on the vocabulary shift from *corporate social responsibility* to *enlightened self-interest* to *corporate social investing*. Are these different ways of expressing the same idea? How do these terms fit in with your own experiences in dealing with corporations?

2. Do the virtues of philanthropy as a gift economy-generosity, charity, compassion, gratitude, and mutuality-have a role in working with corporate donors? In what ways?

3. What do you think of the analogy between cause-related marketing and businesses using celebrity figures in advertising? Is the analogy appropriate? With cause-related marketing, are nonprofits essentially functioning as "marketing arms" of for-profit businesses?

4. In this chapter, a major concern with cause-related marketing is that many people who participate have false impressions regarding how cause-related marketing works. What particular measures should nonprofits and businesses take to clear up these false impressions?

5. The NSFRE Code of Ethical Principles states that its members adhere "to the absolute obligation to safeguard the public trust." With nonprofit participation in joint ventures, do you think that the public's cynicism about corporate greed and self-interest will rub off on nonprofits, weakening public trust in philanthropy?

CASE STUDIES

Tobacco Toll. Addiction, heart disease, cancer—the toll of tobacco on health is well known. Yet, tobacco companies' money has funded vital services through many nonprofits. For example, Philip Morris has given substantial amounts to programs helping hungry people. Cash grants totaling $50 million will go primarily to groups feeding the elderly and people with acquired immune deficiency syndrome (AIDS). The company will donate $50 million worth of food, to be distributed through Second Harvest's network of food banks.[38] Is it consistent with their missions for the following types of organizations to accept grants or sponsorship from a tobacco company?

a. Children's health clinics
b. General population health clinics
c. Children's educational or recreational organizations
d. Drug rehabilitation centers
e. Faith-based housing rehabilitation programs
f. Arts organizations
g. Food banks and soup kitchens

Announcer or Advertiser? A local theater company has had a long and satisfactory relationship with a local radio station. The station frequently sponsors productions, and one of the morning talk show personalities often welcomes the audience to performances. The station asks if while introducing the next performance, the personality, in addition to giving his name and station affiliation, could also announce that the morning show has a contest going. People who call in with the correct answers to trivia questions will receive a Las Vegas vacation package. You value the relationship between your theater and the station, but worry that this crosses the line from sponsorship into outright advertising. The station manager argues that by sponsoring the production, the station bought the right to announce the contest. What are the ethical concerns here?

Fund Raising or Entrepreneurship? The president of your volunteer association comes to you, out of breath and all excited. She says that she has just signed up with Expansive, a new long-distance telephone service, which may in the future branch into on-line services and gas and electric service. The company does not advertise, but individuals who sign up as agents get a percentage for enrolling new customers. The volunteer organization president tells you that her organization wants to sign up new customers and donate their percentages to your organization. Do you see any ethical problems with this arrangement?

Cozy Business. A member of the faculty of a two-year community college phones the advancement officer with an idea for supporting the college's annual fund. This faculty member has a print and frame shop that she runs "on the side." (Many other faculty members also have businesses.) She suggests that she bring a selection of inexpensive prints to her office for a couple of days and, through the college's e-mail system, invite faculty and staff to come to her office and look at what she has for sale. She says her e-mail message will state that 10 percent of all sales will go to the college's annual fund. Do you see ethical problems with this arrangement?

Corporate volunteers. A corporation has offered its employees the opportunity to volunteer for your nonprofit on company time. The company has prepared some flyers and email messages to use in recruiting its employees. Some company representatives bring the literature by your office before distributing it, in keeping with the original agreement. The only reasons for volunteering that it mentions are self-interested ones: networking with other business professionals, developing leadership skills, lowering work-related stress levels, and so on. The company representatives are uninterested, and even a bit turned off, by your attempts to insert language about philanthropic motivation. They tell you, "All that philanthropic touchy-feely stuff won't sell at our company. The most important thing is moving up the corporate ladder, and the employees we attract share this perspective." How do you respond?

Social Justice Troubles. You work for a large religious organization that has an active social justice department. You have been working with the local plant division of a multinational corporation and are close to closing a gift for a large donation to your urban youth literacy and recreation program. You happen to overhear a conversation in which you learn that your organization's social justice department is planning to target that plant's corporate headquarters in New York for bringing in illegal aliens from Central America and working them under poor safety conditions, at less than minimum wage. You do not know whether there are any such workers at the local plant. What do you do?

NOTES

1. Jerome L. Himmelstein, *Looking Good & Doing Good: Corporate Philanthropy and Corporate Power* (Bloomington: Indiana University Press, 1997), p. 16.
2. Craig Smith, "The New Corporate Philanthropy." *Harvard Business Review* (May–June, 1994), p. 107.
3. Supreme Court of New Jersey, *A.P. Smith Manufacturing Co. v. Barlow,* 98 A 2d 581 (1953). Opinion of Judge J. Jacobs; excerpted in Tom L. Beauchamp and Norman E. Bowie (eds.): *Ethical Theory and Business,* 5th ed. (Upper Saddle River, NJ: Prentice Hall, 1997), pp. 110–112. See also Jerome L. Himmelstein, *Looking Good & Doing Good: Corporate Philanthropy and*

Corporate Power (Bloomington: Indiana University Press, 1997), pp. 21–22.

4. Quoted in Jerome L. Himmelstein, *Looking Good & Doing Good: Corporate Philanthropy and Corporate Power* (Bloomington: Indiana University Press, 1997), p. 25.

5. John A. Yankey, "Corporate Support of Nonprofit Organizations: Partnerships Across the Sectors." in Dwight F. Burlingame and Dennis R. Young, (eds.): *Corporate Philanthropy at the Crossroads* (Bloomington: Indiana University Press, 1996), p. 9.

6. Curt Weeden, *Corporate Social Investing: The Breakthrough Strategy for Giving and Getting Corporate Contributions* (San Francisco: Berrett-Koehler, 1998), p. 39.

7. Jerome L. Himmelstein, *Looking Good & Doing Good: Corporate Philanthropy and Corporate Power* (Bloomington: Indiana University Press, 1997), pp. 32–33.

8. Curt Weeden, *Corporate Social Investing: The Breakthrough Strategy for Giving and Getting Corporate Contributions* (San Francisco: Berrett-Koehler Publishers, 1998), p. 36.

9. Pablo Eisenberg, quoted in Kathleen Kelly, *Effective Fund Raising Management* (Mahwah, NJ: Lawrence Erlbaum Associates, 1998), p. 596.

10. Craig Smith, "The New Corporate Philanthropy." *Harvard Business Review* (May–June, 1994), p. 112; Curt Weeden, *Corporate Social Investing: The Breakthrough Strategy for Giving and Getting Corporate Contributions* (San Francisco: Berrett-Koehler, 1998).

11. Adam Smith, *An Inquiry into the Nature and Causes of the Wealth of Nations* (1776); reprint ed., abridged by Laurence Dickey (Indianapolis: Hackett, 1993), p. 11

12. Adam Smith, quoted in Amartya Sen, "Does Business Ethics Make Economic Sense?" *Business Ethics Quarterly*, vol. 3, no. 1 (1993), p. 47.

13. Amartya Sen, "Does Business Ethics Make Economic Sense?" *Business Ethics Quarterly*, vol. 3, no. 1 (1993), pp. 45–54.

14. Lester M. Salamon, *America's Nonprofit Sector: A Primer* (New York: The Foundation Center, 1992); Lester M. Salamon and Helmut K. Anheier, The Emerging Nonprofit Sector: An Overview (New York: Manchester University Press, 1996).

15. Timothy Smith, "Sponsorship Guidelines Are a Moral Necessity." *The Chronicle of Philanthropy*, vol. 10, no. 24 (October 8, 1998), p. 56.

16. Al-Ghazáli, *The Faith and Practice of Al-Ghazáli*, trans. by W. Montgomery Watt (Oxford, Oneworld Publications, 1994) p. 148.

17. *Id.*, pp. 147–8.

18. This is Curt Weeden's central argument in *Corporate Social Investing: The Breakthrough Strategy for Giving and Getting Corporate Contributions* (San Francisco: Berrett-Koehler Publishers, 1998). See chapters 2–4.

19. Kathleen Kelly, *Effective Fund Raising Management* (Mahwah, NJ: Lawrence Erlbaum Associates, 1998), p. 596.

20. Patricia Martin, "In the Company of Sponsors." *Advancing Philanthropy* (Spring 1996), p. 30.

21. Quoted in Irving Warner, "Marketing Deals Shouldn't Be Child's Play." *The Chronicle of Philanthropy*, vol. 10, no. 23 (September 24, 1998), p. 52.

22. John A. Yankey, "Corporate Support of Nonprofit Organizations: Partnerships across the Sectors." in Dwight F. Burlingame and Dennis R. Young, (eds.): *Corporate Philanthropy at the Crossroads* (Bloomington: Indiana University Press, 1996), p. 12.

23. Maurice Gurin, "Phony Philanthropy?" *Foundation News* (May/June, 1989), p. 32.

24. Don L. Riggin, "Cause-Branding: Next Step or Misstep?" in Dwight F. Burlingame and Warren F. Ilchman, (eds.): *Alternative Revenue Sources: Prospects, Requirements, and Concerns for Nonprofits. New Directions for Philanthropic Fundraising*, no. 12 (Jossey-Bass, Summer 1996), p. 136.

25. Boys and Girls Clubs Web site: www.bgca.org/html/partnershipindex.html.

26. "Marketing Deals May Reap $1 Billion." *The Chronicle of Philanthropy*, vol. 11, no. 9 (February 25, 1999), p. 40.

27. Curt Weeden, *Corporate Social Investing: The Breakthrough Strategy for Giving and Getting Corporate Contributions* (San Francisco: Berrett-Koehler, 1998), p. 163; Susan Gray, "Charities' Income From Sponsorships Up 10%." *The Chronicle of Philanthropy*, vol. 10, no. 11 (March 26, 1998), p. 20.

28. Craig Smith, "Desperately Seeking Data: Why Research is Crucial to the New Corporate Philanthropy." in Dwight F. Burlingame and Dennis R. Young (eds.): *Corporate Philanthropy at the Crossroads* (Bloomington: Indiana University Press, 1996), p. 4.

29. Maurice Gurin, "Phony Philanthropy?" *Foundation News* (May/Jun, 1989) p. 32.

30. *Id.,* p. 33.

31. William Schulz, "Tips on Ties to Corporate Sponsors." *The Chronicle of Philanthropy,* vol. 10, no. 21 (August 27, 1998), pp. 39–40.

32. If Barbie were 5'4" tall, the average height for women in the United States, her waist would be 17 inches, her chest would be 32 inches, and her hips would be 28 inches, which surely would qualify her as clinically anorexic. See Jacqueline Urla and Alan C. Swedlund, "The Anthropometry of Barbie." in Jennifer Terry and Jacqueline Urla (eds.): *Deviant Bodies: Critical Perspectives on Difference in Science and Popular Culture* (Bloomington: Indiana University Press, 1995), pp. 277–313.

33. For an excellent discussion of the ethics of cause-related marketing, see Peggy H. Cunningham, "Sleeping with the Devil? Exploring Ethical Concerns Associated with Cause-related Marketing." in Margaret M. Maxwell (ed.): *Marketing the Nonprofit: The Challenge of Fundraising in a Consumer Culture. New Directions in Philanthropic Fundraising* vol. 18 (San Francisco: Jossey-Bass, Winter 1997), pp. 55–76.

34. Vince Stehle, "Pipeline Company's Role in Smithsonian's Alaska Exhibit Fuels Criticism." *The Chronicle of Philanthropy,* vol. 10, no. 4 (November 27, 1997), p. 36.

35. Maurice Gurin, "Phony Philanthropy?" *Foundation News* (May/June, 1989) p. 33.

36. For an insightful discussion of how advertising and marketing commodify inherently non-market values, see John Waide, "The Making of Self and World in Advertising." *Journal of Business Ethics,* vol. 6 (1987), pp. 73–79.

37. Jon Van Til, "What a Mesh: Crossing the Borders or Just Grinding Gears?" *NonProfit Times* (May 1999) pp. 47, 48.

38. Marina Dundjerski, "Philip Morris Pledges Millions to Fight Hunger." *The Chronicle of Philanthropy,* vol. 11, no. 11 (March 25, 1999), p. 14.

Fostering Diversity

"NSFRE members foster cultural diversity and pluralistic values, and treat all people with dignity and respect." This statement is included in NSFRE's "Statements of Ethical Principles," a part of the ethics code that every member signs as a condition of membership. What does this statement mean? What are NSFRE members committing themselves to do when they sign this statement? In this chapter, we will use this statement to explore the ethical dimensions of diversity. The specific actions fund raisers should take to foster cultural diversity will vary, depending on their agency's geographic location, the specific population served, community demographics, and so on. This is not a how-to chapter; instead, it undertakes a broader philosophical exploration of what it means to foster cultural diversity. The resources in the conceptual toolbox will point us toward attitudes and approaches through which to foster diversity and treat all people with dignity and respect.

9.1 WHY DIVERSITY?

Why should fund raisers be so concerned with diversity? Demographics are a good place to start. The membership of NSFRE is 95 percent white. In 1998, 74 percent of the U.S. population was white, non-Hispanic; this number will drop to 53 percent by the year 2050.[1] The United States accounts for only 5 percent of the world's population; the so-called developed countries account for only 20 percent. With changing demographics and increasing interest in international philanthropy, dealing with diversity is inescapable.

Aside from demographics, there are additional reasons why we as individuals and as members of nonprofit organizations should welcome diversity in our work and lives. Jane Addams gives a particularly clear statement of how enriching diversity can be. When she started Hull House, her concern for her immigrant neighbors was genuine, although at the time Addams thought of her role in terms of bringing the arts, culture, and orderliness of American middle-class life to the chaotic conditions she found in the neighborhood. But by living there and interacting with her neighbors as neighbors and not as "charity cases," Addams learned a great deal. The more she tried to understand her neighbors within their own cultural contexts and perceptions of the world, the more she realized what treasures they had to share. Addams explains, "We may make their foreign birth a handicap to them and to us, or we may make it a very interesting and stimulating factor in their development and ours.... I believe that we may get, and should get, something of that sort of revivifying effect and upspringing of new culture from our contact with the groups who come to us from foreign countries, and that we can get it in no other way."[2] With minor adjustments in vocabulary, this quotation could pass as a contemporary affirmation of the value of diversity. Imagination, intellectual agility, and emotional receptivity can all be enhanced through engagement with diverse cultural practices.

The most important reason for fostering cultural diversity is given in the statement from the NSFRE ethics code: to treat all people with dignity and respect. Recall that in Chapter 3, we defined respect in terms of three dimensions: fundamental moral worth, attention to particularities, and generosity in judgment. We demonstrate respect for people's fundamental moral worth through paying attention to the particularities of their individual lives as situated within their cultural contexts, and responding to our mutual encounters in a spirit of generosity.

Diversity is hard to talk about. Sessions on diversity are often poorly attended, and those who participate in them are often already well-aware of diversity issues. Why is diversity so hard to discuss? Fear and discomfort account for part of it. We do not want to embarrass or offend others; we are afraid of being misinterpreted. Diversity issues go right to the core of people's own sense of identity and their fundamental beliefs. Our social skills, so finely tuned to our everyday environment, become awkward and we feel incompetent outside of our usual arenas of comfort. So we avoid these problems by staying away.

Diversity is also hard to talk about because it is so complicated. Here are three of the complications; simply identifying them may help make discussions of diversity a little easier.

1. *Definitions.* Discussions of diversity are difficult because people often define central terms too narrowly. When I tell my students that we are going to talk about gender, they start talking about women. When I say we will discuss diversity, they assume I am referring to people of color. I have to remind them that middle-class white people have a culture, although because it is so dominant, people living inside it sometimes mistake their own culturally shaped perspectives for "the way things are" for everyone. Also, men have gender, as well as women. Men and women both go through gender socialization while growing up and both face social resistance if they press accepted gender boundaries very hard.

2. *Culture and individual personalities.* It is hard to talk about diversity because of the complex, convoluted ways in which culture and individual differences intertwine as they together shape our personalities. Cultural differences among different cultural groups are real, yet within a given cultural group there is enormous individual variation. We should always hesitate to judge individuals on the basis of group membership alone, yet we should also hesitate to say "that's just a matter of individual personality," as if cultural differences were insignificant.

3. *Multiple group memberships.* Think of the diversity check-off lists: ethnicity, economic class, gender, sexual orientation, age, religion, physical ability, plus all the other categories diversity workshop leaders worry about forgetting when they put this list on the flipchart. Diversity would be a lot easier to talk about if we could just divide up the population, put each person into one of these boxes, and then start studying their traits. Unfortunately (or fortunately), it is not this easy because every individual has multiple memberships, participating in most of the categories on the list. This is further complicated by the fact that people can change some of their memberships. They can switch religions, marry into and raise children in a different ethnic group, get older, become more or less able-bodied, and so on. Multiple membership is why the phrase, "women *and* minorities" is so ironic. In people's zeal of trying to be inclusive, the women who *are* members of a minority group tend to be overlooked. We can appreciate that wonderful book title, *All the Women Are White, All the Blacks Are Men, But Some of Us Are Brave.*[3]

In this chapter, the dimensions of ethics as narrative will be used to elaborate on what it means to foster cultural diversity, with sections devoted to diversity and sympathetic understanding, diversity and temporal context, and diversity and social context. Each section contains a fairly lengthy example. The statement about diversity in the NSFRE ethics code refers to treating all people with dignity and respect. Because one component of respect is attention to particularly, each example contains enough detail to make the point that respect for diversity is not just an attitude, but brings with it responsibilities for knowledge and engagement. Throughout these sections, we will see how valuable the process skills of playing with polyrhythms and appreciating astigmatism can be. In the concluding section of the chapter we will again consult Jane Addams for ideas on how to go about fostering cultural diversity.

9.2 SYMPATHETIC UNDERSTANDING OF DIVERSE GIVING TRADITIONS

This section uses an extended discussion of giving traditions among Japanese-Americans and a brief discussion of age discrimination to illustrate how important sympathetic understanding is for treating people with respect. Without sympathetic understanding, that is, without knowledge and appreciation of a particular group's history and culture, people outside that culture are apt to misunderstand and misinterpret the group's practices. This may well lead to disrespectful attitudes and actions.

One common misperception is that white Americans are philanthropic, giving generously to help the needy and to build community institutions, while ethnic groups in America are less philanthropic. Statistics on charitable giving and volunteering to nonprofit organizations reinforce this misperception. Some surveys report that white Americans give twice as much as Hispanics and African Americans, relative to income.[4] In light of such statistics, one can imagine some fund raisers complaining, "Why don't they give more?" with "they" being a fill-in-the-blank name for a cultural group different from the fund raiser's own. Applying the perspective of ethics as narrative by using sympathetic understanding will help us correct these misperceptions in the survey data.

In *Philanthropy in Communities of Color,* Smith, Shue, Vest, and Villareal report the findings of their extensive research into the giving patterns of eight ethnic communities in the San Francisco area, including Mexican, Guatemalan, Salvadoran, Filipino, Chinese, Japanese, Korean, and African American groups. Their findings show the bias in the statistics referred to above. They write, "The present study suggests that the *amount* (relative to personal resources) of minority giving may be roughly consistent with that of white America but that the *forms and beneficiaries* of minority giving may be quite different."[5] In their report, the authors stress that in order to understand giving patterns in a given community we need to understand how its members construct reality in very basic ways. Conceptions of what "family" means and of what responsibilities belong to the family and to the state vary significantly among different communities and so suggest distinctive frameworks for each group's giving traditions.

One of these communities, that of Japanese Americans, will be discussed to illustrate how we can use the ethics as narrative perspective to approach the question, "Why don't they give more." But first a caveat: This is not a thorough analysis of giving traditions among Japanese Americans; that would require volumes. In a few pages, the best we can do is hint at complex realities. This discussion will point out the sorts of information and attitudes that accompany attention to particularity, an aspect of treating people with respect. As you read through the discussion of Japanese American giving traditions, keep in mind that the point of the discussion is to illustrate in a concrete way the sorts of philosophical, religious, and historical background we need to know and appreciate in order to foster cultural diversity. You can use this discussion as a model for the types of information to seek when learning about other cultural groups.

We can approach this task by asking two questions: First, who are "they"; that is, what is their world view and what is their historical experience? Second, what are their giving traditions? These questions have both philosophical and historical components, so some background is in order.

(a) Giving Traditions Among Japanese Americans

First, who are "they"? Tu Wei-ming, a contemporary Confucian scholar, claims that "Confucianism is the cultural DNA of East Asian Societies."[6] To understand giving patterns in East Asian societies, we start with the basic Confucian world view. Confucius (551–479 B.C.E.) was born into a China that was fiercely divided and disorganized. Surrounded by the slaughter and cruelty of war, his central question became, "What would a harmonious society look like, and how could it be achieved?" This was no mere academic exercise, but an intensely practical concern. Confucius spent his life as an itinerant teacher; like Socrates, he posed many questions, gave few answers, and wrote nothing down. Yet his wisdom has provided guidance for over two millennia.

Confucianism is better understood as a moral and social philosophy rather than a religion. Stated simply, Confucius's pattern for a harmonious society is that of hierarchically ordered units with reciprocal duties at every level. The key to a harmonious society, and not merely an orderly one, is cultivation of virtuous character. The foundation for a harmonious society is the family. "Only when families are regulated are states governed," *The Great Learning* begins.[7] Children owe parents loyalty and filial piety, with particular attention to and respect for the elderly. Parents in turn are to treat their children with benevolence and give particular attention to moral education. When families are well regulated, their harmony will radiate out to villages, districts, and throughout the state. Rulers in turn have the duty to treat the people with benevolence and regulate public policy in ways that supports harmony throughout the state.

Human-heartedness is the most fundamental value in Confucianism. It is a complex concept, difficult to translate. It is often described in terms of benevolence, empathy, a sincere concern for others' well-being, and a sincere, life-long cultivation of virtues in oneself. Human-heartedness is not a kind of altruistic love for humankind in general. Rather, it begins as particularized love within one's family, and then extends outward as branches from a tree.[8]

Rituals are the behavioral counterpart to human-heartedness. With a thoroughly disorganized society as his context, Confucius believed that people needed external forms through which to express human-heartedness, forms that others would recognize and interpret as outward manifestations of inward benevolence and respect. Rituals of gift-giving are particularly important for sustaining familial and social harmony. These rituals indicate what to give, on what occasions, to which people, and how one should reciprocate. Rituals without human-heartedness are empty and hypocritical; human-heartedness without rituals cannot by itself lead to harmony. A well-functioning harmonious society needs human-heartedness as its foundation, expressed through well-recognized rituals of behavior.

This is the Confucian pattern: a well-ordered family, its members highly responsive to and responsible for each others' well-being, branching outward to a state that is benevolent and paternalistically responsive to and responsible for its citizens. Notice that gifts of goods and services are deeply entwined within the reciprocal obligations of each level of society. If families and government each do their part, there is no need for formal philanthropic institutions. All of the needs that nonprofits address in Western society would be handled either by family, extended family, village, or state.

Of course, this discussion of Confucianism is just the beginning. To understand fully giving traditions among Japanese people, we would need to study the contributions of Buddhism, Shintoism, the physical character of Japan as an island sitting on faultlines with relatively little agricultural land, and many other factors.

Knowing a cultural group's history is also important for understanding its giving traditions. Japanese people first arrived there in the late nineteenth century. First-generation immigrants, called *issei*, were typically farmers, and, faced with social and legal discrimination, they formed mutual aid societies that provided housing, credit, and other forms of assistance. These societies replicated many of the familial and communal forms of giving found in Japan. Some formal associations were started, including the Japanese Association of America at the turn of the century and the Japanese American Citizens League in 1930. Many of their associations, as well as their agriculturally based livelihoods, were completely disrupted when the U.S. government placed Japanese American citizens in internment camps during World War II. After the war, second-(*nisei*) and third-generation (*sansei*) Japanese Americans began anew to construct their place in society and to reconstruct patterns of giving. Although many Japanese Americans have entered professional and managerial ranks and many contribute to mainstream philanthropic organizations, patterns of giving from their Confucian and Japanese heritage are still influential. Many of the people interviewed for *Philanthropy in Communities of Color* stressed how important familial and extended family obligations were to them, particularly caring for the elderly. They consider Japanese American associations to be important for preserving Japanese cultural identity, which some fear will be lost through assimilation and intermarriage. One of those interviewed noted, "I think there are a lot of differences due to internment. There is a cautiousness in Japanese Americans that is not in mainstream communities.... They have a very insular identity; there is us and them."9

This brief summary points toward a response to our hypothetical fund raiser's question, "Why don't they give more?". "They" are multifaceted people with individual and generational differences who share a heritage of philosophical world views and historical experiences. They *do* give more and they give generously. But giving through family networks and to ethnic associations rather than formal nonprofits accords better with the philosophical orientation and historical realities of their experiences as Japanese Americans. These stand in contrast to the conceptual and historical experiences of those Americans of European descent that Alexis de Tocqueville observed forming "moral associations" so busily. To treat Japanese Americans with respect, people from other traditions need to know enough about their history and culture to be able to enter their perspective sympathetically and imaginatively. Analogously, fostering cultural diversity and treating all people with dignity and respect entails that we learn a great deal of specific information about a given group's philosophical, religious, and historical backgrounds.

Appreciating diverse giving traditions is a form of playing with polyrhythms. I once participated in a workshop on African music in which the facilitator helped us in literally playing with polyrhythms. One section of the group clapped out the first rhythm, which was interesting in itself. A second section layered a very different rhythm on top of that. Initially, it took a great deal of concentration not to be distracted by the first rhythm, but after a while, we were able to clap our own pattern while enjoying the interplay. Then, a third and a fourth group added their own distinctive rhythms. When all the individual rhythms are layered together, the distinctive qualities of each become more salient; how each contributes to the whole ensemble is more apparent. We can think of each giving tradition as a rhythm distinctive in itself. In learning other cultures' patterns of giving, one's own tradition goes from *the* way of giving to being simply one pattern in interplay with others. We can enjoy the unique character of each and appreciate the rich layering of them all.

(b) Sympathic Understanding and Diversity Among Generations

We often think of diversity in terms of various ethnic groups, but there are plenty of diversity concerns *within* a given ethnic group. Generational differences, for example, often bring tensions which call for sympathetic understanding. In *Beyond Race and Gender*, R. Roosevelt Thomas gives the example of a plant manager who reported that the greatest cultural gap in his workplace was not among ethnic groups, but between senior and junior white male managers.[10] Age discrimination is not new. Some of us remember when most airline passengers were businessmen and flight attendants were stewardesses: thin, attractive, and single. If a stewardess lost any of those qualifications, she was fired. By age 32, women faced mandatory retirement, as they were considered too old to be stewardesses. When their policies were challenged in court, the airlines tried to argue that these qualities were bona fide occupational requirements. Their customers wanted it that way, and the airlines wanted to keep their customers happy. The airlines lost the case. The airlines may have been right in the sense that some of their customers might have been disgruntled when older, shorter, heavier, married, and sometimes even male flight attendants brought them beverages and assisted them to emergency exits. But the airlines had to rethink just what services their flight attendants were supposed to offer, and what specific qualifications correlated with those responsibilities.[11]

Consider this scenario:

> **Age-old Relevance:** An arts organization with an aging membership wants to appeal to a younger audience. There is an opening on the development staff, and the hiring committee of which you are a member is debating whether age is a bona fide qualification for the position. One member argues that a young person will establish rapport with younger prospects and give a living message that the organization is genuinely interested in age inclusivity. A 58-year-old committee member confesses discomfort, thinking of several of his highly competent peers, who are being treated as irrelevant in today's job market. What can you contribute to this conversation?

Before making any decisions, the committee should use sympathetic understanding to enter the perspectives of workers at various stages of their careers. Here, sympathetic understanding and attention to context can help us think beyond the confining box of "young people establish rapport with younger prospects." Of course, this statement is true. But extend sympathetic understanding to aging fund raisers, remembering that all fund raisers are aging fund raisers, and all will get old unless they die first. While appreciating the easy rapport young peers establish among themselves, the committee should also consider the shape of the society that makes this rapport so easy. The dominant culture in the United States is segregated by age to a significant extent, compared with many other societies. As many members of ethnic groups interviewed for *Philanthropy in Communities of Color* commented, American culture has a widespread lack of respect for older people. This is a society in which looks and glamour are often accepted as substitutes for experience and wisdom. To make hiring decisions based on age-related rapport reinforces this context of age discrimination, rather than working to change it. Hiring decisions are complex, but this sort of consideration, as an aspect of treating people with respect, should be part of the conversation.

In this section we have looked at Japanese American giving traditions and concerns about age discrimination to illustrate how important sympathetic understanding is to fostering cultural diversity and treating all people with dignity and respect. In her article on diversity for *Advancing Philanthropy*, Janice Gow Pettey writes, "I have learned to wear the shoes of the residents of the communities I'm in as it is their footprints that will head the way to successful fund raising."[12] This is a lovely expression of how sympathetic understanding of diverse giving traditions can facilitate fund raisers' work in the philanthropic gift economy.

9.3 DIVERSITY, RESPECT, AND ATTENTION TO TEMPORAL CONTEXT

The second component of ethics as narrative directs us to pay attention to social and temporal contexts. This section will look at an example of temporal context, or the historical dimensions of cultural diversity.

Historical factors are centrally important in creating cultural diversity, and so understanding history is crucial to being able to foster cultural diversity. It is hard to confront the fact that so much of the history that shaped present-day cultural diversity is a history of oppression, exploitation, and cruelty. Very little of the globe was untouched by European imperialism of the fifteenth to the twentieth centuries. Very few of today's diverse peoples are free of its scars. Treating people with respect and paying attention to particularity means we must pay attention to painful historical realities. To illustrate this point we will place in historical perspective one fund raiser's dilemma in filling out a grant application.

The voices of history cry out in the response Darrell Kipp of the Blackfeet tribe wishes he could make on grant application guidelines. "When they tell us 'Describe the problem you are working on,' I want to say '*I* am the problem. *I am inside the problem.*' ... It is almost that we cannot write with the strength needed to fully describe us. What in the world are you supposed to say when you live in the poorest neighborhood in the poorest town in the poorest county in the United States—in the richest country in the world?"[13] How can the enormity and the tragedy of 500 years of grotesque cruelty be condensed into a two-page proposal summary?

How do we tell the story from before 1492, when Native Americans possessed all of the land, to today when reservations occupy only 2.3% of the United States?[14] The question itself is not posed correctly; "possessing" land is a Eurocentric concept, contrary to native understandings of the earth as sacred, a life-giving mother who could not be divided and certainly not a commodity to be bought and sold.

Darrell Kipp is a member of the Blackfeet Nation, a confederation of three tribes who share language and culture. Many of their members live on reservations in northwest Montana, spreading up into Canada. Much of Kipp's reservation in Montana is high rolling prairie. A rural area, the Blackfeet there are farmers and ranchers, with some involved in oil and natural gas production.[15]

Blackfeet have not always been farmers. Like other Native Americans of the Great Plains, they were a nomadic people. Until the 1830s, they lived in harmony with the bison. And the bison were plentiful. It is estimated that there were 30 million of them on the Great Plains in the early nineteenth century and the bison deeply influenced Blackfeet cultural patterns. The bison has been called "a veritable commissary," and the Blackfeet used every part of the ones they killed. The grazing patterns of the bison determined the tribe's travels. Gender roles were defined in terms of the bison, with men as hunters and women making clothing and shelter out of the skins. Although gender roles were differentiated, men and women shared a large measure of equality. Women had significant political influence and dominated camp life while the men were away hunting. The bison were sacred; their spiritual significance was reflected in ceremonies, rituals, and the tribe's oral literature. Particularly impressive and important for tribal harmony was the Sun Dance, a spiritual ceremony and celebration that lasted many days.[16]

The Blackfeet had had contact with white people before the 1840s. Native peoples had obtained horses from the Spanish, and the Blackfeet had traded furs with the French and British. Native and European concepts of trade did not coincide; the Indians of the Plains thought of trade in terms of reciprocity and sharing and did not understand why market values and property accumulation were so important to their European counterparts.[17] As they traded with whites and acquired horses and guns, the native people's social system became less equalitarian, and accumulating individual possessions assumed greater importance. In the late 1830s, some deckhands on a steamboat brought smallpox to the Great Plains.[18] In 1837, two thirds of the Blackfeet died of the disease. Throughout the rest of the nineteenth century, several more smallpox outbreaks visited the tribe. Try to imagine how death on such a scale would disrupt tribal social and economic patterns.

During the mid-nineteenth century, white Americans were flooding the plains. Concerned that native peoples were increasingly in the pioneers' way, Congress passed the Indian Appropriation Act in 1851, which gave the government power to create reservations and gave the United States Army power to enforce native settlement.

The indignities continued. In 1883, the Code of Religious Offenses outlawed most native dances, including the Sun Dance.[19] Children were taken off the reservation and placed in schools run by missionaries, where native languages were prohibited and assimilation to white culture was the goal. A visitor to the Blackfeet reservation in the 1890s said that the people there were "crowded into a little corner of the great territory which they once dominated." They had to "give up inherited habits, ... to break away from all that is natural to them, ... to reverse their whole mode of existence."[20]

Further encroachment on tribal concepts and ways came in 1887 with passage of the General Allotment Act. Reservation lands were divided into individual plots, in disregard of the native communal use of sacred land. Individually owned lots could be sold to whites; between 1887 and the law's repeal in 1934, the size of the native reservations was reduced by 70 percent.[21]

Now one can see why Darrell Kipp and other Native Americans find grant applications so baffling. Attention to temporal context shows us the enormity of Kipp's sense of dislocation, trying to squeeze all of this history into how he defines "the problem" on the grant proposal application. The difficulty is compounded when we compare the definition of rationality presupposed in many grant applications with that of Native American cultures. Grant proposals give a good example of how unconscious assumptions about the way the world works wiggle their way into the daily details of fund raising. To some people, the questions posed and the calculations asked for in grant proposals follow directly from the requirements of logic and efficiency. The grant requirements seem necessary in order to demonstrate an agency's ability to meet its objectives. Native Americans sometimes find these requirements jarring. These proposals are not rational, logical, or efficient in light of native world views. Rebecca Adamson of the First Nations Development Institute points out how conventional categories that separate environment from education, rural from urban programs, and so on do not make sense in terms of native ecological patterns of thinking. "The conventional mainstream philanthropic or grantmaking categories are not necessarily relevant because Indian people don't think in those categories. Indian people are brilliant systems thinkers—because they have a profound understanding that all things are related, there can be no such thing as a single intervention strategy. These problems in all communities are interrelated."[22]

How can non-native funders, fund raisers, and others concerned with the gift economy of philanthropy respond? Several mainstream foundations do have native people on their boards and involved in grantmaking decisions. This enables the foundations to adjust grant proposal and funding requirements to native worldviews, thus fostering cultural diversity and respecting people of Native American heritage.[23] Responding with sympathetic understanding and with attention to temporal context calls upon so many of the virtue clusters discussed in chapters 2, 3, and 4. We should call on compassion in the face of centuries of oppression and suffering, and mutuality in finally confronting that native and non-native fates are tied together, but that they have been yoked most unjustly. We can call on fairness in the sense of assuming responsibility and equal concern for growth of all people's potential. Finally, we should remember Niebuhr's understanding of responsibility, which ties knowledge of and response to the past with a solidarity which looks toward the future.

9.4 DIVERSITY, RESPECT, AND ATTENTION TO SOCIAL CONTEXT

Cultural diversity emerges out of historical contexts, but it has a continuing social presence. Respecting diversity includes attending to the social contexts through which diverse peoples experience their world.

Occasionally, fund raisers tell stories like this: A radio station sells tapes of its popular morning talk show. The station offers to donate the proceeds to nonprofit organizations that sign up. Humor is the talk show hosts' staple, particularly lewd comments about women's bodies. Fund raisers also relate stories on this theme: A fund raiser is planning a golf tournament. The majority of the golfers will be prominent men in the professional and business community. A particularly influential businessman says, "Get some of those real good looking young things to work this event. You know—tight shirts and all." And then there is this variation on the same theme: A nightclub in town features topless dancers. The club offers its dancing staff to do a car wash, a walk-a-thon, or some other public event for your nonprofit.

As we think about how to respond to requests such as these, we need to think about what sorts of images of women's bodies we want associated with our nonprofit organizations. This concern arises in media presentations as well as in actual participatory events. There are many ways of responding. We can talk about the women them-selves who participate and how they may feel about how they pres-ent themselves. We can talk about the people who enjoy these sorts of displays and try to figure out why they find them appealing. We can talk about the other women who are attending events such as these and ask whether they feel embarrassed or insulted. We can talk about the many men at these events who think of their own wives, daughters, and mothers and feel insulted and embarrassed on behalf of the women they love. These are important lines of thinking to pur-sue and will teach us much about respecting donors, volunteers, col-leagues and community members.

It is also important to place these fund raisers' stories within the larger social context in which they take place. When we get to a rel-evant point in the semester, I ask my students to tell me, just off the top of their heads, what they do on a daily basis to protect themselves from sexual assault. The women in the classroom immediately give me a lengthy list: don't walk alone at night; if you have to walk alone, be acutely aware of your surroundings, noting every shadow, every movement; carry a whistle or a can of mace; keep your dorm room door locked and never open it until you are sure of who is there; don't consider taking a job off campus at night. The list goes on. The men in the classroom sit in utter amazement. One male student said, "It never even occurred to me to think about it." The only answer I ever got from a man was, "Try to stay out of prison."

This exercise affects my students deeply. They can then see clearly that men and women on the very same campus, of the same age and background, live in very different worlds. For men, the phys-ical space they occupy is benign. It is simply the territory in which their comings and goings take place, full of possibilities for explo-ration and growth. For women, the physical territory is terrain to be crossed at their peril, full of potential danger, where the only rational attitude is to be wary and suspicious. If they ignore the danger and proceed with the obliviousness of their male colleagues, they face this drill: "What were you doing, staying at the library so late?" "Why did you take that job; didn't you know it isn't safe?" "Why did you open your door to that person? Don't you know any better?" My female students do know better and their knowledge haunts them. As they walk warily down the street at night, they cannot at the same time mull over how to revise that paper they need to hand in to me the next day. They do not stay those few extra hours in the library, dedicated though they may be to thorough and accurate research.

My female students are not paranoid. One-third of the women in the United States are sexually assaulted at some point during their lives; over 75 percent of them by someone they know. One out of four college women experiences rape or attempted rape during her college career, usually by someone she knows and thinks she can trust.[24] The ones who are willing to talk about it come to me and ask for a paper extension, or they ask if they can take the test another time because they have not slept in a week or they have a court appearance the next day. Others prefer to keep silent out of fear or shame. They decide they would rather have professors think they are lazy and irresponsible than reveal the real reasons. Because of rape and the threat of rape, college women who pay the same tuition, study in the same library, and take classes from the same professors do not have an equal opportunity to learn as their male colleagues, simply because they have female bodies.

Harm and the threat of harm curtail women's freedom and their ability to explore their world and to live freely in it. Their perceptual world—the world as they know it—is stunted by the reality of sexual violence. Most men are not rapists and would never sexually assault another person. Yet, they too are harmed by women's perceptual world. It is rational for women to be suspicious of men they do not know; it is rational to be very slow to trust men that they do know. Yet how does a decent man feel when he walks onto an elevator and the lone woman in it gives him a furtive look, or averts her eyes altogether, or quickly tries to decide if she should push the button and escape to the next floor? How does it feel to an honorable man to be such an object of suspicion? How can relationships between men and women be healthy and forthright when this kind of suspicion is rational? As long as sexual violence against women is as prevalent as it is today, men and women of goodwill and honest intentions will find it difficult to treat and know each others as equals.

This is one dimension of the social context of women's lived experience. Topless dancers at a car wash, "cute young things" scantily clad at golf outings, and sexually demeaning humor on morning talk shows do not exist in social vacuums. They feed the hostile environment against which my female students try so diligently to protect themselves. When we think about what "fostering cultural diversity" and "treating people with dignity and respect" mean, we need to place these phrases within the particular social contexts within which people actually live. If these contexts are ones of injustice and harm, then adhering to these phrases entails a commitment to rectify these conditions.

9.5 FOSTERING CULTURAL DIVERSITY

Just as this book has not been a how-to manual with specific answers for handling specific ethical quandaries, so this chapter is not a how-to guide on fostering diversity. Many organizations offer workshops on diversity, and there is quite a bit of literature available with specific suggestions and exercises. But here are a few reflections on the sorts of mental and emotional orientations that can contribute to fostering cultural diversity. We can again turn to Jane Addams's experiences with diverse groups to guide our own learning.

(a) Keen Awareness of Opportunity

Diversity gives us an unparalleled opportunity for reciprocal learning. There is so much to be learned *by* people of diverse backgrounds *from* people of diverse backgrounds. Addams was exasperated by many Chicagoans' attitudes toward immigrants. While generally very gracious, on one occasion Addams spoke bluntly: "All the members of the community are equally stupid in throwing away the immigrant revelation of social customs and inherited energy."[25] From Addams, this is strong language and reflects her assessment of the invaluably educative effects of fostering cultural diversity.

Nonprofit organizations are particularly well suited as locations for fostering cultural diversity. Most nonprofit missions transcend lines of class, gender, ethnicity, and so on, and thus can give a unifying focus for people who come from diverse backgrounds and have diverse beliefs. Addams, a skillful coalition builder, noted that labor union activity united immigrants from many ethnic groups. She remarked that in her work for women's suffrage, she saw women from every social sector all focusing their energies on the task that lay before them. This sort of coalition building, even around a shared goal, is not easy. Writing of her work with dozens of peace groups, she repeated Emerson's comment that "the test of a real reformer is his ability to put up with the other reformers."[26] Nonetheless, with sympathetic understanding into others' perspectives, working with diverse groups can enrich all of our imaginations and thus increase our abilities to further the purposes of philanthropy.

(b) Keen Awareness of Responsibility

Addams made this wise observation, "We are under a moral obligation in choosing our experiences, since the result of those experiences must ultimately determine our understanding of life."[27] If we mean what we say about fostering cultural diversity, then it is our responsibility to learn the specific history, customs, and ways of various cultural groups.

In Chapter 4, we discussed what responsibility means in terms of responding to current conditions, being able to give account, and working toward social solidarity. Gaining facility in more than one culture's social skills and being comfortable in more than one cultural setting are components of fostering diversity, and we are each responsible for acquiring these abilities. This is particularly a responsibility for many middle-class, white Americans. People of color, gays and lesbians, and so on live every day in more than one culture. They are culturally bilingual of necessity. They must know the rhythms of the dominant culture as well as the patterns of their own. Thus, the responsibility lies more heavily on members of the dominant culture to broaden their own cultural skills. Anthropologist Mary Catherine Bateson made this comment about American professors teaching in the Philippines who, after a brief attempt, refused to learn the native language. "That was the end of their effort to learn the language, for the professors were prohibited by their status from making fools of themselves. Wealth and power are obstacles to learning. People who don't wear shoes learn the languages of people who do, not vice versa."[28] For members of the dominant culture to exercise power by asking others to conform to their own patterns of thought and work is arrogantly disrespectful. Fostering cultural diversity is a responsibility of everyone, but it is especially a responsibility of those whose lives have been ones of social privilege.

(c) Freedom from One's Own Ideas

Let us collect several themes from previous chapters. Remember the "moderate man" from the *Tao*. His mark is freedom from his own ideas. He is "tolerant like the sky" and "supple like a tree in the wind." Recall Dewey's invitation to cultivate the whole world as our garden. Add to these the Buddhists' insight that as they become more compassionate, the boundaries of their own selves become more permeable. All of these images suggest the cognitive fluidity and emotional nondefensiveness that enable us to acquire new cultural languages.

But how do we go about learning these languages? One way is by listening and watching, and sometimes by being very small until the sense of another cultural pattern reveals itself. I know a man, a retired corporate executive deeply involved and utterly committed to philanthropic work in his community. I asked him once how his work with a grassroots inner-city school reform group was going. "It's hard; they are so emotional," was his reply. I smiled, thinking about how part of professional socialization in the United States is learning to impose tighter and more rigid control over one's own emotional expressiveness. I have watched in professional philosophy conferences the academic equivalent of violent barroom brawls. No voice elevates as much as a decibel; no facial muscle twitches more than 5%; hands remain neatly folded on the podium; all sentences, dripping with invective, are exquisitely crafted. I wished the gentleman with the school reform project had seen the group's emotionalism as a welcome contrast to his own highly restrained demeanor. Playing with the polyrhythms of diversity comes more easily if one has both a sense of distance and a sense of humor about one's own, internalized, cultural habits.

Our commitment to fostering cultural diversity and treating all people with dignity and respect is no easy matter. We cannot simply adjust our attitudes toward others and say we have thereby fulfilled our pledge. Instead, this commitment entails learning many particular things and undergoing varied experiences, many of them uncomfortable. It is helpful here to remember Addams's words, "All the members of the community are equally stupid in throwing away the immigrant revelation of social customs and inherited energy."[29] Through experiencing diverse ways of living in the world we gain access to cultural and personal treasures which can be found in no other way.

We can think of our responsibility to foster cultural diversity as an opportunity to enter settings in which all of the tools of the conceptual toolbox can be intensely practiced and finely honed. Appreciating astigmatism will give us the patience not to run away from a sense of dislocation, of not understanding, of not being in control. Playing with polyrhythms will help us endure the disjunction of varied cultural patterns until endurance gives way to delight. Sympathetic understanding and attention to social and temporal context will carry us into the process more deeply and help us inculcate the virtue clusters of philanthropy, of relationships, and of integrity. Fostering cultural diversity is one of our most difficult challenges; it is also one of our finest opportunities.

DISCUSSION QUESTIONS

1. The central argument of this chapter is that treating others with respect is not just a matter of attitude but involves a good deal of specific knowledge about and appreciation for other individuals and groups. Do you agree with this claim or is it going too far?

2. Reflect on the ways that a person's own sense of self changes as he or she fosters diversity through cultivating sympathetic understanding and paying attention to temporal and social contexts.

3. In what specific ways should diversity be reflected in the composition of nonprofit boards? Consider the following:

- Diversity among clients the agency serves
- Socio-economic diversity
- Age
- Gender
- Other dimensions (specify)

In light of nonprofit organizations' desire to have people on the board who have the financial capability to give sizable gifts and who have influential contacts in the community, how should concern about board diversity be addressed?

4. Think of diversity issues in your own workplace and community that are difficult. Make a list of particular things about yourself and your own cultural background that you think it is important for others to know and appreciate with sympathetic understanding. Also make a list of things about others you should come to know and appreciate with sympathetic understanding.

CASE STUDIES

Tokens Only? You have learned that a large, local corporation with a long history of commitment to diversity is offering a very large grant to establish job training programs for welfare recipients. You are confident that the social service agency of which you are executive director has an excellent chance of winning the grant. Your director of development reminds you that there are no women on your board, and she suggests that you ask the nominating committee to bring some women onto the board right away. The finance director throws up her hands in disgust, and says, "I've been a token on enough boards and it's the pits. If you really want women on the board, fine. But, don't just add them as window-dressing." What do you decide to do?

Tipping Point. You are executive director for a private stroke rehabilitation center located in a wealthy suburb. The center has traditionally received most of its financial support and its clients from the white, Anglo-Saxon, Protestant segment of the population, which has been the majority since as far back as anyone can remember. Over the past decade, the demographic mix has changed and your base of support is now in the minority. Few members of the new majority are wealthy.

Your organization has prided itself on the fact that several of the trustees are "minority" (ie, "new majority") members. A spot on the board has come open, and there is considerable support for recruiting a long-time resident from the wealthy Kings Estates neighborhood. A young member of your board is urging you to recruit a representative of the new majority. A few long-time, loyal supporters have a quiet chat with you. Their implicit message is, "Okay, you've played the diversity game and we have supported you. But we have reached the tipping point. One more of 'them' on board, and the organization won't be 'ours' any more." When the board asks for your recommendation, what will you tell them?

Market Images. You are driving down the highway. A billboard flashes by; on it you see a young woman's naked back turned ever so slightly, ever so seductively. At first you think it is one of those ads for bath gel. You are doing 65 mph, so the only words you catch are: "Join me at the Opera." Are images like this appropriate for nonprofit marketing?

How Much Heritage? Cultural heritage tours have been very successful for your cultural history museum. As development director you are planning a trip to Brazil and want to stop at an indigenous village known for its fine native crafts. The mayor of the town is very excited that you want to stop at his village, and writes, "Just bring that tour bus right into our town, and I'll take you personally to the finest weavers and potters we have." However, the potter you have been in contact with lets you know that several of the artists are tired of being stared at by tour crowds, tired of the megaphone noise, and tired of the way the mayor uses the artists to augment his own prestige. "We aren't exotic animals in a zoo and we are tired of being treated that way," he tells you. What do you do?

Funding Pensions. Your grassroots community organizing agency is now 15 years old. Some of the leaders who founded the organization as starry-eyed idealists have now turned 40 and have families. They are urging the board to adopt some sort of a pension plan. They argue that low salaries are evidence enough of their dedication; to ask them not to make provisions for the future is asking too much. Several board members are angry at this request. They live in the community and argue that they and their neighbors work at low-wage jobs that do not offer pension plans and they are all vulnerable to layoffs. They do not see why the community's donated money should go to the staff pension funds, while they do not have any such option. How would you respond to them?[30]

NOTES

   1. National Society of Fund Raising Executives, *Membership Survey Profile: 1995* (Alexandria, VA: NSFRE, 1996), p. 2; Mark S. Littman (ed.): *A Statistical Portrait of the United States: Social Conditions and Trends* (Lanham, MD: Bernan Press, 1998), p. 18; Thomas M. McDevitt, *World Population Profile: 1998* (Washington: Bureau of the Census, 1999), p. 12.
   2. Jane Addams, "Widening the Circle of Enlightenment: Hull House and Adult Education." *Journal of Adult Education,* vol. 2 (1930), pp. 276–279; reprinted in Jane Addams, *On Education,* Ellen Condiffe Lagemann (ed.): (New Brunswick, New Jersey: Transaction, 1994), pp. 209–210.
   3. Gloria T. Hull, Patricia Bell Scott, and Barbara Smith, *All the Women Are White, All the Blacks Are Men, But Some of Us Are Brave* (Old Westbury, NY: Feminist Press, 1982).
   4. Bradford Smith, Sylvia Shue, Jennifer Lisa Vest, and Joseph Villarreal, *Philanthropy in Communities of Color* (Bloomington: Indiana University Press, 1999), pp. 5–6.
   5. *Id.,* p. 6. See also James A. Joseph, *Remaking America: How the Benevolent Traditions of Many Cultures Are Transforming Our National Life* (San Francisco: Jossey-Bass, 1995).
   6. Mary Evelyn Tucker, "A View of Philanthropy in Japan: Confucian Ethics and Education." in Warren F. Ilchman, Stanley N.

Katz, and Edward L. Queen (eds.): *Philanthropy in the World's Traditions* (Bloomington: Indiana University Press, 1998), p. 170.

7. Quoted in Tu Wei-Ming, ed., *Confucian Traditions in East Asian Modernity* (Cambridge, MA: Harvard University Press, 1996), p. 8.

8. Confucius, *Analects* 1:6, quoted in Mary Evelyn Tucker, "A View of Philanthropy in Japan: Confucian Ethics and Education," in Warren F. Ilchman, Stanley N. Katz, and Edward L. Queen (eds.): *Philanthropy in the World's Traditions* (Bloomington: Indiana University Press, 1998), p. 173.

9. Bradford Smith, Sylvia Shue, Jennifer Lisa Vest, and Joseph Villarreal, *Philanthropy in Communities of Color* (Bloomington: Indiana University Press, 1999), p. 125. See pages 121–134 for many specific examples of giving traditions among Japanese Americans.

10. R. Roosevelt Thomas, *Beyond Race and Gender* (New York: American Management Association, 1991). p. 11.

11. Author's communication with Mary Converse, Research Manager, Association of Flight Attendants, Washington, DC.; See also Katharine T. Bartlett and Angela P. Harris, *Gender and Law: Theory, Doctrine, Commentary,* 2nd ed. (New York: Aspen Law and Business, 1998), pp. 166–167, 172–177.

12. Janice Gow Pettey, "Cultivating the Field of Diversity." *Advancing Philanthropy* (Spring 1999), p. 6.

13. Ronald Austin Wells, *The Honor of Giving: Philanthropy in Native America* (Indianapolis: Indiana University Center on Philanthropy, 1998), p. 51.

14. Klaus Frantz, *Indian Reservations in the United States* (Chicago: University of Chicago Press, 1999), p. 39.

15. Malcolm McFee, *Modern Blackfeet: Montanans on a Reservation* (New York: Holt, Rinehart, and Winston, 1972), p. 24.

16. Paul H. Carlson, *The Plains Indians* (College Station: Texas A&M University Press, 1998), pp. 17–40.

17. *Id.,* pp. 125–126.

18. *Id.,* p. 132.

19. *Id.,* p. 165.

20. *Id.,* p. 168.

21. *Id.,* pp. 176–177.

22. Ronald Austin Wells, *The Honor of Giving: Philanthropy in Native America* (Indianapolis: Indiana University Center on Philanthropy, 1998), p. 52.

23. *Id.,* pp. 47–50.

24. Statistics from the National Center for Victims of Crime, 2111 Wilson Blvd., Suite 300, Arlington, VA 22201; http://www.ncvc.org.
25. Jane Addams, *Newer Ideals of Peace* (New York: Macmillan, 1906), p. 79.
26. Jane Addams, "Patriotism and Pacifists in War Time." *The City Club Bulletin,* vol. 10, no. 9 (Chicago, June 16, 1917), p. 2.
27. Jane Addams, *Democracy and Social Ethics* (New York: Macmillan, 1907, reprint ed., Cambridge, MA: Harvard University Press, 1964), pp. 9–10.
28. Mary Catherine Bateson, *Peripheral Visions* (New York: HarperCollins, 1994), p. 69. Bateson's book gives particularly insightful reflections on experiencing diverse cultures.
29. Jane Addams, *Newer Ideals of Peace* (New York: Macmillan, 1906), p. 79.
30. Thomas J. Billitteri, "A Safety Net for Aging Activists." *The Chronicle of Philanthropy,* vol. 11, no. 8 (February 11, 1999), pp. 27–28.

Appendix:
Ethics Education
Committees

Ethical reflection is often enhanced by stepping back a bit from the day-to-day frazzle of events and thinking things through slowly. Doing this alone is valuable; without labeling it as such, I suspect many people use walks, jogs, swim time, and the drive home from work as their time for ethical reflection. Thinking alone often takes the form of a dialogue with oneself, engaging the voices of the various parts of oneself, the voices of colleagues and friends, and perhaps the voices of antagonists.

A.1 WHY ETHICS EDUCATION COMMITTEES

This appendix will point out ways in which an ethics education committee can be beneficial for members of local NSFRE chapters. Valuable as solitary ethical reflection is, working through ethically troubling situations and issues in a group setting also brings insight. When an atmosphere of trust and respect exists among the participants, ethical reflection can be a process of thinking things through together out loud. As sympathetic understanding of each person's perspective develops, the diverse viewpoints can enrich each member's own repertoire of ideas. John Dewey wrote, "Democracy is the faith that the process of experience is more important than any special result attained, so that special results achieved are of ultimate value only as they are used to enrich and order the ongoing process.... All ends and values that are cut off from the ongoing process become arrests, fixations."[1] Although Dewey was describing characteristics of a democratic society in this passage, his observation applies just as well to ethical reflection; the process is just as important, if not more important, than the outcome. NSFRE Chapter ethics education committees can be fruitful settings for thinking matters through together, and being enriched by the process as well as the decisions made.

Engaging in ethical reflection is inherently participatory. It is like eating supper and getting exercise: No one else can do it for you. You can ask others how they do it for themselves, but they cannot do it for you. There are no ethics experts who can come in, analyze a problem for you, and then tell you what to do. The whole notion of expertise is incompatible with the activity of ethical reflection. "Expert" has a ring of authority. It says, "I know what I am doing more than you do. I have esoteric knowledge, which you will not have without special training. I have authority, so you can do as I say without being able to construct the reasoning by which to reach the same conclusion." To put oneself in the position of relying on expert authority is to step outside the activity of ethics. Now I suppose that people who have been reflecting on fund raising and ethics for a long time have gained some facility in identifying ethical issues and placing daily concerns within the larger framework of philanthropy. But John Stuart Mill had a point when he said, "With respect to his own feelings and circumstances the most ordinary man or woman has means of knowledge immeasurably surpassing those that can be possessed by anyone else."[2] No one has access to the vitally important details of a situation's social and temporal contexts comparable to that of its hands-on participants. Here, it is helpful to remember the philosophies of Aristotle, Confucius, and the Akan. For them, ethics was not done by consulting experts. Ethics was a matter of developing virtues as deeply internalized personality characteristics. In a dialectical way, ethical reflection both grows out of already internalized virtues and aids in internalizing them more fully.

A.2 SUGGESTIONS FOR ETHICS EDUCATION COMMITTEES

Participating in an ethics education committee is an excellent way to foster ethical reflection. Here are a number of suggestions for what local chapter ethics committees can do.

(a) Work with the Ethical Decision-Making Chart

Many sample case studies are provided in this book. Using the ethical decision-making chart takes some discipline; by sticking to it, the group is forced to think slowly and carefully. Nuances of the three basic value commitments to organizational mission, relationships, and integrity will emerge with clarity as you work your way systematically through the chart. Also, when one thinks slowly, imaginative and courageous solutions are more likely to present themselves.

Another value to following the chart is that it helps to keep discussions from polarizing. Some people enjoy debating ethical questions. They may have highly honed debating skills from high school and college clubs, or they may simply prefer to stick with their initial inclinations because it is hard for them to admit they might be wrong. Some people learn well through debate, but too often, debates solidify oppositional positions rather than provide a method for exploring a range of options. It is true that in a well-structured debate, one must learn to listen carefully to the opposition and respond. Yet the debate format does not encourage people to enter sympathetically into another's way of experiencing the world. Instead, one tends to enter only as far as necessary to find a way of saying why the other's position is wrong. Evaluating alternative courses of action from the perspectives of organizational mission, a variety of relationships, and personal integrity fosters collaborative work and imaginative thinking more effectively.

(b) Develop Your Own Bank of Case Studies

The best source for identifying ethically troubling issues in fund raising, of course, is fund raisers themselves. You can bring events that occur in your offices, change them to preserve confidentiality, clarify them by discarding purely idiosyncratic components, and then generalize them, as you recognize that the same kinds of issues occur in other settings. Doing all of this is "ethics work"; in many instances, the largest part of working through an ethical dilemma is figuring out what the issues are and clarifying what values are at stake. This also will give you a bank of cases to use in serving the chapter and the community.

(c) Work through Various Codes of Ethics

You might want to discuss one or two of NSFRE's Statements of Ethical Principles or Standards of Professional Practice at each meeting. Paraphrase the statements, think of instances in which those standards apply, and discuss why NSRE considers these standards so important. More fund-raising ethics codes and mission statements can be found by visiting these websites:

NSFRE:
http://www.nsfre.org/welcom/code.html

The Council for the Advancement and Support of Education:
http://www.case.org/about/mission.htm

The Association for Healthcare Philanthropy:
http://www.go-ahp.org/membership/profstandards.html

National Committee on Planned Giving:
http://www.ncp.org/stds.html

Association of Professional Researchers for Advancement:
http://www.APRAhome.org/apra_statement_of_ethics.htm

(d) Discuss an "Article of the Month"

The Chronicle of Philanthropy, Advancing Philanthropy, and many other publications that fund raisers read regularly often raise ethical issues. Committee members could bring copies of a provocative article for spontaneous discussion or distribute them ahead of time to other members of the committee. One of our most vigorous committee discussions was about Maurice Gurin's article on cause-related marketing, "Phony Philanthropy."[3]

(e) Reflect on the Larger Framework of Philanthopy

Ethics education committee meetings are an excellent place to step back and explore questions about philanthropy that are broader than individual case studies. Examples include: Why is diversity important? Has the use of business vocabulary in fund raising altered our focus away from philanthropy as a gift economy? To what extent is it a fund raiser's responsibility to foster philanthropic values of generosity, compassion, mutuality, and so on? The discussion questions at the end of each chapter give you a good place to start.

(f) Formulate a Mission Statement for the Committee

This is not a task for the first meeting. Mission statements are reflective and imaginative. Often, you need to have an experiential base before formulating one so that it reflects the needs and interests of your particular community and chapter.

The Miami Valley Chapter Ethics Education Committee spent portions of several meetings developing a mission statement. Here is the final outcome:

> The mission of the Miami Valley NSFRE Chapter Ethics Education Committee is to protect the integrity of fund raising:
> —by providing a clear focus on ethical values, as exemplified in the NSFRE Code of Ethics;
> —by providing opportunities for ethical reflection and dialogue; and
> —by acting as an educational resource on ethics for the philanthropic community.

The process of developing this statement was valuable, for all the reasons given in all those management books about the process of developing a mission statement. We had to think through what we as a committee could accomplish and separate it from what was outside our domain. Adjudication of ethics code violations, for example, should be handled by the national NSFRE office. Chapter committees should focus on educational activities and services. In the process of developing the committee mission statement, we reflected on what we had done and we imagined possibilities for future endeavors. In formulating the statement, our goals included stating our connection with the NSFRE Code of Ethics, keeping philanthropy in central focus, affirming the value of reflection and dialogue, and stating our mission to serve the community, in addition to discussing ethical issues among ourselves.

A.3 SERVICE TO THE CHAPTER AND THE COMMUNITY

There are many ways in which an ethics education committee can serve the chapter and the community. Preparing these projects is also of value to the committee members, as it provides an opportunity for them to draw their thoughts together in a focused way. Here are some of the things our local Miami Valley NSFRE Ethics Education Committee has done for our chapter and community.

(a) Programs for Chapter Meetings

Our ethics committee is responsible for a monthly chapter program about once a year.[4] Generally, we take a theme, for example, commission-based pay; privacy and prospect research; or same town, new job, and build a program around that. Often, one member starts by laying out the central issues, such as why privacy is important or why commission-based pay is a serious matter. If there is time, a committee member explains how to use the ethical decision-making Chart. One format is to give each table a few case studies to discuss and then ask them to report back to the whole group.

Another format is to have the committee do a role play. Here is an example of a role play that provoked vigorous discussion.

Cast of Characters:
Angela Blackburn: Mayor of the City of Wortham
Carla Birch: Public Relations Director for Puffalot, Inc.
Barry McEwen: Small-business owner, Wortham Community Center (WCC) board member
David Nehring: Community nurse and WCC board member
Robin Paris: Executive Director of WCC
Chapter meeting attendees: Citizens of Wortham

Scenario:
The Wortham Community Center is holding a public forum to present its dilemma to the people of Wortham and to hear community opinions. The WCC is an important fixture in Wortham and offers residents of this working-class city of 50,000 people programs in health, recreation, education, the arts, and so on. The WCC also lets outside groups such as the Girls Scouts, Boy Scouts, and church groups use its facilities.

For the past 20 years, the WCC has held a basketball tournament, which typically brings in $15,000 for operating expenses. Unfortunately, the faithful corporate sponsor just sold his business and retired to North Carolina. With the tournament fast approaching, the WCC is trying hard to find a new sponsor. Ms. Birch brings a proposal from Puffalot, Inc., a local cigarette manufacturer. The company offers to sponsor the tournament, provide T-shirts for all the participants, and design a banner for the tournament site, with Puffalot's name and logo on the shirts and the banner. Puffalot wants the WCC to include its name and logo on all publicity and to thank the company publicly at the start of each tournament game.

Scene One:

Mayor Blackburn opens with a brief introduction, describing the city of Wortham and saying how important the WCC is to the city.

Executive Director Paris describes the WCC's current predicament.

Public Relations Director Birch lays out Puffalot's offer, reminding them of how Puffalot employs many of the city's residents and noting that it is making this offer as a gesture of good corporate citizenship.

Business owner McEwen explains why he, as a life-long resident of Wortham, supports Puffalot's offer. He and his family use the WCC extensively.

Nurse Nehring gives an impassioned speech on how accepting the offer will make it difficult for him to offer health workshops on the dangers of tobacco for schoolchildren and to continue to offer his stop-smoking clinic at the WCC.

Scene Two:

Executive Director Paris invites questions and comments from the audience.

The audience response was so vigorous and spontaneous that afterwards some people asked if we had "plants." (We didn't.) Much of the debate focused on whether the mission of the center would be compromised by accepting Puffalot's sponsorship or whether the offer should be accepted as a demonstration of corporate community citizenship. One audience member stood up, dramatically offered $100 to the WCC, and challenged the rest of the audience to do likewise. Although we did not use the ethical decision-making chart, virtually all of the points emerged during the session that would have been brought up in a more structured discussion.

(b) Mentoring Roundtables

Our chapter also hosts a series of stand-alone mentoring sessions on various topics. The ethics committee has offered a number of sessions on ethics in this series. In these sessions, there is generally more time to analyze cases systematically using the ethical decision-making chart.

(c) Chapter Newsletter

Our ethics committee submits cases studies to the chapter newsletter. If readers give us feedback, it is published in the next issue. However, just printing the cases sparks some reflection among readers.

(d) Service to the Community

There may be opportunities to do sessions similar to ethics chapter programs as workshops at various nonprofit organizations in the area. Our committee has given workshops at the local community college and at a nonprofit resource center. We also gave a presentation in a university class on marketing and nonprofits.

Our ethics committee meets once a month. In spite of the demands of development work and the way emergencies seem to arise at the last minute, the committee members are remarkably faithful and have been most gracious in teaching me about the joys and challenges of their work. I always look forward to the ethics committee meetings and always leave them energized, my admiration for philanthropic fund raisers affirmed. I hope these suggestions help to enable others to have experiences as rich as those our committee shares.

NOTES

1. John Dewey, *The Moral Writings of John Dewey*, revised ed., James Gouinlock (ed.): (Amherst, New York: Prometheus Books, 1994), p. 271.
2. John Stuart Mill, *Utilitarianism* (1861) (reprint ed., Indianapolis: Bobbs-Merrill, 1957), p. 74.
3. Maurice Gurin, "Phony Philanthropy?" *Foundation News* (May/June 1989), pp. 32–35.
4. Members of the national NSFRE Ethics Committee are also available to speak at local chapters.

Bibliography

Addams, Jane, *Democracy and Social Ethics* (New York: Macmillan, 1907; reprint ed., Cambridge, MA: Harvard University Press, 1964).

Addams, Jane, *A Modern Lear.* Survey 29 (1912); pp. 131–137; reprinted by Jane Addams's Hull House Museum, 1994.

Addams, Jane, *A New Conscience and an Ancient Evil* (New York: Macmillan, 1912).

Addams, Jane, *Newer Ideals of Peace* (New York: Macmillan, 1906).

Addams, Jane, "Patriotism and Pacifists in War Time." *The City Club Bulletin,* Vol. 10, no. 9 (Chicago, June 16, 1917).

Addams, Jane, *The Second Twenty Years at Hull House* (New York: Macmillan, 1930).

Addams, Jane, *The Spirit of Youth and the City Streets* (New York: Macmillan, 1909; reprint ed., Urbana: University of Illinois Press, 1972).

Addams, Jane, *Twenty Years At Hull House* (New York: Macmillan, 1912; reprint ed., Urbana: University of Illinois Press, 1990.)

Addams, Jane, "Widening the Circle of Enlightenment: Hull House and Adult Education." *Journal of Adult Education,* vol. 2 (1930), pp. 276–279; reprinted in Jane Addams, *On Education,* Ellen Condiffe Lagemann (ed.): (New Brunswick, New Jersey: Transaction, 1994), pp. 204–211.

Addams, Jane, et al. *Philanthropy and Social Progress* (Montclair, NJ: Patterson Smith, 1893; reprint ed., 1970).

Al-Ghazáli, *The Faith and Practice of Al-Ghazáli,* trans. by W. Montgomery Watt (Oxford, Oneworld Publications, 1994).

Anderson, Lisa, "Charity's Probe Finds Sponsors Funded at Least 24 Dead Children." *Chicago Tribune,* Sunday, March 15, 1998, Section Two, Special Report, pp. 1, 13.

Annas, Julia, *An Introduction to Plato's Republic* (New York: Oxford University Press, 1981).

Aquinas, Thomas, *Summa Theologica* (New York: Benziger Brothers, 1947). p. 851.

Arendt, Hannah, *Eichmann in Jerusalem: A Report on the Banality of Evil* (New York: Penguin, 1964).

Aristotle, *Nicomachean Ethics*, trans. by Terence Irwin (Indianapolis: Hackett, 1985).

Arjomand, Said Amir, "Philanthropy, the Law, and Public Policy in the Islamic World before the Modern Era," in Warren F. Ilchman, Stanley N. Katz, and Edward L. Queen (eds.): *Philanthropy in the World's Traditions* (Bloomington: Indiana University Press, 1998), pp. 109–132.

Avery, Laura J., and John L. Gliha, "Computer-Assisted Prospect Management and Research," in James D. Miller and Deborah Strauss (eds.): *Improving Fundraising with Technology, New Directions in Philanthropic Fundraising*, vol. 11 (San Francisco: Jossey-Bass, 1996), pp. 85–104.

Baier, Annette C. *Moral Prejudices* (Cambridge, MA: Harvard University Press, 1995).

Bateson, Mary Catherine, *Peripheral Visions* (New York: Harper Collins, 1994).

Batt, Sharon, "'Perfect People': Cancer Charities," in Rose Weitz (ed.): *The Politics of Women's Bodies* (New York: Oxford University Press, 1998), pp. 137–146.

Bartlett, Katharine T. and Angela P. Harris, *Gender and Law: Theory, Doctrine, Commentary*, 2nd ed. (New York: Aspen Law and Business, 1998).

Benedict, *The Rule of Saint Benedict in English*, Timothy Fry, ed. (Collegeville, MN: The Liturgical Press, 1982).

Bethune, Mary McLeod, "A College on a Garbage Dump," in Gerda Lerner (ed.): *Black Women in White America: A Documentary History* (New York: Vintage Books, 1972), pp. 134–143.

Billitteri, Thomas J., "A Safety Net for Aging Activists." *The Chronicle of Philanthropy*, vol. 11, no. 8 (February 11, 1999), pp. 27–28.

Black's Law Dictionary, 5th ed. (St. Paul, MN: West, 1979).

Blum, Debra E., "Raising Funds over the Long Run." *The Chronicle of Philanthropy*, Vol. 11, no. 8 (February 11, 1999) pp. 23–26.

Bok, Sissela, *Lying: Moral Choice in Public and Private Life* (New York: Vintage, 1978).

Boys and Girls Clubs Web site: *http://www.bgca.org*.

Bremner, Robert, H. *American Philanthropy*, 2nd ed. (Chicago: University of Chicago Press, 1988).

Brenkert, George G., "Privacy, Polygraphs, and Work," *Business and Professional Ethics Journal*, Vol. 1, no. 1 (1981), pp. 19–35.

Calhoun, Cheshire, "Standing For Something." *Journal of Philosophy*, Vol. 92, no. 5 (May 1995), pp. 235–260.

Card, Claudia, "Gratitude and Obligation." *American Philosophical Quarterly*, Vol. 25, no. 2 (April 1988), pp. 115–127.

Carlson, Paul H., *The Plains Indians* (College Station: Texas A&M University Press, 1998).

Chan, Wing-Tsit (trans. and compiler), *A Source Book in Chinese Philosophy* (Princeton, NJ: Princeton University Press, 1963).

Coontz, Stephanie, *The Way We Never Were: American Families and the Nostalgia Trap* (New York: Basic Books, 1992).

Cunningham, Peggy H., "Sleeping with the Devil? Exploring Ethical Concerns Associated with Cause-Related Marketing." *New Directions in Philanthropic Fundraising: Marketing the Nonprofit: The Challenge of Fundraising in a Consumer Culture*," Margaret M. Maxwell (ed.), vol. 18 (Winter 1997) (Jossey-Bass), pp. 55–75.

Curry, Thomas J. *The First Freedoms: Church and State in America to the Passage of the First Amendment* (New York: Oxford, 1986).

de Tocqueville, Alexis, *Democracy in America*, vol. II, 1835 (New York: Schocken Books, 1961).

Denny, Frederick M., *An Introduction to Islam*, 2nd ed. (New York: Macmillan, 1994).

Dewey, John, *Art as Experience* (1934); reprinted in Jo Ann Boydston (ed.): *John Dewey: The Later Works, 1925–1953*, vol. *10* (Carbondale and Edwardsville: Southern Illinois University Press, 1987).

Dewey, John, *Context and Thought* (1931); reprinted in Jo Ann Boydston (ed.): *John Dewey: The Later Works, 1925–1953*, vol. *6* (Carbondale and Edwardsville: Southern Illinois University Press, 1985).

Dewey, John, *Democracy and Education* (1916); reprinted in Jo Ann Boydston (ed.): *John Dewey: The Middle Works, 1899–1924*, vol. *9* (Carbondale and Edwardsville: Southern Illinois University Press, 1985).

Dewey, John, *Human Nature and Conduct* (1922); reprinted in Jo Ann Boydston (ed.): *John Dewey: The Middle Works, 1899–1924*, vol. 14 (Carbondale and Edwardsville: Southern Illinois University Press, 1988).

Dewey, John, *Individualism Old and New* (1930) (New York: G.P. Putnam & Sons, 1962).

Dewey, John, *The Moral Writings of John Dewey*, revised ed., James Gouinlock (ed.): (Amherst. NY: Prometheus Books, 1994).

Dewey, John, *The Public and Its Problems* (1927); reprinted in Jo Ann Boydston (ed.); *John Dewey: The Later Works, 1925–1953.* vol. *2* (Carbondale and Edwardsville: Southern Illinois University Press, 1988).

Dickey, Marilyn. "Fund-Raising Friction." *The Chronicle of Philanthropy.* vol. 10, no. 24, (October 8, 1998), pp. 33, 38.

Dundjerski, Marina, "Philip Morris Pledges Millions to Fight Hunger." *The Chronicle of Philanthropy* (vol. 11, no. 11) (March 25, 1999), p. 14.

Dundjerski, Marina, "Rabbi Nurtures Young Jews' Quest for Faith and Service." *The Chronicle of Philanthropy* (vol. 11, no. 6) (January 14, 1999), pp. 15–16.

Emerson, Ralph Waldo, "Gifts." *The Essays of Ralph Waldo Emerson*, 1844 (Cambridge, MA: Harvard University Press, 1987), pp. 309–314.

Emerson, Ralph Waldo, "History." *The Essays of Ralph Waldo Emerson*, 1841 (Cambridge, MA: Harvard University Press, 1987), pp. 1–23.

Emerson, Ralph Waldo, "Self-Reliance." *The Essays of Ralph Waldo Emerson*, 1841 (Cambridge, MA: Harvard University Press, 1987), pp. 25–51.

Epicurus, *The Epicurus Reader*, trans. by Brad Inwood and L. P. Gerson (eds.): (Indianapolis: Hackett, 1994).

Esposito, John L., *Islam, the Straight Path* (New York: Oxford University Press, 1988).

Femenía, Nora Amalia, "Argentina's Mothers of Plaza de Mayo: The Mourning Process from Junta to Democracy." *Feminist Studies* vol. 13, no. 1 (Spring 1987), pp. 9–18.

Fiser, Karen, "Philosophy, Disability, and Essentialism," in Lawrence Foster and Patricia Herzog (eds.): *Contemporary Philosophical Perspectives on Pluralism and Multiculturalism* (Amherst: University of Massachusetts Press, 1994), pp. 83–101.

First Peter 4:10, Revised Standard Version.

Flanagan, Joan, "Horizon Hospice: From Zero to $2.7 Million a Year," in Michael Seltzer (ed.): *Fundraising Matters, New Directions for Philanthropic Fundraising,* no. 1 (San Francisco: Jossey-Bass, Fall 1993), pp. 111–125.

Frantz, Klaus, *Indian Reservations in the United States* (Chicago: University of Chicago Press, 1999).

Frost, Robert, "The Death of a Hired Man," in *Robert Frost's Poems* (New York: Washington Square Press, 1970), pp. 160–167.

Gardner, John W., "Summary of Statement to IS Committee on Values and Ethics," in *Ethics and The Nation's Voluntary and Philanthropic Community: Obedience to the Unenforceable* (Washington DC: Independent Sector, 1991).

Giddings, Paula, *When and Where I Enter* (New York: Bantam, 1984).

Gilligan, Carol, *In a Different Voice* (Cambridge, MA: Harvard University Press, 1982).

Goodwin, Beverly, "Ethics in the Research Office," in Marianne G. Briscoe (ed.): *Ethics in Fundraising: Putting Values into Practice. New Directions in Philanthropic Fundraising,* vol. 6 (San Francisco: Jossey-Bass, Winter 1994), pp. 87–104.

Govier, Trudy, *Social Trust and Human Communities* (Montreal: and Kingston McGill-Queen's University Press, 1997).

Grace, Kay Sprinkel, *Beyond Fund Raising* (New York: John Wiley & Sons, 1997).

Gray, Susan, "Charities' Income from Sponsorships up 10%." *The Chronicle of Philanthropy* Vol. 10, no. 11 (March 26, 1998), p. 20.

Greenfield, James M., "Professional Compensation." *NSFRE Journal* (Summer 1990), pp. 35–39.

Griswold v. Connecticut, 381 US 479 (1965), U.S. Supreme Court, excerpted in David M. Adams (ed.): *Philosophical Problems in the Law* (Belmont, CA: Wadsworth, 1992), pp. 160–165.

Gurin, Maurice, "Phony Philanthropy?" *Foundation News* (May/June, 1989), pp. 32–35.

Gyatso, Geshe Kelsang, *Ocean of Nectar: Wisdom and Compassion in Mahayana Buddhism* (London: Tharpa Publications, 1995).

Gyekye, Kwame, *African Philosophical Thought: The Akan Conceptual Scheme,* revised ed. (Philadelphia: Temple University Press, 1987).

Hack, Vanessa, *Targeting the Powerful: International Prospect Research* (London: Association for Information Management, 1997).

Hall, Holly, "Two Fund-Raising Groups Denounce Commission Payments to Gift-Annuity Advisors." *The Chronicle of Philanthropy*, Vol. 11, no. 5 (December 17, 1998), p. 30.

Hands, A.R., *Charities and Social Aid in Greece and Rome* (Ithaca, NY: Cornell University Press, 1968).

Higgins, Kathleen Marie, *The Music of Our Lives* (Philadelphia: Temple University Press, 1991).

Himmelstein, Jerome L., *Looking Good & Doing Good: Corporate Philanthropy and Corporate Power* (Bloomington: Indiana University Press, 1997).

Hine, Darlene Clark, "'We Specialize in the Wholly Impossible,' The Philanthropic Work of Black Women," in Kathleen D. McCarthy (ed.): *Lady Bountiful Revisited* (New Brunswick, NJ: Rutgers University Press, 1990), pp. 70–93.

hooks, bell, *Ain't I a Woman* (Boston: South End Press, 1981).

Hull, Gloria T., Patricia Bell Scott, and Barbara Smith, *All the Women Are White, All the Blacks Are Men, but Some of Us Are Brave* (Old Westbury, NY: Feminist Press, 1982).

Jacobi, Peter, *The Messiah Book* (New York: St. Martin's, 1982), p. 37; cited in Joan Flanagan, *Successful Fundraising: A Complete Handbook for Volunteers and Professionals* (Chicago: Contemporary Books, 1993), pp. 54–55.

Jones, Adrienne Lash, "Philanthropy in the African American Experience" in J.B. Schneewind, (ed.): *Giving: Western Ideas of Philanthropy* (Bloomington: Indiana University Press, 1996), pp. 153–178.

Joseph, James A., *Remaking America: How the Benevolent Traditions of Many Cultures Are Transforming Our National Life* (San Francisco: Jossey-Bass, 1995).

Kant, Immanuel, *Groundwork of the Metaphysic of Morals*, trans. by H.J. Paton (New York: Harper & Row, 1964).

Kelly, Kathleen, *Effective Fund Raising Management* (Mahwah, NJ: Lawrence Erlbaum Associates, 1998).

King, Martin Luther, "Letter from a Birmingham Jail," http://www.msstate.edu/Archives/History/USA/Afro-Amer/birmingham.king.

Kozlowski, Gregory C., "Religious Authority, Reform, and Philanthropy in the Contemporary Muslim World," in Warren F. Ilchman, Stanley N. Katz, and Edward L. Queen (eds.): *Philanthropy in the World's Traditions* (Bloomington: Indiana University Press, 1998), pp. 279–308.

Lao-tzu, *Tao te Ching*, trans. by Stephen Mitchell (New York: Harper & Row, 1988).

Littman, Mark S. (ed.), *A Statistical Portrait of the United States: Social Conditions and Trends* (Lanham, MD: Bernan Press, 1998).

Locke, John, *The Second Treatise of Government*, 1690 (Indianapolis: Bobbs-Merrill, 1952).

Lugones, María, "Hispaneando y Lesbiando: On Sarah Hoagland's *Lesbian Ethics*." *Hypatia* Vol. 5, no. 3 (Fall 1990), pp. 138–146.

"Marketing Deals May Reap $1 Billion." *The Chronicle of Philanthropy* Vol. 11, no. 9 (February 25, 1999), p. 40.

Martin, Mike W., *Virtuous Giving* (Bloomington: Indiana University Press, 1994).

Martin, Patricia, "In the Company of Sponsors." *Advancing Philanthropy* (Spring 1996), pp. 30–35.

Mauss, Marcel, *The Gift: The Form and Reason for Exchange in Archaic Societies* (1925), trans. by W.D. Halls (New York: Norton, 1990).

May, Larry, *The Socially Responsive Self: Social Theory and Professional Ethics* (Chicago: University of Chicago Press, 1996).

McDevitt, Thomas M., *World Population Profile: 1998* (Washington: Bureau of the Census, 1999).

McFee, Malcolm, *Modern Blackfeet: Montanans on a Reservation* (New York: Holt, Rinehart, and Winston, 1972).

McKay, John P., Bennett D. Hill, John Buckler, *A History of Western Society*, 4th ed., vol. 1 (Boston, MA: Houghton Mifflin, 1991).

Mill, John Stuart, *On Liberty, 1859* (reprint ed., Indianapolis: Hackett, 1978).

Mill, John Stuart, *Principles of Political Economy*, 1848 (reprint ed., New York: Augustus M. Kelley, 1965).

Mill, John Stuart, *Utilitarianism*, 1861 (reprint ed., Indianapolis: Bobbs-Merrill, 1957).

Miller, Michael Page, "Nine and a Half Theses about Fundraising Benefits: Rationalizations, Indulgences, and Opportunity Costs," in Dwight F. Burlingame & Warren F. Ilchman (eds.): *Alternative Revenue Sources Prospects, Requirements, and Concerns for Nonprofits. New Directions for Philanthropic Fundraising*, no. 12 (San Francisco: Jossey-Bass, Summer 1996), pp. 109–117.

Monroe, Kristen Renwick, *The Heart of Altruism: Perceptions of a Common Humanity* (Princeton. NJ: Princeton University Press, 1996).

Murphy, Robert F., "Social Distance and the Veil," in Ferdinand D. Schoeman (ed.): *Philosophical Dimensions of Privacy: An Anthology* (New York: Cambridge University Press, 1984), pp. 34–55.

National Society of Fund Raising Executives, *Membership Survey Profile: 1995* (Alexandria, VA: NSFRE, 1996).

Niebuhr, H. Richard, *The Responsible Self: An Essay in Christian Moral Philosophy* (New York: Harper & Row, 1963).

O'Connell, Brian, *Philanthropy in Action* (New York: Foundation Center, 1987).

O'Neill, Michael, "Fundraising as an Ethical Act," in Marianne G. Briscoe (ed.): *Ethics in Fundraising: Putting Values into Practice, New Directions for Philanthropic Fundraising*, no. 6 (San Francisco: Jossey-Bass, Winter 1994), pp. 3–14.

Odendahl, Teresa, *Charity Begins at Home: Generosity and Self-Interest among the Philanthropic Elite* (New York: Basic Books, 1990).

Ostrander, Susan A., *Money for Change* (Philadelphia: Temple University Press, 1995).

Payton, R., *Philanthropy: Voluntary Action for the Public Good* (New York: Macmillan, 1988).

Pettey, Janice Gow, "Cultivating the Field of Diversity." *Advancing Philanthropy* (Spring 1999), pp. 4–7.

Pincoffs, Edmund L., *Quandaries and Virtues* (Lawrence: Kansas University Press, 1986).

Plato, "Ion," *The Dialogues of Plato*, vol. trans. by Benjamin Jowett (London: Begelow, Smith & Co., n.d.).

Plato, *"Phaedrus,"* R. Hackforth, tr., *Plato: The Collected Dialogues*, Edith Hamilton and Huntington Cairns (eds.): (Princeton, NJ: Princeton University Press, 1961), pp. 475–525.

Plato, *Republic*, trans by G.M.A. Grube (Indianapolis: Hackett, 1974).

Pomeroy, Sarah, *Goddesses, Whores, Wives, and Slaves: Women in Classical Antiquity* (New York: Schocken Books, 1975).

Poneman, Daniel, *Argentina: Democracy on Trial* (New York: Paragon House, 1987).

Rahula, Walpola Sri, *What the Buddha Taught*, revised ed. (New York: Grove Press, 1974).

Riggin, Don L., "Cause-Branding: Next Step or Misstep?" in Dwight F. Burlingame and Warren F. Ilchman (eds.): *Alternative Revenue Sources: Prospects, Requirements, and Concerns for Nonprofits. New Directions for Philanthropic Fundraising*, no. 12 (San Francisco: Jossey-Bass, Summer 1996), pp. 133–141.

Rinpoche, Sogyal, *The Tibetan Book of Living and Dying* (New York: Harper-Collins, 1992).

Roberts, Suzanne, "Contexts of Charity in the Middle Ages: Religious, Social, and Civic," in J.B. Schneewind (ed.): *Giving: Western Ideas of Philanthropy* (Bloomington: Indiana University Press, 1996), pp. 24–54.

Ruddick, Sara, *Maternal Thinking: Toward a Politics of Peace* (New York: Ballantine, 1989).

Ryan, Alan, "The Philanthropic Perspective after a Hundred Years," in J.B. Schneewind (ed.): *Giving: Western Ideas of Philanthropy* (Bloomington: Indiana University Press, 1996), pp. 76–97.

Salamon, Lester M., *America's Nonprofit Sector: A Primer* (New York: The Foundation Center, 1992).

Salamon, Lester M., and Helmut K. Anheier, *The Emerging Nonprofit Sector: An Overview* (New York: Manchester University Press, 1996).

Schneewind, J.B., "Philosophical Ideas of Charity: Some Historical Reflections," in J.B. Schneewind, ed., *Giving: Western Ideas of Philanthropy* (Bloomington: Indiana University Press, 1996), pp. 54–74.

Schneider, Susan Weidman, and Gretchen von Schlegell, "Richness in Diversity," in Abbie J. von Schlegell and Joan M. Fisher (eds.): *Women as Donors, Women as Philanthropists, New Directions for Philanthropic Fundraising*, No. 2 (San Francisco: Jossey-Bass, Winter 1993), pp. 135–141.

Schoeman, Ferdinand D., *Privacy and Social Freedom* (New York: Cambridge University Press, 1992).

Schulz, William, "Tips on Ties to Corporate Sponsors." *The Chronicle of Philanthropy*, vol. 10, no. 21 (August 27, 1998), pp. 39–40.

Scott, Anne Firor, *Natural Allies: Women's Associations in American History* (Urbana: University of Illinois Press, 1992).

Sen, Amartya, "Does Business Ethics Make Economic Sense?" *Business Ethics Quarterly* Vol. 3, no. 1 (1993), pp. 45–54.

Shantideva, *The Way of the Bodhisattva*, trans. by the Padmakara Translation Group (Boston, MA: Shambhala, 1997).

Smith, Adam, *An Inquiry into the Nature and Causes of the Wealth of Nations*, 1776; reprint ed. abridged by Laurence Dickey (Indianapolis: Hackett, 1993).

Smith, Craig, "Desperately Seeking Data: Why Research is Crucial to the New Corporate Philanthropy." in Dwight F. Burlingame and Dennis R. Young (eds.): *Corporate Philanthropy at the Crossroads* (Bloomington: Indiana University Press, 1996).

Smith, Craig, "The New Corporate Philanthropy," *Harvard Business Review* (May–June, 1994), pp. 105–116.

Smith, Bradford, Sylvia Shue, Jennifer Lisa Vest, and Joseph Villarreal, *Philanthropy in Communities of Color* (Bloomington: Indiana University Press, 1999).

Smith, Timothy, "Sponsorship Guidelines Are a Moral Necessity." The *Chronicle of Philanthropy* vol. 10, no. 24 (October 8, 1998), p. 56.

Stehle, Vince, "Pipeline Company's Role in Smithsonian's Alaska Exhibit Fuels Criticism." *The Chronicle of Philanthropy* vol. 10, no. 4 (November 27, 1997), p. 36.

Supreme Court of New Jersey, *A.P. Smith Manufacturing Co. v. Barlow.* 98 A 2d 581 (1953). Opinion of Judge J. Jacobs; excerpted in Tom L. Beauchamp and Norman E. Bowie, (eds.): *Ethical Theory and Business*, 5th ed. (Upper Saddle River, NJ: Prentice Hall, 1997), pp. 110–112.

Taylor, Diana, "Spectacular Bodies: Gender, Terror, and Argentina's 'Dirty War,'" in Miriam Cooke and Angela Woollacott, (eds.): *Gendering War Talk* (Princeton, NJ: Princeton University Press, 1993), pp. 20–40.

Thomas, R. Roosevelt, *Beyond Race and Gender* (New York: American Management Association, 1991).

Tu Wei-Ming (ed.), *Confucian Traditions in East Asian Modernity* (Cambridge, MA: Harvard University Press, 1996).

Tucker, Mary Evelyn, "A View of Philanthropy in Japan: Confucian Ethics and Education," in Warren F. Ilchman, Stanley N. Katz, and Edward L. Queen (eds.): *Philanthropy in the World's Traditions* (Bloomington: Indiana University Press, 1998), pp. 169–193.

United Nations, "Universal Declaration of Human Rights." *http://www.un.org /Overview/rights.html.*

Unno, Taitetsu, "Karuṇā" in Mircia Eliade (ed.): *Encyclopedia of Religion*, vol. 8 (New York: Macmillan, 1987), pp. 269–270.

Urla, Jacqueline and Alan C. Swedlund, "The Anthropometry of Barbie." in Jennifer Terry and Jacqueline Urla (eds.): *Deviant Bodies: Critical Perspectives on Difference in Science and Popular Culture* (Bloomington: Indiana University Press, 1995), pp. 277–313.

Van Til, Jon and Associates, *Critical Issues in American Philanthropy* (San Francisco: Jossey-Bass, 1990).

Van Til. Jon, "What a Mesh: Crossing the Borders or Just Grinding Gears?" *NonProfit Times* (May 1999), pp. 47–49.

Velasquez, Manuel G., *Business Ethics: Concepts and Cases*, 4th ed. (Upper Saddle River, NJ: Prentice Hall, 1998).

Verbitsky, Horacio, *The Flight: Confessions of an Argentine Dirty Warrior* (New York: The New Press, 1996).

Walker, Margaret Urban, *Moral Understandings: A Feminist Study in Ethics* (New York: Routledge, 1998).

Waide, John, "The Making of Self and World in Advertising." *Journal of Business Ethics*, vol. 6 (1987), pp. 73–79.

Walzer, Michael, *On Toleration* (New Haven, CT: Yale University Press. 1997).

Warner, Irving, "Marketing Deals Shouldn't Be Child's Play." *The Chronicle of Philanthropy* vol. 10, no. 23 (September 24, 1998), pp. 51–52.

Weeden, Curt, *Corporate Social Investing: The Breakthrough Strategy for Giving and Getting Corporate Contributions* (San Francisco: Berrett-Koehler, 1998).

Wells, Ronald Austin, *The Honor of Giving: Philanthropy in Native America* (Indianapolis: Indiana University Center on Philanthropy, 1998).

Wells, Ronald Austin, "'The Future Is in Our Minds': The American Indian College Fund," in Michael Seltzer (ed.): *Fundraising Matters, New Directions for Philanthropic Fundraising*, no. 1 (San Francisco: Jossey-Bass, Fall 1993), pp. 73–92.

Westin, Alan F., *Privacy and Freedom* (New York: Atheneum, 1970).

Whitman, Walt, "Song of Myself," in Sculley Bradley and Harold W. Blodgett (eds.): *Leaves of Grass* (New York: W.W. Norton & Co., 1973).

Wisdom of Solomon 9:1–4; an apocryphal book, noncanonical for Jews and Protestants, canonical for Roman Catholics.

Yankey, John A., "Corporate Support of Nonprofit Organizations: Partnerships across the Sectors," in Dwight F. Burlingame and Dennis R. Young (eds.): *Corporate Philanthropy at the Crossroads* (Bloomington: Indiana University Press, 1996), pp. 7–22.

Young, Dennis R., "Nonprofit Organizations and Business: The Conflict and Confluence of Managerial Culture," in Royster C. Hedgepeth (ed.): *Nonprofit Organizational Culture: What Fundraisers Need to Know, Fundraising Matters, New Directions for Philanthropic Fundraising*, no. 5 (San Francisco: Jossey-Bass, Fall 1994), pp. 81–94.

Zaehner, R.C. (trans. and ed.), *Hindu Scriptures* (London: Everyman's Library, 1966).

Index

Visit us on the World Wide Web

NONPROFIT
Resource Center

www.wiley.com/nonprofit

Our nonprofit website features:

• **A nonprofit catalogue** where you can order and search for titles online. View book and author information about our management, law/tax, fundraising, accounting and finance titles.

• **A threaded discussion forum,** which will provide you and your colleagues with the chance to ask questions, share knowledge, and debate issues important to your organization and the sector.

• **Over 500 free forms and worksheets** to help run any nonprofit organization more efficiently and effectively. Forms are updated monthly to cover a new key area of nonprofit management.

• **Useful links** to many nonprofit resources online.

The Wiley Nonprofit Series brings together an extraordinary team of experts in the fields of nonprofit management, fund raising, law, accounting, and finance. This website highlights our new books, which present the best, most innovative practices being used in the nonprofit sector today. It also highlights our established works, which through their use in the day-to-day operations of thousands of nonprofits, have proven themselves to be invaluable to any nonprofit looking to raise more money or improve their operations, while still remaining in compliance with all rules and regulations.

For nearly 200 years, Wiley has prided itself on being a publisher of books known for thoroughness, rigor, and readability. Please browse the website. You are sure to find valued titles that you need to navigate the new world of nonprofit action.

Wiley Nonprofit Series